For
Notre Dame Fans
<u>Only</u>

The New Saturday Bible

by Rich Wolfe

Published by Lone Wolfe Press, a division of Richcraft. Distribution, mar-keting, publicity, interviews, and book signings handled by Wolfegang Marketing Systems Limited—But Not Very.

ISBN: 0-9729249-9-X

Interior Design: The Printed Page, Phoenix, AZ
Author's Agent: T. Roy Gaul
Chapter heading photos courtesy of Jim Augustine

The author, Rich Wolfe, can be reached at 602-738-5889.

Page Two. Following Notre Dame's miracle comeback in the 1979 Cotton Bowl, legendary announcer Harry Caray narrated a documentary about the game entitled "Seven and ½ Minutes to Destiny…" In 1941, the news director at a small radio station in Kalamazoo, Michigan hired Harry Caray who had been employed at a station in Joliet, Illinois. The news director's name was Paul Harvey. Yes, that <u>Paul Harvey</u>! "And now, you have the rest of the story…… ➡

DEDICATION

To

The incredible Subway Alumni

and

To my parents, Melvin and Frances Wolfe,
who had the foresight to make sure I attended
Notre Dame and the thoughtfulness not to
name me after my father.

GENESIS

THE PREFACE

Could my mother be serious? What she just told me was preposterous. It was the fall of 1953. Iowa was playing against the number-one team in the country, Notre Dame. Iowa, a huge underdog, was leading 7-0 shortly before halftime. With just a few seconds remaining in the half, a Notre Dame player faked an injury to stop the clock. On the next play, Notre Dame quarterback Ralph Guglielmi threw a touchdown pass to tie the game. I am in the kitchen of our farmhouse in Iowa—going crazy! There was a man from a neighboring town who was working on the cabinets in the kitchen that day—the only day in the hundred-year history of that house that anyone ever worked on the cabinets.

My mother was in the dining room. She called for me. Whenever she said, "Richard," I knew I was in trouble. I venture into the dining room, not imagining what I had done—well, actually, I imagined a lot of things I had done, but I did not think she knew about any of them. There was a swinging door that closed behind me, so the cabinetmaker supposedly could not hear what we were saying. She said, "Richard, you must root for Notre Dame." I said, "What did you say?" She said, "You must root for Notre Dame." Fortunately, at that stage of my life, I had not yet heard the old adage: "If you can't laugh at yourself, laugh at your mother!" I thought she was just playing a joke. It became apparent she was serious. I said, "Why would I possibly root for Notre Dame? You know what an Iowa fan I am." She said, "You'll root for Notre Dame because you're 100% Irish and you're Catholic." I said, "What does that have to do with the price of tea in China? I don't care about that. I'm an Iowa fan. I'm rooting for Iowa." She said, "No, you won't." I said, "Yes, I will. I'm rooting for Iowa." In those days, it was very unusual to disobey your mother. I had not only just committed a venial sin; I was well on the way to a mortal sin on this deal. No amount of Hail Marys, indulgences or donations to pagan babies could rescue me now. I had said my piece and counted to three. At least, she did not play the "I wouldn't want to be in your shoes when your father gets home" card.

In the second half, Iowa takes the lead 14-7. With seven seconds remaining in the game, ND has the ball. A Notre Dame lineman fakes an injury, stopping the clock—Mavraides and Varrichione are names that will live in Hawkeye infamy. On the last play, Guglielmi throws another touchdown pass to tie the game 14-14. By this time, I'm completely unglued. My mother's ready to shoot me. The cabinetmaker is smirking.

That night, we are watching the news. The TV station had a taped interview with Iowa Coach Forest Evashevski as he disembarked the airplane in Cedar Rapids. The interviewer asked, "Coach, what do you think about what happened in South Bend today?" Evashevski, paraphrasing the famous Grantland Rice poem, said, "When the One Great Scorer comes to mark against your name, He'll mark not if you won or lost, but how you got screwed at Notre Dame." I turned to my mother and said, "What does that mean?" She said, "Nothing. He's just a sore loser." I said, "But we didn't lose." She said, "Well, I don't want to talk about it." The next day in the *Des Moines Register*, there was a cartoon in the Peach Section. It showed the clock atop Notre Dame Stadium indicating seven seconds left in the game. Underneath the clock there was an old man—the timekeeper—with a long beard leaning back in a chair, snoring. There were cobwebs in the clock where the seven seconds were marked.

Seven years later, my mother's prayers were answered when I enrolled at Notre Dame. Freshmen could not play varsity sports until 1972. Nevertheless, the freshmen football players came in two weeks before the rest of the freshman class. One of my friends, Jack Barnard, was on the team. Jack said that the first night the freshmen football players were there, they were all sitting around the locker room. One player said, "Hey, let's go all around the room, stand up, introduce ourselves, say where we're from and what we did in high school football last year."

The number-one recruit in the country that season was a running back from Clarksburg, West Virginia, named Bobby Secret. Notre

Dame won the recruiting war. When it was his turn, Barnard stands up and says, "My name is Jack Barnard. I'm from Kansas City, and I was Mr. Kansas City Football last year when I scored 26 touchdowns." Barnard then said the leader continues around the room and eventually got to Bobby Secret. He stands up and says, "My name is Bobby Secret. I'm a running back from Clarksburg, West Virginia, and last year I scored 13 touchdowns…"

Barnard said he was sitting there thinking, "This is the number-one running back in the country, and he only scored 13 touchdowns—some hillbilly from West Virginia—and I scored 26 touchdowns in Kansas City." But, then, Bobby Secret finished his sentence. He said, "I scored 13 touchdowns on pass interceptions, and 51 altogether." The bottom line to that story is that Bobby Secret rarely played at Notre Dame and ended up transferring to Pitt.

Fast forward over two decades, we are living in Scottsdale, Arizona. I am not only a Notre Dame fan, but a season ticket holder for Arizona State University. ASU's hated rival is the University of Arizona. It's October, '82 and Arizona is playing at Notre Dame. Now, this is a double whammy. Not only, if Notre Dame gets beat is it disastrous, but if they get beat by the University of Arizona, it is a calamity! It was a beautiful, beautiful day in Scottsdale, and all the windows were open. There was a nice breeze wafting through the house. The problem was the game was not nationally televised. We could pick up a Tucson station, but it came in very snowy and fuzzy. Arizona won the game when the Notre Dame quarterback threw his bazillionth interception of the day.

When that happened, I lost it. I screamed at the TV as loud as I could every profanity I have ever known in my entire life. It was language not heard on this planet for thousands of years. Certainly, it was a lot more profanity than God wants to hear from a football fan during peacetime. It was an awful conclusion to a game—the worst nightmare—U of A beats Notre Dame *in South Bend.*

About five minutes later, there is a knock on the door. It is my neighbor, Roland, from across the street. He said, "Hey, Rich, can I talk to you for a minute?" I said, "Sure." He said, "Can I talk to you *outside* for a minute?" I said, "Sure." I stepped outside. He, obviously, was agitated. He said to me, "What kind of argument did you and your wife have?" I said, "Argument? When?" He said, "About five minutes ago." I said, "Roland, I've been here all afternoon by myself. There's nobody else here. Why do you ask?" "Why do I ask? I'll tell you why I ask. As you know, I've been trying to sell my house for seven months. I just had this older couple spend two hours inside the house. We were out in front, and we shook hands on a deal when, all of a sudden, he hears this would-be, across-the-street neighbor yell out threats that he's going to kill people in the house and someone was the only abortion ever to live." I said, "Oh, no, Roland, I've been here by myself. I was just watching the Notre Dame football game." He said, "You were just watching a football game. That's all you were doing—just watching a football game?" I said, "Yep. Notre Dame got beat." It took Roland another eight months to sell the house, and he never talked to me the entire time.

One of the great things about Notre Dame is the stories you hear over the years. You think they are true. Some may be apocryphal, but they're all fun. When I was a freshman, a senior was telling a Paul Hornung story. In those days, most athletes did not smoke or drink. Apparently, Hornung was standing on the Quad, talking to some of his friends, when one of his buddies whispered, "Paul, Paul, here comes Coach Leahy." Hornung dropped the cigarette he had been smoking. Leahy comes up, points at the cigarette on the ground and says, "Paul, do you see what I see?" Hornung makes an exaggerated effort of looking down at the ground and said, "I see it, Coach. But, you saw it first. You can have it."

Stories like these became the genesis of this book. Whenever they were told, the listeners would always volley with similar tales of their own. Publishers were not interested in doing a series of books involving the fans of certain teams. They laughed and said no one would be interested in other fans' stories.

Upon becoming my own publisher six years ago, that concept seemed like a good idea to test. The first scheduled fans book was to be about Notre Dame fans but it was shelved when *"Win One for the Gipper"* was replaced by *"Just Win One."* The actual first "Fans" book, *For Yankee Fans Only,* sold out. The second, *For Red Sox Fans Only,* sold out immediately. Twenty thousand more were reprinted. The book *For Cub Fans Only* not only became the best-selling book in the history of the Cubs, it sold over three times the previous record.

Publishing can be a vicious business with phony reviews and spurious stories constantly planted on the Internet by publishers trying to protect their investments and new releases. The trade-off is that "the more you get ripped, the better you're doin'." Their shenanigans do not bother me since I cannot type, have never turned on a computer and have never seen the Internet. The closest that I have ever come to the Internet is material given me concerning the wonderfully-done, "Call-For-Change campaign" on the NDNation web site. Perhaps I am a Luddite at heart, but one thing is certain: the only critics who count are the readers like you.

Since the age of ten, I have been a serious collector of sports books. During that time, my favorite book style has been the eavesdropping-type where the subject talks in his or her own words without the "then he said" or "the air was so thick you could cut it with a butter knife" waste of verbiage. Books such as Lawrence Ritter's *Glory of Their Times* and Donald Honig's *Baseball When the Grass Was Real*. Thus, I adopted the style of these books when I started compiling oral histories of the Mike Ditkas and Harry Carays of the world. I am a sports fan first and foremost—I do not even pretend to be an author. This book is designed solely for other sports fans. I really do not care what the publisher, editors or critics think. I am only interested in Notre Dame fans having an enjoyable read and getting their money's worth. Sometimes, a person being interviewed will drift off the subject, but if the feeling is that Irish fans would enjoy the digression, it stays in the book.

In an effort to get more material into the book, the editor decided to merge some paragraphs and omit some of the commas, which will allow for the reader to receive an additional 20,000 words, the equivalent of 50 pages. More bang for your buck...more fodder for English teachers...fewer dead trees.

There are three things that make shivers run down my spine when I hear them played: "My Old Kentucky Home" at the Kentucky Derby, "Pops Goes the Fourth" by the Boston Pops celebrating the Fourth of

July at the Esplanade on the Charles River, and the "The Victory March" by the Notre Dame marching band on football weekends.

The first two happen once a year. The latter? "Too much ain't enough!" If a sign said the Notre Dame band would play "The Victory March" as many times as you wish for a thousand bucks, I would order two thousand dollars worth. Every Friday before a home game, I make sure to watch the band's final rehearsal. Last year, the day before the famous Southern Cal game, the band started playing "The Victory March"…out of the scrapbook of my mind popped 45 years of Notre Dame football weekend memories…the first memories come from my freshman year in 1960 when Purdue handed us our worst defeat ever, the first of a school record eight losses in a row…a football season ticket cost about $20 total that year…the 25,000 empty seats for a home game against North Carolina in '62…by my senior year Notre Dame was moving closer to the fork in the road where academics went left and football went Dixie…our class had the dubious distinction of being the first class never to experience a winning season… returning for an extra semester in the fall of '64 when Ara answered our prayers…the images kept coming….faded games and faded memories, how they linger in the mind.

Davie and Willingham, coupled with miles and years, have played this Domer like an old melody—out of tune and out of time. It would be great to turn back the clock and return to those halcyon fall days of '64, but the sun does not back up for any of us. Sometimes, the things we want most are the things we once had.

The band continued to play "The Victory March." I closed my eyes and, in my mind, I was a student again. It was easy to do because Notre Dame memories—like Notre Dame heroes—never grow old. It was then that I realized that for four-and-a-half years, I had gone through Notre Dame and, for 45 years, Notre Dame had gone through me.

….And to think that back in '53, Mom thought my life wasn't going to work out.

Go now.

Rich Wolfe

I Chronicles

II Chronicles

Chapter 1

Proverbs

...and a Couple of Converbs

Proverbs

"Prayers work better when the players are big."

—Frank Leahy

***

"The thing that I'm most proud of in my life is, simply, being a priest."

—Father Theodore Hesburgh, C.S.C.

***

"I'd rather have a slow guy going in the right direction than a fast guy going in the wrong direction."

—Lou Holtz

***

"No one relishes a pickled driver."

—Sgt. Tim McCarthy for the Indiana State Police

***

"You know what dad says:
Having a dream is what makes life tolerable."

—Sean Astin in the movie "Rudy"

***

"Let me tell you something. If you or any of your people ever violate NCAA rules, you'll be fired! Period! You'll be out of here by midnight."

—Father Hesburgh to new Athletic Director, Gene Corrigan, 1981

***

The Notre Dame hierarchy desperately wants to avoid the jock-factory image, but the fact is few people would know how tough Notre Dame is academically if it wasn't for all the constant talk about how difficult it is to enroll athletes into Notre Dame. In reality, sports greatly enhances Notre Dame's intellectual reputation.

—Andrew Pongracz, Ohio State fan from Plymouth, MI

***

"Notre Dame's no better than New Mexico State."

—Texas Tackle, Clarence Martin, after Notre Dame beat Texas, 1996

***

"When other coaches are playing checkers, Charlie Weis is playing chess."

—Mike Leep, Notre Dame Monogram Club

***

"…my husband hasn't satisfied me in years."

"Yeah, that's how I feel about Notre Dame football."

—Homer Simpson's reply to a woman
in a 2004 episode of "The Simpsons"

***

"…It doesn't take much biology to know it's a baby. It's basic science. It's not a value judgment."

—Student, Claire Johnson, in the 1995 book, *The Domers*

***

"Your value to the team depends on how far from the football you are."

—Lou Holtz

***

"George Zipp said to me, 'Doc, some day when the crew is up against it and the breaks are beatin' the boys, tell them to get out there and give it all they got to win just one for the Zipper. I don't know where I'll be then, Doc, but I won't smell too good, that's for sure.'"

—Scene from the movie *Airplane*

Chapter 2

Pharisees and Wannabes

Put Me In, Coach

WHERE WERE YOU WHEN KENNEDY DIED? YOU'RE KIDDIN'— TEDDY DIED?

SENATOR TED KENNEDY

Notre Dame football makes strange bedfellows. Believe it or not, Ted Kennedy once played football for Notre Dame. He played in the 1953 Varsity vs. Old-Timers game as a defensive back. Senator Kennedy, now 74, lettered in football at Harvard in 1955, even though, technically, he graduated with the Harvard class of 1954.

My family has had a long and wonderful association with Notre Dame University. My father was on the Lay Trustees Board for many years. My brother, Jack, received an honorary degree from Notre Dame...*and he constantly reminded us of it.*

The legendary football coach, Frank Leahy, would come to our house in Palm Beach to relax for about a week at the end of each season. He and my father were very close friends. Also, Father Cavanaugh, the president of Notre Dame, was one of my father's best friends.

One of Jack's fondest retorts occurred during the Notre Dame-Iowa game in South Bend in the fall of 1958. He was being interviewed at halftime by a legendary Iowa announcer, and he didn't want to say anything that would alienate the people in Iowa. Iowa was beating Notre Dame by the score of 25-0 at halftime. The Iowa announcer asked Jack what he thought of the game. Jack replied, "I'm rooting for Iowa...and I'm praying for Notre Dame."

It was the spring of 1953, and I had just gotten out of the Army, after having served for a couple of years. I went to visit Notre Dame. While I was there, I discovered that they were going to play the Old-Timers game in the next day or so. I heard Frank Leahy and Father Cavanaugh talking about the game and about the Old-Timers who would be coming back to the campus. I went out to watch the teams practice, and Frank Leahy said, "Would you like to play with the Old-Timers?" I said, "That would be the greatest thrill of my life."

When we were dressing out in the visitors' locker room, I said to Jerry Groom, "What do you want me to do?" Jerry said, "Stay out of the way so you don't get killed." The Old-Timers were playing the varsity team, which was loaded with players like Johnny Lattner and Ralph Guglielmi. But the old timers had a loaded team, too—we had Leon Hart, Jim Martin, Bob Williams, and Frank Tripucka.

So, at the Old-Timers' game, I played defense for the Old-Timers team for four or five series of downs. I was surrounded by great All-Americans. Jerry Groom was really my life-saver that day. A couple of years before this, he was a team captain and an All-American. He had just finished his second year in the NFL—and today he is in the NFL Hall of Fame. My Notre Dame friends from the Boston area had spoken highly of Groom, and he was the one who took me into the locker room and introduced me to the other former players who had come back to play in the game.

One of spectators sitting on our bench that day was Charles O. Finley, who was a close friend of Coach Leahy. In fact, they were almost neighbors—each living about an hour west of Notre Dame. Leahy took me to the firehouse on campus and showed me his little apartment he lived in weeknights during the football season.

A couple of years later, when Finley bought the Kansas City A's— now the Oakland A's—he changed their colors to green and gold because he loved Notre Dame so much. Coach Leahy told me that the Green Bay Packers used green and gold because Curly Lambeau had played at Notre Dame and really liked the green and gold colors.

It was a beautiful sunny day. There may not be any place on this planet that is prettier than Notre Dame. So, for someone who loved Notre Dame and loves football and who had such high regard for Frank Leahy…it was the thrill of a lifetime. Who else can say they have played in the Notre Dame Stadium…and, who else has had the thrill of playing against the Fightin' Irish? It was a great day!

RUDY??
IT WAS EASY FOR RUDY.
HE WAS *ON* THE TEAM.

MIKE BROOKS

These days, Mike Brooks is a respected doctor in Prince Frederick, Maryland...but as a wide-eyed Notre Dame freshman, 30 years ago, out of Grosse Ile, Michigan, he was determined to be in a Notre Dame uniform on the sidelines on game day. The only thing holding him back was the fact that he wasn't on the team.

I played sports in high school in a small Class B school, nothing real big. I was a good athlete in ninth grade and probably could have played college football at some very small college in Michigan but I'd grown up dreaming of going to Notre Dame. My mother was born in Ireland, and from the moment she stepped foot in America, she always had an idea that I was going to go to Notre Dame.

I had gone down to Notre Dame about a month of two before classes were to start freshman year. Still in the back of your mind, as you walk around campus, you think, "I could do this. I could play football here. I could be a star." They were putting us up in Alumni Hall. There was a huge door there. I was banging on it, trying to get someone to open it up. The door opened—Jeff Weston was the guy who was there letting people in and out. He was the starting defensive tackle for a couple of years. He was the biggest person I'd ever seen in my life—he was huge—he was chiseled with muscle. All he was wearing was tight little gym shorts. I was just awe-struck. My jaw dropped. I looked at him. All I could think of to say was, "Do you play football?" When he nodded, or grunted, "Yeah," I said, "Oh my god, that's it." Immediately, my dream was gone that I would play football at Notre Dame.

Going to college, I knew I wasn't going to play at Notre Dame, but I still wanted to see what the football experience was about. I even told people about it freshman year, "I am going to go on that field some day." They would laugh and laugh and laugh. I played interhall football for a while until I realized I was going to have to get serious about my studies in order to be in pre-med. I kept hanging onto that sidelines dream, though, and, people kept reminding me of it.

I lived in Dillon Hall for four years and became real good friends with Dave Huffman, the starting center on the football team. He was a consensus All-American our senior year in '78. He was a wonderful, great guy. The summer before senior year, Dave worked in a liquor store. He said, "I don't know many Irishmen on the Notre Dame football team, but I met a lot at that job." He went on to play several years with the Vikings. Unfortunately, he was killed in a car accident a couple of years ago. We were always doing something in our dorm. I developed this plan over a couple of years that I was going to try to get on the field with the team and see what it was like to be down there. By the time I got to be a senior, it became 'put up time' to do it. A friend of mine had been egging me on—not believing I would do it.

I'm not really sure what I envisioned doing if I ever got on that field. The whole goal first was to get on the sidelines and not get caught. The second goal was not real clear. I wasn't going to go onto the actual playing field or do anything stupid because I knew that would be a very bad thing. I just imagined it more as a harmless prank—just wandering the sidelines, seeing what the experience was like down on the sidelines, looking back up at 50,000 fans and the band being there. I had told other people about this dream, "Before I graduate, I'm going to do that."

It became time when I had to pick a game. At the time, the interhall teams were all full-equipment teams. Everybody who plays on the dorm teams has a full set of equipment. I was able to put together a uniform from a combination of places. My friend, Dave Huffman, loaned me his #56 jersey. It was actually the jersey that Dan Devine had given him—the famous Southern Cal green jersey. The players had all been given one from the '77 season, and he loaned his to me. I was able to get socks and gold pants and a gold helmet and the whole deal so I had the whole uniform together. We finally picked the Tennessee game of our senior year.

We divided up things. I put on shoulder pads and all the football uniform and then pulled some bib blue jeans overalls over it and then pulled over an old football parka that I had left over from high school. Some other guys carried in the helmet. Once we got inside the gate, I got the helmet and other things and went to where the freshman section was. Before the renovation of the stadium, down in the northwest corner, you could easily get over the wall. Students would storm the field all the time by doing that. It was a custom that, when the team was coming through the tunnel, a lot of kids would go over the wall and would make a human "tunnel" for the players to run through. Then, they would climb back over the wall, go back into the stands. It was never a big deal at that time.

Notre Dame was getting ready to run onto the field. I got down next to the wall. Just as the Irish started to come out, everybody stood up and was cheering. I stripped off the parka, put on the helmet, pulled off the overalls and went over the wall just as the team ran out. I ran down with them past the band and the cheerleaders. I got on the sideline as people got all settled in waiting for the kickoff. I just stayed there on the sidelines as long as I could. I was extremely nervous. Getting on the field without a hitch went perfectly smooth—going over the wall and through the people and nobody really took notice. Other people were also coming and going over the wall to cheer the team on—I had counted on that. When the team and the cheerleaders run onto the field, nobody notices what's going on by the wall.

I was down on the sideline and tried to pick a place that was not too close to the majority of the players...but, not too far away, just on the side closest to Touchdown Jesus at the periphery. I just stood there with the rest of the team during kickoff, and nobody really paid much attention to me. The whole team had the green jersey on and that's what I had on, too. They'd worn the green jerseys in '77 and had worn them in '78, which was when this happened. They wore green jerseys every game.

I saw Huffman and went over and talked to him for a little bit. He just nodded his head—he couldn't believe I had actually done it. He edged over with the offensive team so he just shot me a wave and then I stayed away from him. I figured that if two '56s' stood next to each other, that wouldn't look good. A lot of times, some of the players would have duplicate numbers. They had no names on the jerseys at that point so his name was not on there. I saw another guy I knew who was one of the senior managers and I talked to him for a little bit. He couldn't believe I was out there. I just mostly tried to stay out of people's way.

Friends in the stands kept running down the aisles and yelling and screaming my name and taking pictures. That may have been why the managers and security guards zeroed in on me. I was trying not to really look too hard at them, but, at the same time, trying to look up at them so I could get some pictures taken. I still have those pictures.

I never got as far as halftime. Probably two-thirds of the way through the first quarter, one manager, who I didn't know, came over and asked me who I was. I just blew him off for a while...but he came back and said, "No, really, what are you doing here?" Then, a security guard came over. I told him I was doing a story for a George Plimpton first-person type story for the *Observer*, just to see what the experience was like. I said that I had permission to do it. That appeased them for another five minutes or so. Then, they *all* came back and said, "No, what are you really doing?" I said, "I'm just here to see what it's all about—no harm intended for this—and I can leave any time." Originally, the student manager backed off and the security guard stood with me the whole time, and then Coach Devine's personal bodyguard came by. He was a sergeant on the South Bend Police Force. He was about 5'6" tall by about 5'6" wide, a really imposing looking guy, who always stood by the coaches. The security guard asked him if it would be okay if I would stay. This guy said, "No! Get him out of here." I said, "Fine, I'll go. I'll climb back up over the wall and go to my seat. I've got my ticket with me." Then, they became alarmed when I said that because it would look bad if suddenly one of the "players" goes climbing over the wall and up into the stands. They said, "No, we've got to get you out of here some other way." The security guard who, at first, was a little angry and gruff, suddenly became more conspiratorial. He said, "I'll tell you what. I'll take you down through the tunnel, and you can get out that way. We'll go down past the band, and you can limp out past everybody." So, I limped my way out.

Huffman later told me one of the offensive coaches—who was up in the press box—came to him and asked if he knew anything about that 'other' 56 who was limping off. He said he just laughed it off—which would have been hard 'cause he was a really chatty person. He was one of the best-known, quoted players during those years. Imagine the consternation of Notre Dame fans nationwide when the television announcers reported that the Irish All-American, Dave Huffman—Number 56—was limping towards the locker room before halftime.

Being down there on the field was very interesting. The enormity of the size of the stadium and the number of people and the sound are unbelievable. Going to a small high school, you might have 500 people at a game, or 1,000 as the most ever for a big game. This was unbelievable. Also, too, you realize how small you are in scope to the stands. When you sit up in the stands and watch the players, it's like they're out there and everybody can see them. When you get down there, you realize you are so small, not only to the rest of the players, but compared to the surroundings around you. I was also amazed at how business-like everything is. Everyone is coming and going, and people are going to a certain place. You realize the organization it takes to do it. But, it was an overwhelming feeling. I was extremely scared and nervous that somebody was going to take this the wrong way so there was a lot of anxiety. There was a lot of adrenalin pumping. My heart was probably beating 140 times a minute and felt like it was going to jump out of my chest. I remember it being a great place to watch the game—to watch the action well. It was an overcast day. More than anything else, it was just a sense of awe and nervousness all rolled into one.

After I got through the tunnel—right outside that—is the gate where they let me out. A couple of people looked at me curiously. I said, "I need to get out. I have to go back to my dorm." I was running back toward Dillon Hall so I could return in time to see the rest of the game. At one point, just as I was coming out of the gate—before I got up to full speed—this little kid said, "Hey, 56, can I have your autograph?" I felt embarrassed and said, "No. None of the toilets are working in the locker room. I've got to go back to the dorm and go to the bathroom." His parents looked at me funny…the kid was just standing there holding his pad and pencil. That's when I took off running and ran all the way back to my dorm. There were people everywhere outside the stadium, and they would see me and yell, "Go. Go. Go." By this time, I was running pretty fast. Nobody else stopped me and asked where I was going. I put different clothes on and went back into the stadium.

I had kept my ticket with me in my game pants on the field because my exit strategy wasn't worked out as to how I would go back to my seat. I thought at some point I could just climb back over the wall and go up to my seat. By this time, we were seniors and had tickets on the 40-yard line. Our seats were literally right behind the players' bench, right exactly where I had been on the field. After I ran back to the dorm, I used my ticket to get back in. I came back into the stadium and got up to my seat just before halftime. Everybody there was going crazy. After the game, we went to the old Senior Bar and had a couple of beers. Huffman was always one for a prank so he thought it was great. He talked to me about it that next week. I didn't get any feedback from any of the other players. My parents found out later, and they thought it was great. They thought it was marvelous. They thought it was the funniest thing ever. It's still a great source of stories. When I go to reunions, people come up and say, "Hey, aren't you the guy…?" And I say, "Yeah, that was me."

Some people called my actions a "Rudy" type of experience. I was a freshman when the actual Rudy event happened. Nobody really had made a big deal about Rudy. It was a small, incidental thing at the time and didn't really strike people that this was really a terrific thing. Living in the dorms, you always knew somebody who was a walk-on, and you always knew the players so it wasn't such a big deal that somebody who was a walk-on actually might get on the field and get to play. I was at the game but don't have strong memories of it. I wish I did. I've seen the movie enough times to think that was the reality of it. I've talked to other people who were there with me— part of the thing was that we were there as freshmen, and, as freshmen, you don't really know anything, can't remember anything— and thus don't have a real strong memory of it. I don't remember him being carried off.

I was confident that Notre Dame would return to prominence in football like we did in 2005. I actually thought it would be under Ty Willingham. I thought he was a great gentleman, and I was sorry for the way it went down. Actually, it was funny— I was back at Notre Dame not long after Ty got fired. I was just checking in at the Morris Inn and went to the car to get my suitcase. This guy in a big, black, Cadillac Escalade was backing up. I looked, and then I looked again, and it was Charlie Weis. He was almost running over me in the parking lot. He was leaned way back in his seat and was talking on his cell phone and backing up—all at the same time. I realized he was going to run me over—he didn't see me at all—so I jumped out of the way and got in front of my rental car which was parked right next to him. After he backed out and left, I jumped in the car and started to back out and thought, "Oh my god, that would have been a great headline. 'Alum comes back and is run over by new coach.'" ...or maybe the headline could have read, "Former player comes back and is run over by new coach."

Joe Montana was in my class, and I had met him, but didn't know him personally. At the time, he was married to his first wife, so he was off by himself. Even though Charlie Weis was in my class then, I did not know him at all. Rusty Lisch was another quarterback when I was there. In fact, he's the answer to a great trivia question because he was the starting quarterback before Montana took over four games into Joe's junior year and then Rusty started again once Montana was gone. A **_SPORTS ILLUSTRATED_** reporter once asked Rusty if he learned anything when Montana played ahead of him. Lisch said, "I learned a lot." "What?" "That I wasn't as good as Montana." Another time, Lisch was being heckled by some fan in the stands. Dave Huffman offered to do something about it. Lisch said, "Don't, it's probably my dad!"

Who was the only Major League Baseball player to grace the cover of the college football edition of _SPORTS ILLUSTRATED_? Bo Jackson? No. Kirk Gibson? No. Rick Leach of Michigan? Yes.

YESTERDAYS TOMORROW

KEITH CROSS

Keith Cross, 33, is the vice president of an optical laboratory near Newton, Massachusetts. Cross was one of the first subway alumni to sign up for the inaugural Notre Dame Fantasy Football Camp in 2003. Notre Dame was the first college to have such a fantasy camp. The first camp had 27 participants, while each camp since has sold out all 50 slots. A recent fantasy camp had 18 former players as instructors including 10 All-Americans. Proceeds from the camps are donated to the Notre Dame Monogram Club's Brennan-Boland-Riehle Scholarship Fund.

Every Saturday morning, when I was a kid, we'd get our $5 a week allowance. My brothers and I would go to downtown Worcester, play around and go to a movie. After the movie, we had to meet my dad at a place called Coney Island—a hot dog emporium. There was no alcohol there, but the priests were allowed to bring in their own alcohol. They would bring in a fifth or a pint, and they'd spice up the hot chocolate and the coffee.

All the Irish-Catholic priests in the Worcester area were all Notre Dame fans, or Holy Cross, which at the time was huge, with a player named Gordy Lockbaum. I would bet, and I would clean house. I would walk out of there with twenty-five bucks. We'd bet on everything from the coin toss to what the first play of the game was going to be. We'd bet nickels and dimes and quarters. I'd get a little gutsy and start reading the paper about Notre Dame 'cause they were one of the few national teams on the upper East Coast—television didn't carry college football like they did in the South and the Midwest and West Coast because there are so many small regional colleges and it isn't as popular. National college football is not that big in New England for whatever reason. The only games we would get would be Notre Dame.

My dad was a huge Notre Dame fan. He looked at it at a different level. He always idolized Notre Dame because he was a single dad, a religious man, and it was mystifying to my father. He looked at Notre Dame as the pinnacle—a Catholic college run by priests. We grew up in an Irish and Italian Catholic neighborhood. My dad worked his rear off just to provide the basics. He always told us that he couldn't give us money, but he could make us smart. "Go to school. Learn. You've got to make something of yourself." Notre Dame, to me, was the pinnacle. No matter what happened—**PATRIOTS** win or lose— it doesn't matter. If Notre Dame wins, it was like Christmas at our house on Sunday. We'd have a boiled dinner. If Notre Dame loses, we'd go to my grandmother's house up the road. My dad would be so bummed out, he wouldn't even want to cook dinner. We'd read the paper and we'd analyze the game. It was a great experience. As a kid, we loved it.

When you're a certain age, 9 or 10, losing doesn't hurt as much. You go on…. You get a bag of candy and forget all about it. But, by '86, I was 13 and just beginning to play organized sports. I agonized over that season and the next couple of seasons. Then, that '88 season meant so much because of the Miami game and the West Virginia game. You've got Tony Rice, Rocket Ismail, all these guys playing. This is the greatest. It was one of those times when you watched the games and you hung on every play. You watched it, and you smelled it, and you tasted it. Because I grew up with it, I matured as a Notre Dame fan during the '86 season.

The first time I went to a game in South Bend was for a Boston College-Notre Dame game in 2000, the last time Notre Dame beat

As a result of a public contest in 1960, the team nickname of PATRIOTS was chosen. Many years later when considering a name change, management decided on the Bay State Patriots, but changed that because they worried about Bay State being abbreviated in headlines.

In the history of the Patriots, they have played home games at Harvard Stadium, Boston University Field, Fenway Park, Boston College and in 1971 they made their debut at Schaefer Stadium in Foxboro. Schaefer was the one stadium to have when you're having more than one.

BC at Notre Dame. I'm young in my career but I've been fortunate to have some success so I was able to take my twin brother as my guest. We took my best grown-up friend and a co-worker who is 18-years my senior but who is my soul mate when it comes to Notre Dame. We joked that the only people who could get to go to Notre Dame games were rock stars and astronauts. We figured that had to be your social status in order to get to go. It's everyone's dream to go. I went on the Internet and punched in "Notre Dame Tickets". I got in touch with a ticket broker who sold me tickets for $50 over face value, which was extremely reasonable. Originally, he wanted $200 over face value. I said, "Listen, I'm going to tell you my story." I told him how much I loved Notre Dame. He said, "For you to love Notre Dame that much, I want to be the guy to let you go." That was my first experience with, not necessarily a fan, but a Notre Dame-type guy. Wasn't that a wonderful thing? They were upper end zone seats—not great seats. He told me we were going to see touchdowns the whole game.

We flew into Chicago, drove to LaPorte, Indiana the night before because I couldn't get a room in South Bend. We arranged ahead of time for a taxi to pick us up at seven in the morning on Saturday. We had a rental car but none of us wanted to drive to the campus on game day. We didn't know where we were going and didn't know where to park. The taxi picked us up and when we got there, the first thing we did was go to the bookstore. I bought a Notre Dame "Rudy" jacket. I shipped my coat home, and we just walked around. We took about eight rolls of film

Words can't describe it. It was magical. It was a thousand times prettier than I expected. On NBC every fall on Saturday morning, you watch the pre-game, and they show the Dome and show the campus. It shows **THE GROTTO**, but being there in person is almost impossible to describe. Everyone was willing to help us and tell us how to get to places we wanted to see. We were walking around with our heads straining, bumping into everybody. We bumped into an older priest who gave us a grand tour of Notre Dame campus. He walked

THE GROTTO is a 1/7 replica of Lourdes. On a football weekend 10,000 candles are lit. In 1985, 1500 candles melted their casings, setting The Grotto on fire and part of it collapsed.

us everywhere for over an hour. He brought us into Leahy's Pub in the Morris Inn, bought us Bloody Marys and took us on our way for the rest of the day.

It was the most magical experience. If you could bottle that moment up, that's every time I step on the campus. You walk in and something magical happens every time you go. That was the first time any of the four of us had been there. We were bouncing around the place. My friend and I didn't leave our seats the whole time. My brother and my best friend, at halftime, came back with hot dogs and sandwiches and said, "You'd probably starve to death and freeze to death if we don't get something for you." But, we didn't want to miss any of it. I wouldn't leave my seat for a second. We told the ushers, when we walked in, that it was our first time at Notre Dame, and they gave us the Lou Holtz prayer card. Everybody who heard that it was our first time at Notre Dame wanted to do something special for us.

You see the sign "Play Like a Champion" and my goal is to 'Live Like a Champion.' Ever since we went to the Notre Dame Fantasy Football Camp and met fabulous guys…if you can imagine a locker room full of those type of guys. That's what it's like. You say to yourself, "Every day, I want to be perfect." That's the standard you try to hold yourself to. It's part of the Notre Dame spirit. Let's try to be perfect. Let's try to be the best possible person we can be today. That little tiny sign at the bottom of the flight of stairs transcends 10,000 undergrads and the fan base.

After going to that first game six years ago, I was smitten. Absolutely. We had thought that trip would be a once-in-a-lifetime experience. Then, I thought, "We can't let this go. How do we get back here next year? How do we do it?" One thing led to another. My brother was working for a company where a guy had gone to Notre Dame. He had played football as a walk-on at Notre Dame for a couple of years, and he was getting tickets. He had a friend at Wellesley who began giving us tickets, and then it just spiraled. I became a member of the O'Hara Society at Notre Dame. You just want to be part of it—not only just the football aspect of it, you want to be a part of the whole atmosphere—what goes on there. When you walk on campus, something happens. It's magical. So, you say, "I want to be a part of this all the time. How do I become a part of this family—this group—all the time." My wife thinks I'm nuts.

Even when Notre Dame was losing, you would look at it and say, "Well, the standards at Notre Dame are high." I like the higher standards. One of the reasons that makes me a Notre Dame fan is that you see a true student-athlete. The kids have to progress with their class. They have to graduate. They're not a third-year football player, but a freshman, academically. That's one of the appeals I've always had with Notre Dame. I hold academics to such a high standard, and they hold it to a higher one. I love the fact that year-in and year-out, we have the hardest schedule in the country. Our kids accept it—to be the best, no matter what, on the football field and off, you have to play the best, you have to beat the best if you want to be the best.

My business partner, John Shanly, is a die-hard Notre Dame fan, and we have all kinds of Notre Dame paraphernalia around the office. About three years ago, we started going through the process of selling our business and brought in a group of potential buyers. One of these guys was a Notre Dame alum…but we didn't know that. He came in and was teasing us, "Oh, you like Notre Dame. Do you know anything about Notre Dame." We started going on and on and talking about it. John and I have an actual Notre Dame game helmet, and it was on my desk. The guy looked at the helmet and said, "Oh, it's a real helmet." John and I have a pact—whichever one of us dies first, the other guy has to bury him with the helmet. Come to find out, his group was in over their heads with the thought about purchasing us so it didn't work out.

About a week later, we get a phone call from that same guy. He said, "I just want to thank you guys. Can I fax over something to you I thought was funny?" We said, "Absolutely." He faxed over an article from one of the *Alumni* magazines that had a brief description about the fantasy camp. He wrote on a note, "Keith, now you and John can suit up for real. Ha Ha Ha!" /s/Paul. We started laughing about it, but I called the number right away. I actually got Pat Steenberge, a former Notre Dame quarterback and the founder of the fantasy camp. He told me all about it. I said, "Pat, this is unbelievable. I'm coming to camp." He said, "We don't have all the details finalized." I said, "I'm in. What do you need?" He said, "Well, I just need the fact that you're interested." I said, "But, I don't want this to go by without me being in." I told Pat I was destined to go to this camp. He was laughing. That was in November, 2002. I get a note from him right around Christmas saying, "Hey, we're going to start finalizing the camp." I was leaving for a family vacation to Aruba. I said, "The area we are going to doesn't have e-mail access so being gone for a whole week will kill me." I couldn't wait to know if I was coming so I mailed him a check for $1,500.00, knowing it was going to be a lot more, but this was just to say, "I want to be in. I'm mailing my check today. I want a spot." Pat and I hit it off, and we talked once or twice a week for the next five or six months up until camp. The excitement was building. It was so stressful, but in a good way.

In high school and in Pop Warner, I had played football and was pretty good. I was able to start on the varsity team my sophomore year, junior year and senior year. We weren't a great team, but I was competitive. I made All-City my senior year. I wasn't recruited by anyone.

The camp cost $3,500 that first year. When I found out the cost, I told Pat, "That's unbelievable." From the things he was telling me, I figured we'd get to visit for five minutes and then we'd have to leave. I thought, for an experience like he was talking about, thirty-five hundred bucks was too cheap. My business partner and I figured at least $10,000. I told my wife—it's easier to beg for forgiveness than it is to ask for per-mission—"I'm doing it. No matter what it costs, I'm going to do it."

Leading up to it, there was a lot of nervous anxiety. We were really anxious. We were working out. We were running and jogging. I wasn't really lifting weights, but I was trying to get my wind. It was not going to be a contact game so I thought if I could outrun some-one, I'd be happy. They were planning to take 50 participants, but when I got information about the camp, they only had 27 people who paid to go. He was willing to accept up to 50. I thought, "You know how many alumni are going to want to go to this!" We thought we'd never get in. I figured my $1,500 would put me on the list somewhere with an asterisk. When Pat called in late February and said, "Keith, you're in. You can pick your number." I was number 9 all through high school because I wanted to be Tony Rice. He was my idol. I'm wearing my high school workout shirt, my high school football jersey with number 9 and my name on it. I'm working out off-season and getting ready for camp. There was such anxiousness not knowing what to expect. We thought we'd probably have a 15-minute game—that they'd walk us around in shirt and ties to see the football field, and we'd have to play on the practice field or on the field where the Interhall dorms play their football games. We're thinking that for this kind of money, it can't be the experience they're talking about—it just can't be.

The camp was held the Fourth of July weekend. We stayed at the Jamison Inn the first year—it was air conditioned, and some of the residence halls are not. Pat wanted everyone to have a hotel-type experience. The camp went from Wednesday to Sunday.

We show up Wednesday afternoon. They have duffel bags with our names on them, with the camp logo engraved on it, our number is on it. Seeing all those little things, I thought, "Wow, this is unbelievable." The bag held all of our practice gear. We had shorts, tee shirts, and baseball hats with the camp logo on them. We also got actual Notre Dame-type cleats that **adidas** gives to the players. Already, this was more than I had expected. I had gone out and bought a pair and brought them with me. Having played high school football, I know running in cleats is a lot different than running in sneakers.

There was a walking tour of the campus. Tony Yelovich gave the walking tour. He started talking about things when he had coached in his early years, just the intricacies of the campus, not just the Grotto, not just the Dome, but all over the place—the statues and The Log Chapel—the little things. We were awestruck. I had tears in my eyes. During the walking tour, some of the other fantasy players thought I had allergies. I told them, "You know what. I'm not ashamed to admit this, but it's tears of joy because I can't believe I'm doing what I'm doing." This was only my second time ever to be on campus. I was so impressed that here was an assistant athletic director, a former coach

"adidas" is named after its founder, Adi Dassler. "adidas" is never capitalized.

here, giving us a tour and patting everyone on the back. You could tell Tony was in a genuinely good mood and happy to do it.

We're scheduled to have the opening-night dinner in the Monogram Room. The biggest deal to me, and I hope I'm not sidetracking, was that one of the coaches, Peter Vaas—a quarterbacks coach under Lou Holtz—was coming back to coach the camp. He had graduated from Holy Cross College, which is in the city of Worcester, Massachusetts, where I grew up. He was also the head coach there when I was in high school. I walk over to him, look at him, and I've got this big smile—he and I had never met other than I had probably gotten an autograph from him when I was about 15-years-old after a Holy Cross game. I said, "Coach Vaas…." He said, "Let me guess. You're Keith Cross from Worcester." I said, "I am." He said, "When I saw the roster, and I saw another guy from Worcester, I said 'I can't wait to meet him.'" I said back to him, "Coach Vaas, I said the same thing. I can't believe you're here." He said, "Will you sit down and eat with me?" We were having dinner, chatting away, he asked me about how things are in Worcester. We forged a great friendship from that night on. That was the highlight so far at camp. I thought, "It can't get any better than this. It just can't." He was then the head coach for an NFL Europe team in Cologne, Germany. Later, he would invite me, my wife and some other friends to stay with him for two weeks in Germany, which we did last year. We went to two games while he was the head coach, and he treated us as though we were family. He arranged everything for us. We traveled with the team, went to the practices, ate meals with the team. My wife and his wife and two daughters have all become close friends. Now, when we get Notre Dame tickets, we stay at Coach Vaas' house for every home game….

A couple of the coaches and **JOHNNY LATTNER** are there signing footballs for everyone. Lattner is just an outgoing guy, a great guy. He's up there in years, but he's got his marbles. He's reciting jokes about Coach Leahy. I'm thinking, "How does it get better than this? It just can't."

> **JOHNNY LATTNER**, the 1953 Heisman Trophy winner from Notre Dame, didn't even lead the Irish in rushing or receiving that season.

Then…in walks Rudy Ruettiger, to give a pep talk to us. The *Rudy*!! He said, "This fantasy camp is like my four years at Notre Dame. You're about to do something for a week that I worked four years for…you're about to do it for four more days." He gave us this great talk. I thought, "I don't believe it—that's Rudy." There wasn't a dry eye in the place when he told us about how tough his road was to get there and how much he envied us for being able to do what we were doing. He was the first real Notre Dame football player to welcome us to the fraternity. Just reciting it right now, I have tears in my eyes. It was such a special moment.

I thought, "How do these people welcome us?" A lot of us had said privately to each other, "Are we infringing? Are we doing something that the people here at Notre Dame are going to think we're sell-outs because we had to pay to do this experience? Or, it's not real because we're not 18-years old? Are we going to be treated less than what the standard should be?" It was the total opposite. Everybody we came in contact with was unbelievable to us. The coaches were amazing.

The 27 guys who attended that first camp were from all over the country. One guy was from England and he has become one of my closest friends. There were only two people at camp who were Notre Dame alumni—the rest were all "subway."

Those coaches beat the crap out of us. The first day of practice, we lost five guys to injuries. One of the alumni tore a calf muscle, stretching. He was an internal medicine doctor from Indianapolis. It was tough. The best way to describe it is—football coaching is football coaching. When you're at that level, and especially at the level of Notre Dame, when they coach, they don't coach half-----. They went after us. If we weren't running full speed, or if we were doing something, and they thought we could give it a little more, especially guys who were a little bit younger, they really pushed you. They were coaching football. It was really great.

Because we only had 27 guys there, we practiced as a total unit until the day before the game. Then, we separated. Everyone had to play both ways and on special teams. Up until the day before the game, we had two practices a day. Jim Russ, the head trainer deserves a ton of credit for keeping us in shape and able to play. It was one hundred degrees that first day of practice.

They let us use the varsity locker room. The first day, Thursday morning, was amazing. We eat breakfast at Jamison and all of us get to walk over as a unit. We walked into *the varsity locker room*. It was amazing to see the **HEISMAN** trophies, to see the plaques. It's an unbelievable experience to see your name on that locker, and your number and your practice jersey hanging up in it. All the athletic trainers were running around helping—taping ankles and knees, giving eye-black—whatever you needed, just like a normal day at practice.

I walked out of the locker room, down the tunnel to see the field. There, of course, was the "Play Like a Champion Today" sign. I thought to myself, "I'm gonna wait to touch that sign until it's my time." I stood at the top of the steps. I walked down to the sign but I didn't slap it. I waited until it was my chance to run down those steps. I was waiting for that moment since the day I signed up for camp. I wanted it to be special—I wanted my hand to touch that sign in the same spirit that everyone who's done it has. It was stellar. *We're in the locker room at Notre Dame.* Guys were taking pictures of everything. Our practice was at 10:00, but they let us in the locker room at 8:30.

They really kept game-day quiet. There wasn't a lot of hype about what was going to happen on game day. We knew we were going to play the game, but we didn't know what to expect. When we walked into that locker room Saturday morning, and saw our jersey hanging up—our game jersey and game pants, and new cleats—everything, wristband, armband—just like a game day. The coaches were wearing their coaches' polo shirt that they would wear for a game.

When we got on that field, it changed. The mentality of what we were doing changed. We thought it was going to be a grab-ass, slap-you-

> **What HEISMAN Trophy winner has made the most money? The 1959 winner, Billy Cannon of LSU, was arrested for counterfeiting in the early '80s and spent almost three years in jail. Technically, he is the only Heisman Trophy winner to ever "make" money.**

in-the-butt game. When we got on that field, you really felt like you were representing Notre Dame, wearing that jersey. How many people have an actual game jersey who didn't play football at Notre Dame? The great thing is that the Monogram Club documented what we were doing because we were the first non-varsity football players to get issued full uniforms by Notre Dame.

We have a Notre Dame Football Fantasy Camp Alumni Association tailgate. We've been tailgating at the baseball field—the right-field foul pole. The Monogram Club has given our Notre Dame Football Fantasy Camp Alumni Association two tailgate passes to every home game. They recognize what a special group we've become. The Monogram Club has really allowed us to become part of the Notre Dame family.

I've already signed up and paid to go to the Fantasy Camp this year. I have a couple of friends who graduated from Notre Dame and I say to them, "The reason I think the Subway Alumni formed such a bond with the university is because if you meet someone who loves Notre Dame, you instantly have something in common." Through that common bond, you tend to build relationships. Even if it's for 20 minutes while you're waiting in line somewhere or sit next to someone at the game, you build a relationship. It's not often—as adults—you extend your horizons and meet new people and make new friends. When you do, and when you have such a common bond, it transcends everything, and you don't want that bond to go away, regardless of what it is. For the Subway Alumni, it's Notre Dame. Every time we go, we make new friends. We meet new people. We have new experiences. It's just one of those things. Why would you want that to go away?

The margin of error in a college football poll is plus or minus 100%

IF GRACE KELLY HAD SEEN THEIR PAD IN WALSH HALL, SHE WOULDA DROPPED PRINCE RAINIER LIKE A BAD TRANSMISSION

JOHN RYAN

John Ryan, Class of 1955, is enjoying retirement in Wheaton, Illinois after a successful career as a physician in Carol Stream, Illinois.

There were four of us, all seniors, and all committed to graduate school, with the last semester off, basically. We were all sitting around in one room, and I was reading the *Chicago Tribune*. I happened to notice a little two- or three-inch column story that Grace Kelly was in Chicago for a press conference related to the release of her latest film, *Country Girl*. This was a gloomy, gray day in February in South Bend. You can imagine what that's like. I read it, and I said, "Listen. I've got an idea. Let's do something today." They said, "Oh, sure, okay, what is it?" I knew one of the fellows had a car stashed. I said, "Let's go to Chicago and interview Grace Kelly. She's at the Ambassador West Hotel." They said, "Yeah, sure." With that in mind, I said, "Well, we can go to the bookstore and buy her something to give her that would put a focus on Notre Dame." They said, "Ah, come on." I said, "All right. I'll be right back." I went downstairs and made a phone call. I called the Ambassador West Hotel and asked for Grace Kelly's suite. Much to my surprise, they connected me. A fellow answered the phone and I said, "I'm a student at Notre Dame. I'm a writer and photographer, and I wanted to come up and do an article on Grace this afternoon." He said, "Sure, come on. When you get to the front desk, give me a ring."

We drove in to Chicago in about three hours. We parked, went into the hotel, walked up to the concierge. We said, "We'd like to speak to Grace Kelly." He dialed the room. Some guy answered, and we explained who we were and what we were doing. He said, "That's fine. We're having a reception. Why don't you come down and have a glass of champagne." Somebody came down and took us into the ballroom of the hotel. It was pretty much filled with people. He said, "We've got to go through this procedure for about half an hour. When we're finished, I'll put you fellows in a side room with Grace, and you can have at her." So, that's what happened. They had a little anteroom off the ballroom.

Grace came in wearing a beautiful white knit dress, with her hair all done up. It made my heart beat a little bit faster. We presented her with the little stuffed dachshund doggie that we had bought for her. It had an "ND" on one ear. "Oh I love him! He's such a darling dog!" She did the typical, "Thank you boys. I enjoyed being with you." We had a chance to ask her questions for about five minutes.

"Miss Kelly, do you follow Notre Dame football? Have you ever seen a game?"

"Yes, I follow the team…I've seen them play in Philadelphia…but, as you know, Penn doesn't do very well against them…. My brother went to Penn and my sister Lizanne is graduating there this year…. She's president of her sorority…but I'm still a fan of the Irish."

In the early 50s, Penn was ranked several years. In '52, Notre Dame and Penn tied 7-7 when both were ranked in the top 12 in the country. Notre Dame had barely beaten Penn in '53 but beat them good the previous fall.

"Miss Kelly, do you take any particular pride in being Irish?"

"Why, yes, of course I do…naturally…."

"Do you really enjoy being in the movies?"

"I like the movies very much…but I have a part in a Broadway play next season. I'm looking forward to it immensely…I've enjoyed all my movie parts so far, with the exception of one…."

"What was it?"

"I'd rather not say…."

"You really don't have to…. We saw *Green Fire* and it seemed to us that you weren't quite thrilled with the part."

"Oh, I didn't know it was obvious."

"Do you have any words of cheer for the five thousand lonely guys down at Notre Dame?"

"You mean they're *all* lonely?"

"Well, no, I guess not."

"I don't have anything special to say except that I love my little Notre Dame dog, and I'll have it with me on every set. Thank you so much."

"Miss Kelly, we would like to have you come down and visit Notre Dame."

"I'd *love* to come for a visit and perhaps later, when I have some time, I'll be able to make it."

That was before she was engaged to Prince Rainier. We had some time with her and then after we came out to the lobby of the hotel, my friend, John O'Brien and I took some pictures of various subjects—ourselves with her and her alone. Initially, I had six or eight different poses that I took, and then after awhile, she went on her way. We went back to Notre Dame and headed straight for the darkroom. There was a weekly magazine, *The Scholastic,* that was published. My friend, John, wrote an article for the feature piece of the magazine, sort of a quasi-editorial, topical. The magazine came out a day or two later. They would distribute it by throwing a copy at everybody's door. It would stay there for a few days until it got walked on enough and, then, the student would pick it up and throw it in the garbage. In other words, there wasn't much readership interest. Those copies hit the floor…and they were gone. There wasn't a single one left after about an hour. We made about two or three hundred dollars that next day selling the pictures. We turned it into a sophisticated, yet tacky, commercial enterprise....Made enough to support us for a month or two.

Grace Kelly came from an Irish-Catholic family in the social headquarters in Pennsylvania, Philadelphia. She was the most elegant woman who ever lived. There was no comparing her to the other girls we knew. She was gracious and just absolutely gorgeous. She was very kind. When we were with her, she was not at all impatient.

In those days, if you wanted to go from New York to Hollywood, you had to take the train. About a year later, she was passing through Chicago, my hometown, on the train. I was engaged at the time. I went downtown. I didn't tell my fiancé I was going down there, because I was supposed to go to her parents' house for dinner. I thought, "I'll just go down and see what happens." My fiancé found out about it several days later. She was really p-----. That should have given me a clue that it wouldn't turn out to be a good marriage, but we were married for almost 25 years.

Ironically, at the rededication of the new Notre Dame Stadium in 1997, Princess Diana was referred to as Princess Grace.

Hey, Tony Roberts...Thanks
You were great!

I TIMOTHY

A CAMEL, A NEEDLE, NOTRE DAME

John Lynch

John Lynch looks like a Notre Dame man. The smilin' Irishman didn't go to Notre Dame, but like thousands of other parents, dreamed of his son matriculating there. After playing collegiate golf at Arizona State, he formed and later sold successful golf publishing and athlete management companies in Arizona. Lynch moved back to his native Chicago and became head of sports marketing for Motorola.

You grow up in Chicago…you grow up Catholic…you're a Notre Dame fan. That's it. Growing up, there was a real mystique about Notre Dame. Every year, maybe twice a year, three or four buses would leave the Catholic Church parking lots and go to games. Your parents are on it, and they're gone all day. It was "Hey, it's Notre Dame." Notre Dame was it.

Everybody and his brother know how hard it is to get into Notre Dame. We found out first hand that it doesn't matter who you know or what you know. If you're a legacy, if your dad or brother or sister went there, you've got a great chance of being accepted.

Our son, Tim, applied. He had a wonderful high school career, being captain and MVP of his high school's basketball and golf teams while maintaining an A- grade average. He attended daily mass, and was committed to the community with charitable involvement and service projects.

He had letters of recommendation from the Cardinal, Bishop George Rassas and several local priests who had graduated from Notre

Dame. He even had a letter from Father John Smyth, who at the time, was honored as the Notre Dame Man of the year.

Timmy grows up in Scottsdale, Arizona, and becomes a Notre Dame fan because his dad is a fan and because you get to watch Notre Dame every Saturday on TV. When we moved back here, we were advised by our good friend and Notre Dame basketball coach, John MacLeod, that Tim would have an easier time getting into Notre Dame if he were to apply from Arizona rather than from the Midwest. He said, "John, it is going to be really tough for Timmy competing against all those Catholic kids from the Midwest." Notre Dame likes to branch out and bring in kids from other areas of the country so you are hurting your chances a little bit." I am sure he was right but we had already moved back.

I took Tim to his first Notre Dame football game in 1994. Here is a little kid, 10 years old, who's heard nothing but Notre Dame. We get there early and the first thing we do is head straight to the Basilica. We walk in and the first thing we see is the entire Notre Dame football team kneeling in prayer service-all dressed in their blue blazers. For a kid who is really a Catholic kid, seeing the entire team in prayer before the game is something special. After the Basilica, it was off to the Grotto and a walk around the lake before returning to the Dome to listen to the Notre Dame band. It's a tradition to play for the fans before marching across campus and into the stadium.

After a short break under the dome, the band reassembled to get ready for their march across the campus. We are all bunched together with the several thousand spectators aligning the sidewalk—all waiting for the leprechaun and cheerleaders to lead the band across campus. The band is playing and everyone is cheering and going nuts. All of a sudden, the leprechaun stops, the band stops. I don't know why, as I have been to over fifty games, but I have never seen the leprechaun bring everything to a complete halt. He reaches down, takes off his hat and places it on Tim's head. They stare at each other, smile and exchange high-fives. People are staring and wondering what is going on. The leprechaun takes his hat, gives a gesture to the band, and it's off down the sidewalk to the tunes of the fight song. Timmy turns to me and says, "Dad, I think it's meant to be." Those were his words. I will never forget it and he will never forget it. From that time on, being back in the Midwest, we knew Tim would be going to Notre Dame.

When Tim applied, we had a golf video completed and sent to John Jasinski, the Notre Dame golf coach. John said, "Your kid looks small, but he's got good fundamentals and seems to have a mature attitude." The tape was a question-answer tape about life, competition, and family, while showing a selection of Tim hitting all kinds of shots. John said that he really liked the tape and wanted to meet with Tim.

After our initial meeting with Coach, a meeting was set up in the admissions office with a guy coordinating admissions for several student athletes. He had reviewed Tim's application, and felt that Tim needed higher test scores on his college boards. The conversation was informative and the criteria for getting into Notre Dame was explained as best as possible.

I sat there sort of begging for Timmy. What if I get a letter from the pope...? I said half jokingly. The advisor said, " John, it doesn't really matter who you have letters from. We look at each kid individually." He talked about the importance of grades, mentioned the legacies (alumni offspring), and the number of international students. I talked about the Catholic element, Tim's leadership roles, his charitable work, and the extra hours spent on high school sports activities. It all seemed for naught. He said, "John, everybody who applies here is a leader, a captain, an MVP, or a homecoming queen. Everybody who applies is the best of the best and we get to take our pick. We have to maintain our standards to compete against Stanford, Duke, Harvard, and Yale. That's just the way it is."

No longer is Notre Dame an all-male university accepting 1,600 young men each year. Now, being co-ed, you can divide that number by two. Take in to account the legacies, the athletes, the international students, and other factors, and you cut that number to 400. That's 400 males out of 17,000 applicants. Wow. Whoever said life would be fair? With faith and acceptance you realize that God has a plan for everyone.

It goes without saying that with each passing opportunity, there is a chance to start something new. Tim is now playing golf and getting a great education at Santa Clara University in California...and despite not being an active part of the Irish Tradition, we still cheer for ol' Notre Dame.

LATE NIGHT BENEDICTION

KEN MacLEAN

Ken MacLean is retired in Boston, Massachusetts, after a long and successful career in the medical supply field. He will never forget an eventful two months in South Bend 40 years ago. One name and one town in this story have been changed to protect the guilty! Everything else is 100% true.

In the early 60s, I played baseball in the Cape Cod summer college league with a Notre Dame player named Dick, who was from a farm town in Iowa. In the fall of '63, I dropped out of college and was moving to California when I stopped at Notre Dame to see my old teammate who was living off-campus at the time.

During the time I was at Notre Dame, we went on a road trip to Iowa City to his home state to watch Notre Dame play Iowa. It was the weekend President Kennedy was shot, and the game was canceled. The Saturday night of the day the game was canceled, we ended up with these girls from the Quad Cities. One thing led to another, and this guy, Dick, ended up having this gal named Suzie paint red toenail polish on his toenails. No big deal…at the time.

We ended up back in South Bend until December 13th, when Christmas break started at noon. My car had broken down in South Bend, so, earlier that day, I had taken the South Shore into Chicago and picked up a brand new Oldsmobile Toronado from a car dealer. We were going to drive this car to California and be paid gas mileage. We're getting ready to leave, and I said to Dick, "Wait a minute. We've been going to Giuseppe's every Friday night since I've been here, and there are always 2,000 Notre Dame guys, all of them better looking than us, and about eight South Bend townies. Why don't we go down there tonight—we'll have no competition." That night we went to Giuseppe's. It was absolutely true. There was no competition.

We didn't get home until five in the morning. What I didn't know is that Dick had told his mother in this little farm town in Iowa that he was going to be there Friday night...and he forgot to call her. Anyway, we don't get up until the middle of Saturday afternoon, and we take off for Iowa.

As we get near Chicago, I told Dick, "I've never seen Chicago. I'd like to see what downtown looks like." He said, "Well, I can show you a great view of downtown Chicago." It ends up that he was there for the Serbian National Convention a couple of weeks before. When I asked him what he was doing at the Serbian National Convention, he said he was chartering an airplane. It ended up he really was, but that's too long a story.

He has me pull up on Michigan Avenue right in front of the Sheraton Chicago Hotel. What we were going to do was go in there, go up as far as the elevator would take us, walk up some other stairs, take another elevator to a penthouse, go up some side stairs to a cupola. As we walk into the lobby, about a half dozen young kids descend on us and ask us for our autograph. We didn't know that the next day the Bears were hosting the Detroit Lions for the right to play in the **NFL** championship game the following week against the New York football Giants. When the kids asked us if we were football players, we said, "Yes." They asked for our autographs. So, Dick signed the name Jim Kelly, who was an All-American end at Notre Dame that year. I signed the name Frank Budka, who I knew was the Notre Dame quarterback that year and a friend of Dick's. So, we signed our names for all these kids, and they're all excited.

Then, we get on the elevator to go up to the cupola area. We could see that the other people in the elevator were looking at us admiringly and trying to figure out which famous football players we were. Again, we didn't know the Lions were staying there. We go up to the cupola—and he was right—it was an incredible view of Chicago,

> **More NFL games have been played in the Meadowlands than any other stadium. Until 2003, Wrigley Field held the record even though Wrigley had not hosted an NFL game since 1971.**

just fantastic. We come back down and exit the elevator on the first floor. There must have been 30 kids waiting for us. So, we suck in our bellies, and we sign "Jim Kelly" and "Frank Budka" again.

There was a bar in the lobby area called Kon-Tiki Ports. We sit in there and are acting like absolute jerks. The NFL draft was five months earlier than it is now, and that particular week, Budka had just been drafted by the Bears, and Kelly had just been drafted by the Dallas Cowboys. We're sitting in this lounge talking real loud like "How much bonus did you get?" and "When are you going to report to training camp?" We were thinking we'd impress somebody and get a free drink. Nobody paid any attention to us, so we paid and left.

In those days, there were hardly any Interstates at all so we had to get on a road called the Congress Expressway West out of downtown Chicago. I'm driving. We turned the corner, and there's a Playboy Club! At that time, in 1963, there were only a handful of Playboy Clubs in the United States and you needed a key to enter. Very few people had a key. It was every kid's dream to get into one of those clubs. I said, "Oh my God, there's a Playboy Club. I'd love to go to one of those." So, Dick, the farm boy from Iowa, said, "Well, park the car. I've got a key." I said, "How'd you get a key?" I should never have asked him that question.

We parked the car, and he said, "Hey, Jim Kelly made Playboy's pre-season All-American team. He was telling me about a party at the Playboy Mansion. Why don't we try to tell the people here at the Playboy Club that we're Jim Kelly and Frank Budka?" I didn't care—that sounded like a good idea. We walk into the Playboy Club. The bunny at the front door says, "Is the key in your name?" He said, "No, my name is Jim Kelly. The key is in the name of Dick so-and-so." That got us in. We go to this one room and sit at a really small table. The tables would seat two people and were very close to each other. We sit down and another bunny comes over and said, "Hi. Is the key in your name?" We went through the same exercise we had gone through at the front door. "No, the key's not in my name. My name's Jim Kelly, and this is my friend, Frank Budka. The key's in the name of Dick so-and-so." She took our drink order and left. We each ordered a beer. We'd had very little to drink in our lives at that time even though we both were seniors in college.

Anyway, at the table next to us, which is inches away, there's this freshly-scrubbed man and this beautiful woman wearing this low-cut dress. He leans over and says to me, "You guys play football for Notre Dame, don't you?" I said, "Yes." He said, "Hi, my name's Jack Crowley. I'm from Jackson, Mississippi. This is my friend Jo Ann." I said, "Oh, Jo Ann, what do you do?" She said, "I'm an actress." I said, "Where?" She said, "Hollywood." I said, "Did you ever do any movies?" She said, "Yes. I just finished doing *McClintock*." This was a new movie starring John Wayne.

Jack Crowley said to me, "Frank, are you color-blind?" I said, "No, why do you say that?" He said, "Well, in that Navy game this year, with the interceptions you threw, I thought you were color-blind. You cost me a lot of money." It ends up that he was a gambler as well as a maverick wildcat oilman. We're getting along great with these people. He said, "Come on with us up to the Penthouse." We go up to the Penthouse, and he introduces us to the maitre-d and the floor manager. We go over to a corner and he said, "What are you guys drinking?" We said, "Oh, we'll just have a beer." He said, "Oh, no, no, no, have a Stinger." We didn't even know what a Stinger was—it ended up being some kind of hard liquor drink with brandy in it. We said, "All right, we'll have a Stinger." The next thing we know, there's a three-piece band on stage and they're getting ready to play. We had told this Jack Crowley that we were on our way to the East-West Shrine game in San Francisco. The emcee stands up and says, "We've got some celebrities in the audience tonight we want you to meet." One of the celebrities was Jimmy Durante. Another was an actor named Robert Morse who was in town performing in *Something Funny Happened on the Way to the Forum*. Then he said, "We have two All-American football players from Notre Dame on their way to the East-West Shrine game in San Francisco, Jim Kelly, the All-American tight end, and Frank Budka, the starting quarterback." The band starts playing "The Notre Dame Victory March." Dick stands up and starts singing it out loud. I'm standing up, but I don't know the words to it so I'm singing that old 'wood alcohol' Notre Dame march from high school. I also had a blazer on. The blazer had my name, "MacLean," on the chest." After we sat down, Crowley said, "Hey, what's that 'MacLean' on your blazer?" I said, "Oh, that's a department store chain down in the Carolinas. The owner loves Notre Dame, and he sent it to me." We're just having a great old time, and these Stingers are starting to take effect. The next thing we know, the emcee says, "Hey, it's Twist Time with the Bunnies. Let's have our All-Americans start it off." Neither one of us could dance worth beans, but we get up and get out on the dance floor. It's just the two of us with these two bunnies. These two bunnies are so gorgeous that the Bishop would kick out a stained-glass window to get a closer look at them....or as Dick the farmboy said, "They were 10 pounds of pretty in 5-pound bags." The one Dick was dancing with had a little button on her hip that said, "June." It ends up it was June Cochran, who, just a few months before, had been voted Playboy's **PLAYMATE OF THE YEAR**, the very first Playmate of the Year in the entire history of *Playboy,* which had been around about a decade by that time. We're having a great old time. We return to our table. I mean, we were having a <u>great</u> time!!!

This big guy comes over and says, "Hi, I'm Jack so-and-so. I'm from Albuquerque, New Mexico. I'm the president of the Homebuilders' Association." Apparently, the Homebuilders' Association was a huge group that had just concluded their annual meeting in Chicago that particular day. It was the same day that it was announced that Ara was leaving Northwestern for the Notre Dame job. Dick was ecstatic because he felt Ara was an excellent coach and couldn't understand the rumors that Northwestern wasn't going to extend his contract. Dick said that he heard that Ara was trying to get the Miami job. Both of those statements later proved to be true. Anyway, this guy, Jack, said, "I love Notre Dame. I always wanted to go to Notre Dame. I want my kids, when they're old enough, to go to Notre Dame. Notre Dame is the greatest school in the country. You guys are so lucky to go there. Is there anything I can do for you?" We said, "No." He said, "Where are you staying tonight?" Then, it occurred to us that we

> **The late Bo Belinsky married 1965 *Playboy* PLAYMATE OF THE YEAR, Jo Collins, in 1968. They were married for five years...Jimmy Connors married the 1977 Playmate of the Year, Patti McGuire in 1978.**

were supposed to be staying in this farmhouse in Iowa that night—actually we had been supposed to be staying in that farmhouse the night before…and we still hadn't called Dick's mother. Dick said, "We're going to the Bears game tomorrow. Frank just got drafted by the Bears." The guy asked, "Where are you sitting?" We said, "We're not really sitting. We've got sideline passes." Jack Crowley leans over and said, "Well, I'll see you on the sideline. Bears' linebacker, Joe Fortunato is from my hometown, and he's got me a sideline pass. This will be great." Dick, recovering quickly, said, "We might be on the sideline, but we might be up in the press box with George Halas, Jr., if it's too cold."

So then, we told Albuquerque Jack, "We really don't know where we're staying tonight. We just got in town." He says, "I'll take care of you. I'm staying at the Conrad Hilton Hotel." He went away, came back and said, "I got you guys the Presidential Suite at the Conrad Hilton Hotel tonight. It's on me. Don't worry about a thing." Now, it's almost four in the morning. He takes us to the Conrad Hilton Hotel. We didn't even have any suitcases with us but he took us to the Presidential Suite with a bathroom way down at one end of the room and another bathroom way down at the other end of the room. He's talking to us, talking football and asking questions. He said, "Listen, I've got to check out of here in the morning. I've got a plane back to Albuquerque…but, you guys stay here as long as you want. Order whatever you want from room service. It's all taken care of. Don't worry about it. If you ever come to Albuquerque, please look me up. Sometime, while you're in the NFL, if I'm in Dallas or somewhere, maybe you can leave me a ticket." We said, "Jack, we'd love to do that." He left and went back to his own room about five o'clock in the morning.

Again, we don't wake up until one or two o'clock in the afternoon. The football game has already started, and the Bears were beating the Lions. We're hungry. We'd never ordered room service before. We didn't really even understand how it "worked" until we read the menu there. I ordered chateaubriand. I didn't even know what chateaubriand was, but it was the most expensive thing on the menu. Then, Dick ordered chateaubriand, too. It was brought up, and we couldn't eat even half of it. Around five o'clock in the afternoon, we decided we had to get on to Iowa.

About 40 minutes later, we're near Aurora, Illinois. There's a huge place there called Mercyville, a sanitarium. It ends up that Dick's aunt was a nun—the head nun at Mercyville and had been there quite a while. When he was at Notre Dame, he would go up there on weekends. He'd take the South Shore to Chicago and then the train out to Aurora. His aunt adored him. He could have the run of the place. He had a key to the gym and could shoot baskets at three o'clock in the morning. He would eat steak for breakfast. This was a sanitarium, and they had psychiatric nurses from an eight-state area that would come there for six weeks of psychiatric training. Those nurses couldn't go off the grounds the entire six weeks…unless they were with Dick. Then, they could go off anywhere they wanted and come back anytime they wanted. So, this was like shooting fish in a barrel. It was like winning the lottery…maybe better. Remember, the priests would preach that sex "kills" so most Notre Dame guys thought they would live forever.

As we get near Aurora, Dick said, "Hey, we've got to stop. I know this neat gal named Diane Matthys there, and I want to say hello to her." So, we stopped in there. It's dark by now. The Bears have already beaten the Lions. This Diane Matthys looks like Grace Kelly—she looks like Grace Kelly as a Breck girl. She looked beautiful. She grabbed a friend, and we went off, and we shot pool. We're having fun, and we got her back about midnight, and we said, "We've got to get going. We've got to go to Iowa."

We finally get to this farmhouse in Iowa at three o'clock in the morning. Dick's mother is up. I guess it's a habit, or a given, that if you go visit a farm, they'll always have a full meal waiting for you if they know you're coming. It's 3:00 o'clock in the morning, and his mother is beside herself. She'd had the state highway patrol out looking in the ditches to see if our car had overturned. She had expected us Friday night, and here it is Monday morning. She said to Dick, "Your father and I are on an 8:00 o'clock plane out of Moline tomorrow morning to Los Angeles," Dick's sister and one of his brothers lived in LA, and that's why he was going to Los Angeles with me for Christmas. She said, "We're going to be on that plane. You just make sure you are in California by Christmas." He said, "Oh, yeah, no problem." His mom said, "I'll believe that when I see the whites of your eyes." Since they left early in the morning, we slept late again.

Late the next afternoon, we take off. We're driving to Los Angeles in this brand new, expensive, one-of-a-kind Oldsmobile Toronado car, the first car to have front-wheel drive. Technically, the Tornado didn't even hit the market until the fall of 1965, but this was a prototype, and we had one of the very, very first ones. So, everybody was intrigued by this car. We decide we're going to head to California on Highway 66, which means we've got to go down to St. Louis.

I fell asleep while Dick was driving, and the next thing I know, we're crossing this big bridge over this big river. The sun is right in my eyes as I leaned up over the back seat. I asked, "Where are we?" He said, "Well, we're going into Memphis, Tennessee." I said, "Memphis, Tennessee! That's not on the way to Los Angeles." He said, "Well, when I was going through St. Louis about five or six hours ago, there was a sign there that said 'Highway 66' west to Oklahoma City, Albuquerque, Los Angeles. But there was another sign there that said, 'Highway 61 South' Memphis, Natchez, New Orleans. I think it's time we go see our buddy Jack Crowley." I said, "Whoa! That's a pretty good idea." We had a brand new car and we're getting our gasoline paid within reason. We stopped and rested by the roadside for a while. We get to Vicksburg, Mississippi, and have lunch with Dave Ellis, who was the Student Body President at Notre Dame that year.

Also, we stopped in a place called Clarksdale, Mississippi. We're in a Rexall Drug Store. I have no idea what we're doing in there. Somehow or other, we're always bragging to people that we're these All-American football players. We're starting to believe our line of bull. The wife of the owner of this drug store got all excited. She said, "Charlie Connerly has a shoe store here around the corner, and we ought to get Charlie over here." Charlie Connerly was a great quarterback for the New York Giants, as was Y. A. Tittle, at the same time. I said, "Oh, no, we don't need to bother Charlie." Anyway, she goes over and gets a box. She takes out a brand new product we've never heard of or seen before—a Polaroid Camera. She had a customer take her picture with her arm around both of us. The picture developed instantaneously, and we couldn't believe it. We'd never seen anything like it in our entire lives.

Then, we get back in the car, heading south. Our gamble was if we got to Jackson and Jack Crowley figured out that we weren't who we said we were, we'd just keep going to New Orleans…neither of us had ever been to New Orleans…and then we'd head west. If he hadn't figured out that we weren't who we said we were, then we were going to have a fun time with him. He had said, "If you guys are ever in the area of Jackson or New Orleans, give me a call. We'll paint the town red." That sounded great because in South Bend we were having a hard time painting the town beige. We pull into the edge of Jackson, just as the sun is setting. We're at a Pure oil station. Dick gets on a phone and calls Jack Crowley, whose number was listed in the phone book.

Crowley gets all excited. He told us to stay where we were, and he'd be over there within ten minutes. A few minutes later, here comes this big, white Lincoln Continental pulling into the gas station. Crowley hops out. He's all excited. He has some guy with him about his same age, named Cotton. Each of them was holding a drink in his hand. They actually had some kind of a mini-bar in this car. They were so excited. They asked us how long we were staying, and we told him we were on our way to the East-West Shrine game—"as you know"—we just decided we'd take the southern route—which made no sense at all…that we were going to fly from New Orleans to San Francisco. He takes us over to a place called Joe Adcock's Belmont Motor Inn. It was owned by Joe Adcock, who was a famous major league baseball player at the time and who was originally from Coushatta, Louisiana, which we assumed wasn't very far from there since Louisiana was just on the other side of the Mississippi River. He told us to get cleaned up and he'd be back to get us and we'd go out that night.

He and Cotton came back shortly, and we go across into what they call the Gold Coast in Louisiana, just across the Mississippi. We go in these places, and they have gambling—slot machines, card gambling. It was unbelievable to us. Dick was really excited because he claimed he had something that none of those guys had—"a system." He didn't hang onto that dream for very long. We were seeing a lot of things that week that we had never seen before. As we walk in, we're introduced to the owner, and Jack told the owner we were All-American football players from Notre Dame. He said, "Oh, my God, Bill Shakespeare just left here not more than ten minutes ago." Bill Shakespeare was a Notre Dame quarterback back in the mid-thirties who had engineered a great upset of Ohio State. I didn't know any of that at that time, but Dick did. He said, "Oh, Bill was here. I hate to miss him. We'll just catch him back on campus." He didn't even know where Bill Shakespeare lived. We're playing slot machines. Crowley says, "I've got a great idea. We've got to have a party for you guys out at the country club."

So, sure enough, the next night at the Country Club, there was a party for us. There were well over 100 people at this party, and we were the guests of honor with a receiving line—a receiving line, for God's sake! While we're there, this man comes up with a microphone in his hand and introduces himself as a local radio sportscaster. He wants to know if he can interview us. We go out into a lobby area where there was a huge fireplace. One of the questions that the interviewer ask to me, "Who are your assistant coaches at Notre Dame?" I didn't know any of the coaches at Notre Dame. I barely knew the name of the head coach—a guy named Hugh Devore. So, what I did was name five of our teammates from our team in the Cape Cod League that previous summer. He bought into it.

We just had a blast. Every night in our room, we'd take out our clothes to wear for the next day. Then, we packed our bags and put them in the trunk of the car. We never knew when we might have to leave town in a hurry. The next morning, the phone rings. I'm watching Dick on the phone, and his face just gets real pale. Jack Crowley was on the other end and said, "Jim, you won't believe what I'm looking at in the paper here." Dick, right away, figured out there was a picture of Jim Kelly working out at the East-West Shrine Game that doesn't look anything like him. Dick is motioning to me to get out of bed and get some clothes on 'cause "we're hitting the road." But Crowley continued—reading the headline in the sports page, "The Pittsburgh Steelers just traded Buddy Dial to the Cowboys for the rights to Jim Kelly and Scott Appleton." Dick says, "Oh, man, that's great. I'm going to play for the Steelers. This is good news." Crowley says, "Yeah, we've got to celebrate. Let's go. I'm going to come out there and get you." Dick said, "That's fine, where are you?"

It ends up, he's right outside in the parking lot. We open the door, and he comes in. He takes one look at Dick's feet, which have red polish on all his toenails from the JFK weekend. He looks at me and he looks at Dick. Dick says, "Oh hey, you're going to love this story. It's not what you think it is." It was a good story, and he bought it. It was a true story.

That day, as Crowley was showing us around, he asked us when we were leaving. We told him we had to leave that day because we're really late getting to San Francisco. School had gotten out on the 13th and this was a week later. We told him we were going to go down to New Orleans and then head west. I said, "We'll park our car in New Orleans and fly to San Francisco 'cause we've got to get out there to practice." He said, "Well, I have an office in New Orleans. I have twin girls there who work for me, and they're beautiful. I'll call them and you can just stay at their place in the French Quarter." We thought that was great. Life is good. Southern hospitality is better. We're gonna win the lottery again. God is good. Two nights before, we had learned that any God is great that makes an ace both a "1" and an "11" at the same time.

We get to New Orleans, and we meet these girls…and they are beautiful. We decided we would go to Pat O'Brien's that night, a famous bar in New Orleans, which at that time and for many years thereafter, served more booze than any single establishment in the world. We let the people there know that we are All-American football players. They had these dueling pianos, and one of the piano players introduced us, and they started playing "The Notre Dame Victory March." Nobody there got very excited. Nothing happened. Except, we're standing by the bar and this guy comes up to us and says, "My name's Joe. I'm from Brookline, Massachusetts, and I'm the biggest Notre Dame fan in the world. I've been in Venezuela this past year, but I'm still well aware of what you guys did, and I just want to hang out with you. You can just call me Joe Sports Fan." We were with the girls so we didn't want to hang out with "Joe Sports Fan."

We decided that since nothing was happening there, we'd better go over to the Playboy Club in New Orleans and try the routine that worked so well for us in Chicago. We get a cab and this guy—*Joe Sports Fan*—is trying to get in with us. We ended up having to literally push him out onto the ground. He was so enraptured with Notre Dame he wouldn't leave us alone. We went to the Playboy Club, and we do the same thing we had done in Chicago, but nobody knew, nobody cared, and nothing happened there. But, these two gals that we stayed with in New Orleans—not only were they beautiful, but, like so many women in the South, as we later found out, were incredible football fans. One morning we woke up, and on the coffee table was the *Street & Smith 1963 Football Annual*. It was turned to the page with the Notre Dame forecast, and there were pictures of Jim Kelly and Frank Budka. Those pictures didn't look anything like us. The gals told us that they knew we weren't who we said we were, but they liked us and they would go along with it anyway.

Even though we weren't Notre Dame players, after a while—when we kept telling people we were—we began to believe it ourselves. We were the same guys throughout the caper, but people sure looked at us and treated us better than if we were just our regular selves. Perception is reality.

Nothing I've ever done in my whole life was more exciting or more fun than my Notre Dame experience. Go Irish!

Oh, yeah, one more thing. We ran out of money in Tijuana on Christmas Eve. When Dick called his parents in Pasadena, they hung up on him. Parents today would send a limousine.

Can you read this? Miami Hurricanes can't.

Chapter 3

Exodus

On the Road Again

CHEERS, CHEERS
FOR OLD NOTRE DAME

GEORGE WENDT

Former Notre Dame student, George Wendt "hit it big" playing the role of Norm Peterson on the TV show, "Cheers." Someone once asked him how he was able to so convincingly play that role, given the fact that he took no acting classes at Notre Dame. Wendt replied that he had practiced the part non-stop in South Bend bars for three years, which explained why he flunked out after his junior year. Wendt was on campus from 1966-'68. He came from Campion Academy in Prairie du Chien, Wisconsin, and lived in Breen-Phillips, Pangborn and off-campus. Before the famous ND-Miami game in 1988, Wendt was one of the main speakers at the pep rally.

When I spoke at the Miami pep rally, I said, "I consider myself an alum of Notre Dame, that is five-sevenths of alumnus. I have some unfinished business, and I'm not referring to my junior year course of studies. I'm not even referring to my honorary degree, which, as we all know, is way overdue." I talked about the unfinished business being against *Miami.* I also said stuff like, "People think I got kicked out in the middle of my junior year, but nothing could be further from the truth. Coach Parseghian called me in to tell me that I'd pretty much taken sitting on a bar stool and drinking as far as I could on an amateur basis and it was time to move things to the next level, and do it professionally."

When I was a student, I never dreamed I would ever be up there talking to the student body. I said, "I promised my poor, dear father, George Wendt, class of '43, that I would go back and get my degree. I've re-applied to Notre Dame every year since. Apparently, I am no longer Notre Dame material." Then, I started screaming, and nobody knew what the hell was going on. I just started screaming. Chris Zorich stood up behind me and started screaming, too. Then, the whole team started screaming, and then the crowd started screaming. I had one of the students bring a red cape out for me and he walked me away from the microphone, like James Brown. I walked a few steps away and then I threw the cape off and ran back to the microphone and started screaming—totally ripped off the whole James Brown gig.

I had a blast doing that pep rally. There's got to be a video somewhere, and I'd love to find it. Bob Wright, the president of NBC, was in the audience that night, which was pretty funny. I saw him, and it was like, "Whoa!" 'cause he was my boss at the time.

I grew up on the South Side of Chicago. You hate to change anything in your life that got you into such a favorable position. I've got a wonderful wife and five wonderful kids and have had a hell of a career. I probably wouldn't have done anything differently, but it had to kill my dad when I left Notre Dame. It was probably, in a passive-aggressive way, some kind of separation ritual that I was doing—flunking out of my dad's alma mater. That's why it was such a great joke, if I may pat myself on the back, to say, "Apparently I'm no longer Notre Dame material." These days, you've got to be the valedictorian of your high school, and you've got to have astronomical boards, or you're not getting in. I still maintain oodles of friends from my days at Notre Dame and still follow Notre Dame. I can discuss all 27 recruits, or whatever they have each year. When Ty came, everyone wanted it to work for all sorts of reasons. The weird thing about Willingham's teams were they would get worse during the course of the season. They showed no improvement. When they laid down against Syracuse that one year—I'm not saying Syracuse in the Carrier Dome is an easy take, by any means—but they ran all over us. That game was maybe the low point of modern Notre Dame football. That game was a disgrace.

I love Notre Dame and was very fortunate to spend three great years there.

THE SECOND GREATEST STORY EVER TOLD

JOE CASEY

Joe Casey graduated from Notre Dame in 1973 and is a noted surgeon in Fort Lauderdale. The Chicago Brother Rice alumnus spends part of the year at his vacation home in Park City, Utah.

I'd always wanted to have a motorcycle. I was raised by a rather strict father in the South Side of Chicago. When I was a kid, I wanted to have drums, and I couldn't have drums. I couldn't have a motorcycle because he thought they were just too dangerous…and only hoodlums rode them. He didn't know that, in my spare time, one of the things we did was that at a friend's house, we used to take old bicycles and bolt on an angle iron and mount lawn mower engines and, basically, make our own motorbikes. But, I could never take one of the motorbikes home because he would just kill me if he ever saw me on one of them. A lot I did subsequently, before I finally got a real job after my surgical residency, probably was a very delayed rebellion against some of the rules of the house back in those days.

In 1992, I got a new Harley-Davidson motorcycle. Harley-Davidson publishes a road atlas every year as part of your membership in their owners group called *Hog—Harley Owners' Group.* This atlas is nicely detailed and has lot of information that's specific for the motorcycle rider. I was mapping out a route to the Rockies—whether to go along Interstate 10 or I-70. I happened to notice a red dot in the state of Kansas. If you looked closely, it said, "K. Rockne Memorial." I said, "I'll be darned. That must be the site where Knute Rockne crashed in 1931." Sure enough, that was the site near Bazarre, Kansas, which is right near Cottonwood Falls. The best resource I could find near the site was the Chamber of Commerce in Emporia,

Kansas. I called and mentioned that I had a map which shows there's a Knute Rockne memorial. I said, "Is that, in fact, a real location?" The woman I was talking to said, "Oh yeah. That's the site of the plane crash. There's a monument there, and people visit it all the time." That was good enough for me. I talked to my wife and told her what I wanted to do. She's learned to give me a little bit of leash in these circumstances as being the best way to handle me so she turned me loose.

I said, "Do you want to go for the ride?" She said, "I'll tell you what. If you make it to Denver, and you're still alive, I'll go the rest of the way with you." The ultimate destination was the Salt Lake City area. "I'll go through the mountains with you if you make it to Denver." That was the time constraint I had. She was going to fly from Ft. Lauderdale to Denver, and I was going to pick her up in Denver at an assigned time. I had a definite goal in terms of having to be there when her plane landed. Off I went. I made it into Georgia the first day. I had a good "long" second day and wound up in southern Illinois.

The next day I headed out on I-70 through St. Louis and across Missouri, through Kansas City, and got to Emporia. I stopped at a gas station there and asked an attendant where the Knute Rockne Memorial was. I got just a totally blank stare. I thought, "Uh-oh, this just might not be so easy." I was 30 to 50 miles from Bazarre. I went to a pay phone and called the Emporia Chamber of Commerce. I asked the fellow there, "I'm trying to find the Knute Rockne Memorial. Can you tell me how to get there?" He said, "I'm not exactly sure. It's out there near Cottonwood Falls somewhere, but I'm not sure exactly where it is, and I'm not sure you can actually see the monument. I think it's on private land." I said, "That's not what I was told when I called the Chamber a few months ago." He said, "That's the best I can do. Just try to go out there to Cottonwood Falls, and maybe somebody can point you in the right direction." I thought, "Gee, that's pretty vague." But, since I had come that far, I thought I might as well give it a shot.

I went to Cottonwood Falls, a little town with one main street. I drove down the main street which had a few little stores and shops. People are looking at me like, "Who's this weird-looking guy on a bike?" I was pretty scruffy looking at that point. I parked the bike and looked around, and for some reason I just wandered into an attorney's office, which is normally the last place that you'd find me—a physician. The attorney was not in town, but his secretary was there. I told her what I was up to, and she said, "Oh yeah, it's just down the road a piece. It's almost across from the Heathman Ranch. Let me call Mrs. Heathman and see if she can help you." She called Mrs. Heathman, and there was no answer. She said she could tell me where the ranch was, so she sketched a little map out for me.

I went down the two-lane paved road south of town—a bend to the right and a bend to the left. I'm going along and seeing these homes that are half-a-mile apart. I finally got to a railroad track and realized I went too far. I had to double back and eventually stumbled upon her farm. I went up, pulled into the long driveway and went up to her house. The windows were open, and the doors were open. I parked the bike and went up the steps and knocked on the door. I thought somebody was home, but there was no answer. I figured they were either not home and had left the doors all open, which, to me, coming from the city for most of my life, you just don't go off and leave your doors open….or else they were inside and hiding. Remember the Clutter family—the Kansas farmers killed in *In Cold Blood*? After knocking a few times, I gave up and was walking down the steps. All of a sudden, I hear a car pull in the driveway, and up rolls this sweet, little, old lady. She skids to a stop and says, "I'm here. I'm here. I'm sorry I wasn't here when you got here." I was just taken aback by how open and friendly she was. I told her what I was up to and that I wanted to see the Knute Rockne Memorial. She said, "Well, come on in. Let's see if Easter's here." Easter is her husband.

We go right on up the steps and into the house. I'm thinking, "This woman does not know me. I got off a big motorcycle. I haven't shaved. I've been wearing the same clothes for three days." I can't even imagine what I smelled like. We walk into the house. She wants to make me coffee. She wants to make me tea. I finally wind up having a soda. She's running around the house yelling for Easter. It turns out that Easter wasn't there. He had gone out to help his son move. She hadn't known exactly when he was leaving, but knew that when he went, he would be gone for a day or two. She said, "I'm sorry. Easter loves to take people out to the monument. He knows the whole story. He's got a key to the lock on the fence. If he was here, he'd sure take you out there. I have no idea where he keeps the key. That's his little thing, and I just let him have it all to himself." She was so friendly. Within a matter of moments, I felt like I knew this lady…she was so disarming. I asked her if she had any idea where the monument is. She said, "Well, I think it's at least a mile back off the road. People think it's right on the road, and you can see it, but you can't."

The Flint Hills is the name of the area out there, and it looks flat as you look at the horizon, but it's wavy, undulating land. It's deceptive. It was a very hot July day—really hot and not a cloud in the sky. She said "I'm worried about you going back there. I'm afraid you'll get lost. It's too hot." She wanted me to stay for a couple of days and wait for her husband to get back. I knew I had to get to Denver so I told her I couldn't stay. I told her I was going to take a chance and try to go back there. She gave me a rough estimate of where she thought it was. "Easter said if you went down the road, there was a corral, and that's where the locked gate is, and if you went straight back in from there, it was in that general area, but at least a good mile back." There was a wood fence all around the big ranch, which was hundreds or thousands of acres. I asked her if she knew the people who owned the land. She said it was a new owner and she knew who he was but didn't know him well. All she knew was that he was from Texas and he wasn't there all the time. She didn't think he was there at that time. I told her I had come 2,000 miles and was just going to take a chance. "I'm going to walk back there. If I get hot and really feel I can't do it, and there's no clue as to where I should be headed, I'll keep track of where the road is and will turn around and come straight back. I just feel like I should try since I've come this far." She says, "Well, all right, good luck, and if you change your mind, come back when Easter's here." She was just a sweetheart, and I thanked her and off I went.

I followed her instructions and saw where the corral was. I got off the bike and pulled it in off the side of the road where it was safe. As long as I'd been on this road, I had never seen a car on it so it was not a well-traveled road. The corral was located about a half-mile from her ranch. The sun is getting lower, but it's still blazing hot. I took my denim jacket and my gloves off and stuffed them in the saddlebag, figuring it was going to be a hot walk. I went to the fence. I was just about to give it a heave-ho and climb up and jump over, when I heard a sharp crack…and then another one. I'm thinking, "What the heck? Is that a gun?" I had asked Mrs. Heathman, "This Texan is not going to shoot me, is he?" She says, "Well, he is a Texan." So, that's going through my head and I'm thinking, "Is that guy firing shots at me?" I backed up and looked around. Finally, on the other side of the corral, there's a guy in a cowboy hat, and he's fixing a crossboard in the corral fence. He's got a mallet in his hand, and he's pounding some nails in. He sees me, and I see him. He starts walking over. He didn't look scared, but I was a little scared. You see a guy walking toward you with a mallet in his hand and he belongs there and you don't…. He had seen me about to climb his fence so I think he definitely had the upper hand. He was probably in his late 50s or 60 and was a wiry guy. He looked like he could handle himself.

I said, "Hi. Is this your ranch?" He just looked at me and said, "You're standing on my land." There was no smile. I'm thinking, "Well, this is the guy Mrs. Heathman was talking about, and I didn't exactly have the best introduction." I hadn't seen him, but he would have heard me coming up on the motorcycle. Having seen me come up on the motorcycle and start to climb his fence, I'm sure he thinks, "He's a trespasser." I quickly tried to disarm the situation by saying that "Mrs. Heathman said I might find you here." I figured he knew who she was and the fact that I knew her might assuage the situation a little bit. I then asked him if the Knute Rockne Memorial was somewhere around here. He said, "Yeah, it's here, back on my land." I asked, "Would you mind if I go see it?" He said, "No, you can't go back there. I've got cattle out there. I've got broken fences. You'll scare the cattle, and I'm not going to lose my cattle." He said, "What do you want to see that for anyway?"

I said, "Well, I'm a big Notre Dame fan. I went to Notre Dame. My dad went to Notre Dame, and my grandfather went to Notre Dame. My dad actually played for Knute Rockne on the freshman team. But, then the Depression hit, and he had to take a year off and try to make some money to get back in school. He carried bricks and mortar for the Notre Dame Stadium. By the time he came back to school, Rockne had died right out here in your field. It was devastating news. My dad was heartbroken because he'd thought the world of Rockne."

He said, "Well, what do you do?" I told him I worked in Ft. Lauderdale and was taking a cross-country motorcycle trip and this was one of the things I wanted to see on my way across the country." He said, "No, what do you do back there in Ft. Lauderdale?" I told him I was a surgeon. He looked at me with a little incredulity, like I was a tree surgeon. He said, "What kind of surgeon—a doctor surgeon?" I said, "Yeah." Just out of the blue, he said, "Where's your liver?" I said, "Really?" He said, "Yeah, where's your liver in your body?" I made the connection—he's testing me here and wants to see if I'm just giving him a line of bull or if I really am telling him the truth. So, I went on to describe where the liver is. He looked at me and said, "Bring your motorcycle down there at the turn-in. I'll meet you down there in my pickup, and I'll take you back." I said, "Back where?" He said, "Well, you want to see the monument, don't you?" I said, "Yeah." He says, "Okay, meet me down there." I said, "Why did you change your mind?" As soon as I said it, I thought, "I shouldn't look a gift horse in the mouth here." He said, "Well, when I first saw you, I thought you were a hippie, but you're a professional man, and you work for a living. You've got a good reason to see it, so bring your bike down there, and I'll pick you up." Sure enough—I went down there, he picked me up in his pickup truck, and we drove back. I could understand what Mrs. Heathman had meant because we went bouncing over little hills and through dry river beds. It was a rocky road and it was a pretty good ways back there.

Finally, we came upon it. To this day, I can still picture it vividly in my mind. I got out of the truck. By that time, the sun was almost at eye level and it's still hot as blazes. The whole place is just lit up with a glow. It's a stone obelisk. On one side, they have the names carved of all those killed in the crash. At that time, it was the largest aviation disaster ever. Eight people were killed. Around that is a fence, about three-feet high. I completely walked around it, just staring at it. I backed off and took several pictures. The man just stood back a ways and was watching me. I just stood there and stared at the site for a few minutes, just taking it all in and looking at the ground and thinking about what had happened there in 1931. I remember being in awe—

like time stood still—of the place and what had happened there and everything associated with it. I snapped out of it, thinking I had no business taking this fella's time like this. I said, "Well, thank you very much. I'd better let you get back to work."

As we were driving back in his pickup truck, I asked him, "What is it like having Rockne's Memorial there?" He knew who Rockne was and knew a little bit about it, but he was a relatively new property owner and didn't know a lot of the details…knew that there were a lot of crazy people who visited the site, usually against his wishes. He pointed out that if you looked at the carving on the monument, like in the "Os" and the "As," that they were chipped away. Souvenir seekers would go up to it and chip away a portion of the monument. I said, "That's a shame that people would destroy the monument." Yet, at the same time…that place and Rockne mean so much to them that they want a piece of it…so I had ambivalent feelings about it. He told me that every March 31, a group goes out there to visit it—and that's with his permission since it's the anniversary of the crash. He was wondering out loud if maybe they couldn't move the site closer to the road so people didn't have to trespass to get out there. I said, "That would be nice, but, at the same time, it's not the place where he crashed." There's just something special about that location. I could understand why he didn't want people traipsing across his property, but, on the other hand, it's less than satisfying to be a mile away from where the actual site is and not see it. I wasn't going to solve that problem for him at that time. We started talking about Rockne and the history of Notre Dame football…how it meant so much to so many people and that's why there are all those crazy people who want to go back and see that site.

I never addressed whether he was a sports fan—a football fan. I felt that if you were a sports fan to any significant degree, you probably know the history of any number of teams. I'm, first and foremost, a Notre Dame fan. On the other hand, I know a fair amount about Texas football, about USC football, Alabama football and college football going back to Amos Alonzo Stagg and Pop Warner. Any football fan is going to have at least a general sense of the history of the game. It was my impression that he didn't have any real depth of understanding.

When we got back to my bike, I thanked him. I told him it really meant a lot to me and how much I appreciated him taking me back there. He said, "Where are you heading?" I told him I had to be in Denver the next day so I was going to head back up to I-70 and get as many miles in as I could that evening. He suggested that I go up north to a junction and take a left and go on some of those state roads. He told me I would see a lot more of the country and see some beautiful land. I took his advice and took some of the state roads, and he was absolutely right—it was Norman Rockwell-scenery. Riding down those two-lane roads, you'd see kids playing and riding their horses alongside the road. There were houses with clotheslines where the mothers were drying their laundry outside in the sunshine. I saw men working on their farms. It was a special experience. That was a beautiful ride for about 90 minutes before I actually got back on I-70.

I'm not sure where that group who visits the monument on March 31 comes from. It may be the Notre Dame Alumni Club in that area. Later, on the phone, Easter Heathman told me one year Knute's daughter came, but, at first, nobody knew who she was. She was just a woman who was there tagging along and wearing black. They all went back into Bazarre and had a communion breakfast afterwards. That's when people began introducing themselves, and she introduced herself as Rockne's daughter. Everyone wanted to talk to her and it became a special thing. It was odd because she said she had never had any desire to visit the site. All of a sudden, she felt that maybe it was the right thing to do…maybe for closure, or whatever. She knew there was a group that went out there, and she just joined in, but she didn't make any fanfare of it

Once we got back home, on a Sunday night, I was getting ready to go back to work the next day. I decided I would call Mrs. Heathman and thank her and tell her what had happened. I got her number from directory assistance, and I called her. I told her who I was and that I wanted to let her know that I had actually run into the Texan and he brought me out to the monument. She said, "Oh, I know." I said, "How do you know?" She said, "Well, this is a small town. Nobody comes in and out of here without everybody knowing about it and talking about you so I know all about that. I'm glad you got to see the monument. The only thing I'm upset about is that you missed Easter. He sure is upset he missed you, and he'd like to talk to you." He was there, so she got him.

This friendly voice gets on the phone and he apologizes for not being there. Then, we got into the story about how he actually saw the crash. He didn't see the plane come down. The story was that he was about 13 years old at the time. They had just come in from morning chores and had gone to a store to pick up some groceries. He was out in their garage putting away some items they had bought at the store. He heard engines revving. He said that young men would race their cars on the highway out there in front of their house. He thought there was a race going on so he ran inside the house and called his two older brothers, "Come on. Come on. There's a race on the highway." All three of them go running out to the fence waiting to see the cars go speeding by. They get out by the road…it's dead quiet. They wait and wait and don't hear a thing so the two older brothers think he was just pulling their leg. They throw him down and put snow down his back. They went back into the house.

Shortly after they got back into the house, the phone rings. It's their uncle calling. He said there was a plane crash just up the highway from them, and they should get over there and see if they could help out. They jump into their father's pickup truck and drive up the road a mile or so when they see other people going out to the crash site. He described the scene in some detail, a mangled mess on the ground. He said there wasn't any fire, just mangled pieces of metal and wood and bodies scattered about. All he remembered was the smell of oil. The other observation he made was that he saw the bodies, and there was no blood. There were cuts on the skin, but there was no blood. He said he could see the fat through the skin like when you skin an animal...but there wasn't any blood whatsoever. He remembers loading bodies on the stretchers.

He said there was one fellow there who had these black rubber bandages around his legs. They had come unraveled and were hanging over the side of the stretcher. He ran over and picked one of these bandages up and stuffed it back up the fellow's leg because he was afraid one of the ambulance drivers would step on it and trip. He found out later that Rockne would wear those because he had phlebitis. So, he assumed that Rockne was the person who needed the bandages stuffed back up the leg.

To him, the most awful thing was the pilots. It was a Fokker Tri-Motor which had one engine in the nose and an engine on each wing, for a total of three engines. Obviously, it came down nose first and the pilots were just driven into that nose engine. Trying to get their bodies out of the mangled mess of the engine was gruesome. They took a lunch break and came back out to the site. He remembered smelling that oil again, and it made him sick. He asked his father if he could go home and his father let him go. He remembers leaving and then the next day learning that it was Rockne, and it hit all the newspapers. All of a sudden, there were newspaper people from all over.

He sent me some articles that indicated this was the first crash of a scheduled commercial airline. Mail planes had crashed and other private planes had crashed, but this was actually a scheduled commercial flight. Fellows from the Commerce Department in Washington came out to investigate the crash and decided that the wooden plywood wings on the plane had rotted and had caused the plane to break apart in flight. After their investigation, one of their suggestions was that— because of the burgeoning aircraft industry—they should create a special department and thus was born the FAA, all as a result of this Rockne plane crash. That was the story I got from Easter. Because it was Rockne and because it was a plane crash involving Rockne, it took on a meaning and importance probably greater than any other would have.

I'm very glad I went there. Sometimes when you're on an adventure or some such thing, you don't realize it at the time. I studied existential philosophy and existential literature as an undergrad at Notre Dame, and that was one of the things I remember. Sartre talking about how our experiences are something we construct in retrospect, and we give them meaning and structure retrospectively. This was one of those things. I had thought this was going to be just a monument at the side of the road. I would pay my respects, I would take it all in and be on my way in a matter of 15—20 minutes. It turned into hours. It took all sorts of unexpected turns, and I met all sorts of unexpected people—colorful people. You go across country, and you get on that Interstate and you see some things and you go some places, but you really don't have any specific memories. I'm thinking about Mrs. Heathman and the Texan. How would I have had this experience except that I was looking for Knute Rockne's monument?

I ran into a PAC-10 referee yesterday. Then, I backed up and ran into him again.

HE'S ONE OF THE BEST UMPIRES IN THE COUNTRY.
THE COUNTRY IS MONGOLIA.

MIKE REILLY

Headline aside, Mike Reilly, of Battle Creek, Michigan, is recognized as among the very elite of major league umpires. Reilly has been a Notre Dame season-ticket holder for decades. His very first Notre Dame game was, arguably, the most famous Notre Dame game of all time.

The first Notre Dame game I was at was that 1966 Michigan State game. My dad was in the insurance business at that time, and he was able to get two tickets. I had four brothers, so our family did a draw out of the hat, and I was the lucky one who got it so my dad and I were there together. It was just the atmosphere of the game—the two biggest teams in college football going at it. The neatest thing was to be there with my father and to be able to beat out my brothers for the ticket. It was perfect!

In those days, teams could be nationally televised three times every two years. Notre Dame was at the limit because our game with Purdue had been televised earlier that season...but the MSU game was televised "regionally." About the only region that didn't get it was Alaska. Notre Dame tickets were $5 each in 1966.

It was a cloudy day. Obviously, the 10-10 tie. The atmosphere was great. That was my first introduction into big-time sports. At that time, I hadn't been to anything of that magnitude where there was so much excitement. Can you imagine the media, with all the media avenues we have now, if that game were held today? Back then, in '66, you had your local newspapers. Didn't have ESPN going like it is now. It was probably 20 years later before I realized that I had been at one of the most famous games in college history. At that time, being 16, and growing up with all those Irish ties, and being a big, big Notre Dame fan, like my dad was, I couldn't wait for Saturdays when Notre Dame would play football....

I can remember being in Puerto Rico in the winter baseball leagues and following Notre Dame football on Armed Forces Network. I was sitting out on a beach with a radio to my ear, getting the Notre Dame scores and highlights. We'd go to the Dominican Republic to umpire in the winter, and they'd have Notre Dame football down there. My mom would send me the clippings of the game a week later so I was still in touch with Notre Dame....

The other umpires give me a hard time about being such a Notre Dame fan, but it's good-hearted. It's funny because I have umpiring colleagues from all the country—we've got Miami fans, USC fans. I would say, we probably have more Notre Dame fans than any other ones. Eric Cooper is on my crew, and he's a big Notre Dame fan. Jeff Kellogg, who lives in Michigan, is on my crew, but the bad thing about him is he's a Michigan fan. My wife is a Michigan grad, but she's forgotten most of those.... I've got Andy Fletcher this year, and he's an Ole Miss grad, and he follows Ole Miss really, really close. Too close. All of us have a lot of fun in the fall, giving each other a hard time. I have Kellogg on the crew, and we've beaten Michigan the last two years, and it's been phenomenal. It's been great.

The first **MAJOR LEAGUE** game I ever worked, I wore a Notre Dame shirt—the old baseball one, white with navy sleeves. I'm very superstitious...so, every game, I wore that shirt. I've been in the big leagues 30 years now, and I had that shirt 26 years. I would work every game in that shirt, and, after 26 years, obviously, I would have to wear a shirt over the top of it. It got so old and had holes. This shirt looked like moths got at it. One game, it slipped off my shoulders and went right down into my underwear. I finally had to say, "I can't wear that shirt anymore." Being the guy that I am, I cut out pieces of the shirt,

> **In 2004, only 17 of the 750 MAJOR LEAGUE baseball players had a college degree. No college had more than Notre Dame....The difference between a .250 hitter and a .300 hitter is one hit per week.**

and, to this day, I carry that in my back pocket. That's my Notre Dame shirt, and, I'll be honest with you, a lot of people think I'm crazy.

I'm so superstitious that one time in Milwaukee they lost my Notre Dame shirt in the locker room. I started ranting and raving. I said, "We can't work this game unless I get my shirt, so you have to go back and go through all those laundry bins and make sure none of those players got it." Sure enough, the clubhouse man came back with my shirt…and we were able to work.

I went to the national championship game in 1977 at the Cotton Bowl, the world's largest ashtray. Our Magic Carpet Line charter plane broke down in Springfield, Missouri, on the way home. We joked that the plane only stopped three times between Dallas and Springfield: once for gas and twice for directions…and that there were decals on the windows from the states Magic Carpet had flown through. There were all Notre Dame fans on the plane. The charter stopped to refuel, took off, had mechanical problems and had to re-land. *Three days later,* we were still in Springfield, Missouri. The marquee of the hotel said, "Notre Dame fans are the best." I was with my brother, Tim, and I said to him, "I know all about this. It's their responsibility. They've got to pay for the hotel. They've got to pay for our food and everything else. Don't put your cash out, just sign everything to your room." So, for three days, we did nothing but eat, drink and have fun with all these people." Now, we're celebrating the national championship when we upset Texas. That was probably the most fun experience I've ever had with Notre Dame. …yet, I don't know how close I came to dying on that airplane. It was a mom and pop operation. Every day, they'd load us on the plane and would try to take off. We were never able to go. Magic Carpet was the name of the travel agency. Finally, they brought in an Ozark airplane to pick us up at Springfield and we went back to Chicago. There's a reason that Ozark spelled backwards is KRAZO!

They were having a snowstorm in Chicago, and we had friends who picked us up at the airport and drove us to South Bend to pick up our cars. The snow was horrendous One of the kids on the charter was a student manager. Instead of my brother Tim and I driving back to Battle Creek, we spent the night in the Joyce Center in his room right in the ACC. I thought I'd died and gone to heaven.

YES, VIRGINIA...
THERE IS A SYSCO KID

ROBBIE HORTON

Robbie Horton is a resident of Suffolk, Virginia, where he is a regional manager for Sysco Food Systems. Horton, 38, attended the first Notre Dame Football Fantasy Camp.

I had just gotten my drivers license when a priest called my parents and said he had an extra ticket to the Notre Dame game and would I like to go with him. My parents said, "Sure, he'd die to go." So, at 16 years old, I drove the priest from Virginia to South Bend. My parents didn't find out that I did all the driving until I got back. We stayed at St. Mary's with the nuns. They had a room for us. From the minute my feet hit the campus, it was like this is the only place I wanted to be.

When I take a group of guys, I always rent a house. It's about a mile from campus. I pay $1500 for a Thursday through a Sunday morning. We have three bedrooms and a basement. With 12 guys, it's tight. The whole trip is about $800 to $1,000—house, car. Working for Sysco, we have some connections in the food business, but I also know one of the coaches very, very well, and they get allotted 20 tickets a game so when I can get tickets from him, I get them. I typically get four or five from him....I had a aunt who is 68-70 years old who, every game, locks herself in the bathroom with her rosary beads saying Hail Marys the whole time. She doesn't have a lot of money so I took her out there years ago. The very first thing she did was kiss the ground.

My oldest dog is named is Rudy and my wife's dog is named Lady because Notre Dame means 'Our Lady.' We had a baby girl in May (2006) and we named her Brady Elizabeth Horton with "Brady" coming from you-know-who.

'TIS BETTER TO TRAVEL WELL THAN TO ARRIVE FIRST

When we went to the Sugar Bowl in 1973, I'd never seen so many good looking girls as the Alabama coeds. We were outnumbered five to one down in French Quarter. There were buses to take us to the Sugar Bowl. The night of the game, it was drizzling. We got into the bus which the hotel had hired so it wasn't affiliated with either school. Just by coincidence—it was all Notre Dame people. As we were about ready to pull away, two good-looking Alabama coeds came running up...one of them very well-endowed. As they get on the bus, they start walking toward the back, and they begin to realize that everyone on this bus is a Notre Dame fan except them. They are wearing bright red. One of the women who, as I said, had oompahs that John Philip Sousa would kill for, had a big button on her chest that said, "Go to hell, Notre Dame!" People were coughing nervously as she's walking toward the back of the bus because that's the only place where there were empty seats. Everybody is giving her dirty looks. Finally, they sit down next to us. My buddy, to break the silence, looks at her and says, "Honey, I can't say that I like your button, but I sure like the way it's mounted. You prove that a girl only gets out of a sweater what she puts into it." The bus went crazy.

——MIKE BUSH, '74, Quad-Cities attorney

The night before the 1963 Navy-Notre Dame game, my uncle took me to The Bellevue-Stratford Hotel in Philly, where Legionnaire's Disease was later found. I met Tommy Longo, and the other guys on the team outside the hotel when they were coming in. Back then, football was not what it is today—it was real football—they blocked and tackled and leveraged. That's what the game was about. Now it's holding and whatever else you want to call it.... A few years ago, some friends painted an old yellow school bus green and gold. They cut a hole in the bus itself so they could relieve themselves as they were driving from Philadelphia to South Bend—they didn't want to stop the bus. They took all the seats out of the bus and got old couches from people who were putting them out in the trash. These guys are so crazy, they had no place to put their luggage…so on top of the bus, they build a rectangular picket fence to hold in their bags. When they went underneath the bridges on the Pennsylvania Turnpike—WHAM! These idiots had no clue. By the time they got to South Bend, the picket fence had been knocked off the top of the bus because they built it too high. So, when they got to South Bend, they had no clothes….

I went to the first football game in '63 at nine years old. I went to my first game at Notre Dame in '67 when we lost to Missouri. I was in seventh grade, and had gone with my two uncles. When I came home, my mother asked me what it was like. I said, "Mom, all I can tell you is I heard words I'd never heard before. I learned words I never knew before, Mom, and your nephew started a fight. We had a ball…."

In '73, Notre Dame played Alabama in the Sugar Bowl. I knew Notre Dame was going to win the game because my uncle told me they'd win the game. My uncle watched a team and could tell you if they were going to win. We got nine points. We won the game 24-23. I won $5,000. I was 19 years old, and I put all the money in the bank. It's not there now!

——**BILL O'LEARY**, Philadelphia area funeral director

I went to summer school at Notre Dame a couple of years. They had a program where students from Xavier University in New Orleans would come up to Notre Dame for the summer. Two Xavier guys, Renaldo Wynn, the defensive end, and I decided to get in this little Ford Escort and drive to Atlanta for a weekend. I'm 6'5" and Renaldo is easily 6'5"—both ways—so we were in the back. It takes two days to drive to Atlanta. Everybody had money except Renaldo. Everybody *barely* had money 'cause we were in college. Renaldo kept saying he had an uncle who would put some money in an ATM machine for him so he should have some money by the time we got to Atlanta. We all told him he had to pitch in on the gas and the food when he got some money. We're driving down. We make our first stop to get gas, "Hey, man, check that ATM machine to see if…." He goes over there and punches in numbers and…nothing yet.

We get all the way to Atlanta, and he never gets any money. It's like *I'm dating this guy!* I'm from Notre Dame, and he's from Notre Dame so the two Xavier cats aren't donating any money for him. Anything we do, I have to pay twice! We go to a club called Club

One-Twelve. I had just turned 21. Renaldo had champagne tastes, but he had a beer budget—no money. We were in the club and he said, "Let's get a drink." I'm thinking, "I'll get a drink…you ain't got no drink money." I didn't know what to get so I told him to order. He goes, "Let's get Long Island Iced Teas." I didn't know what it was so I asked this girl what was in it. She says, "Twelve liquors," and she named them all. I asked how much it cost, and she said, "$12 something." I said, "NO. NO. I don't want it." I didn't know you can't return drinks. As soon as I say I don't want it, the drinks hit the bar, both of them. This was a black nightclub. The bartender snaps his fingers two times. Lights shine on both me and Renaldo. Security guards are coming from every direction ready to throw us out. All this because Renaldo, our big football stud, didn't have any money. I go, "Alright, I'll pay." It was the saddest thing. I'm a college student—I paid in single bills, quarters, nickels and dimes in this black nightclub. You could hear the "clink," "clink," "clink" of change falling out…even tokens from the La Fortune Center. It was so sad…no women would talk to us 'cause we were clearly broke. I drank that drink—I nursed it—I drank it so slowly because it had cost all the money I had because I'd been buying our meals and stuff the whole time. After we got back to Notre Dame, I was with him the whole year and we got that same story, "My uncle still hasn't…." We played Bookstore Basketball all that year—not a dime. He went to the NFL and was in the Pro Bowl. If I had his money, I'd burn mine. So, my point is, Renaldo owes me $60. He is an established NFL player, and he plays for the Washington Redskins, my home town team. Please put that story in the book to show that Renaldo Wynn owes me $60. Maybe, it'll shame him into being an honest man.

——OWEN SMITH, '94, Los Angeles, comedian

Nebraskans are the most amazing fans I've ever seen. When Notre Dame played at **NEBRASKA**, every single person in Lincoln wore red from shoes to hat, and they were the loudest fans I've ever heard from start to finish. They won in a rout so there was really no need to

> **Academic All-American teams have been picked every year since 1952. NEBRASKA leads all colleges by a wide margin in number of players selected.**

continue their exuberance. They were the most polite fans I'd ever seen. They couldn't have been nicer to us. When we came out of the locker room and marched to the field, a very long distance through the concourse, through thousands of fans—Nebraska fans—they were saying "Good luck, Irish." The worst thing you heard them yell was something like, "Go Huskers." There was no taunting. That's the way it should be, but the way it isn't. They were the most outstanding fans I'd ever seen. When I "advanced" the security, their security and crowd management were woefully inadequate, yet entirely unnecessary, which was amazing. I wouldn't have tolerated the preparations they made for us except I'd developed a good relationship with the Nebraska Athletic Department, and they convinced me—and I believed them—that it just wouldn't be necessary. Ironically, the following week, we go down to Texas A&M—and same thing—tremendous fans, very rabid, very respectful, and nothing like the amount of crowd management and security that I would deem acceptable—but unnecessary. That Nebraska game in 2001 was amazing because they slaughtered us. It clearly was a depressing loss for Coach Davie. He was the last one to leave the locker room. Everyone else is out on the buses as he and I are making a long, slow walk to the buses. There is nobody around us. We were probably walking 100 yards or so. You know he can't be happy about the loss, not just the loss, but getting embarrassed. Just before we get on the bus, he turns to me and says, "How about those fans?" They were that impressive that even with the loss, you had to make a compliment to the caliber of the fans.

——*CAPPY GAGNON*, Notre Dame security

Name the Stanford coach. Win valuable prizes.

Chapter 4

Numbers

(Leviticus is on Vacation)

Buenos Noches, Coaches

PAUL HORNUNG WAS JUST A REGULAR GUY...WHO, SOME DAYS, WORE A CAPE

#5 PAUL HORNUNG

Few Notre Dame alumni have given more back to their university than Paul Hornung. No Notre Dame alumnus has been the subject of more tall tales, wild stories and fantasies than the Golden Boy from Louisville. He still holds the NFL record for most points scored in a season.

At Notre Dame, Hornung played quarterback, halfback and defensive back, punted, kicked off, kicked field goals, kicked extra points, ran back punts and returned kickoffs. He won the Heisman Trophy in 1956, playing the toughest schedule, in the nation, including the #1, #2 and #3 ranked teams. He ran a quarterback sneak 80-yards in Iowa City, and, in his final collegiate game—against USC—he had a 95-yard kickoff return and 215 yards, despite playing the entire game with two broken thumbs. He was Frank Merriwell, Horatio Alger and Jack Armstrong rolled into one. He even played basketball his sophomore year and did quite well.

Hornung sold his Heisman Trophy for a quarter of a million dollars in order to endow scholarships for Notre Dame students.

Hornung's 2004 comments that Notre Dame should use affirmative action for recruits just as Michigan and other big football powers do, created an uproar...and brought thousands of Notre Dame alumni to his defense.

The rumor, for years, had Frank Leahy saying, "Boys, there's a front door and a back door to the NFL. Notre Dame is the front door."

"Not so." said the very cooperative Hornung.

They closed my alma mater, Flaget High School in the mid-sixties. Senior year, my Flaget teammate, Sherrill Sipes, and I went to the USC-ND game. It was colder than s---. We didn't have a topcoat. We were freezing there on the sidelines. We're lined up with all the other recruits-to-be. We're going in after the game to see Coach Leahy. We were recruited by this ex-Marine sergeant, a great guy, I forget his name. Coach Leahy looked at me, and he looked at Sipes, and he said, "You two'd look good in green." We shuffled on away because there was a line of recruits behind us. I looked at Sherrill. I had to laugh and say, "We come all the way up here, and I guess this is supposed to be special." We didn't even get a chance to talk to the head coach. When I look back on Leahy, I thank him very much because he really came out with some strong language about me when I was a freshman. People have said, "He put a lot of pressure on you from what he said." He was quoted as saying, "He's the best football player I've ever seen come in here." He had me kicking against the varsity, doing kickoffs, punting. Johnny Lattner was like my big brother. Lattner would say, "Keep that 'g--d-----' Horning down on that freshman team. Don't let him come up and punt. He makes me look bad."

I knew of a couple of other guys who sold their Heisman Trophies. A couple of them needed the money, which was fine. I don't care what they do with their trophies. It's their trophy. When it came time for me, I was going to give some money to Notre Dame. They're in my will pretty good, or, at least, they were. I told Angela, "Look, honey, I can sell this trophy for about 250,000 dollars…. I want to give the money to Notre Dame, and I'll just get another copy." That's exactly what I did. I sold the trophy to a big Notre Dame fan in Jersey named Walsh. He bought it for 250. The stipulation was he'd give the money to Notre Dame—or I would give the money to Notre Dame so I could have the write-off. We did that. It worked out that Notre Dame got the scholarship money and I had a copy of the Heisman made and gave it to my wife, and we have it here at home.

I've been working with Notre Dame all these years to get some kids from Louisville. I wanted them to take this Brohm kid, Jeff's brother, Brian. He'll be a #1 pick in the NFL. There's no question about it. He didn't want to go to Notre Dame. He wanted to stay home and his mother and father wanted him to stay home. The point is they never did a g--d--- thing about going after him or calling him. They didn't recruit him. We had a couple of kids. Louisville's got a kid named Mike Bush. I told Notre Dame this kid could play anywhere. "Aw, he has to improve on his grades. If he improves 20 percent on his grades, he can come here." I said, "Would you give him a scholarship?" Notre Dame said, "H--- yeah." He improved 20 percent, and they never called him…never called him. I called them up three times and said, "You told me if this kid improved his grades 20 percent, he could get a scholarship." "Oh, I don't know if we can give him a scholarship now." They didn't give him one. I guarantee you one thing—if he'd gone to Notre Dame, he'd have been the best running back right now on that football team. They were absolutely strange when it came to giving out scholarships, and, as far as recruiting is concerned, the last few years before Weis were disastrous. They don't show a tremendous amount of interest, I don't think.

I tried to get Lombardi to go up and talk to Notre Dame after he stepped down as Packers coach. They didn't want to talk to him. This was after he decided to leave Green Bay. He was giving Edward Bennett Williams a "yes" in Washington. He hadn't signed yet. I had talked to him about a year before when he was with the Packers as a General Manager. I said, "S---, Coach, there's only one place for you, the best place in the world." I went to Notre Dame. I said, "Hire Lombardi in some capacity. He was the best coach in the history of football. He would be the most perfect match for Notre Dame." Of all the people, in the last 40 years, he'd have been the perfect match. He loved his Catholicism. He would have been the greatest image they could have hired. They wouldn't even talk to him. They had people running that university that knew nothing about what was happening in the world.

The people at Notre Dame wouldn't back me up during our little "dust-up." They jumped on the bandwagon when they said that what Hornung said was…. Hornung didn't say anything untrue, when you really look at it. If you're an urban football player, black or white—that's all I would have had to say *black or white*—you've got a tough time getting in Notre Dame if you play football in the cities of most of the United States. Jim Morse, my old teammate, stood up and talked at one of the dinners. He gave Notre Dame about seven million to build one of the buildings up there that's named after him. When he speaks, they listen. He got up and said, "This is ridiculous. We know Paul, and Paul's this kind of guy. He's done a world of good for the university. He's tried to recruit kids that would help out. To accuse him of being a racist is stupidity."

It was like Mitch Albom. I read an article after that fiasco that said, "Paul Hornung is not a racist. I've had dinner with him. I know him. I've known some of his friends. He's anything but a racist. His peers love him." In the very next paragraph, Mitch says—right in the article, "Well, what do you expect of a 65-year-old guy from Kentucky?" He's doing the same thing I was accused of. He turns around and generalizes that the whites in Kentucky are stupid.

I knew Charlie Weis would turn it around. I'm a big backer of Charlie. He's got one whole wall of Lombardi in his office about the habit of winning. These days, Notre Dame is going out and recruiting the way you should recruit. Weis made over 200 visits to high schools all over the country...and they're urban high schools. He's introduced himself to all the right schools. He's touching base with all these kids, literally touching base with them. That's going to help out tremendously. Kids are going to want to go to Notre Dame again, especially if you're an offensive football player. You'd be crazy not to want to go and learn college football under Charlie Weis because that's the quickest step to the pros. That's the most important thing these green kids want. They want to be able to get to the professional ranks. To go to Notre Dame, and to play in that system that he has, is the best way.

Before Weis, Notre Dame didn't make four visits to Louisville here in five years. There were six players who could have played at Notre Dame in a New York minute who came out of here. They never even once decided to put some emphasis on this area. It used to p--- me off.

THE LAST SUPPER

#85 Jack Snow

BOB ARBOIT

Jack Snow, the 1964 All-American Notre Dame receiver, passed away in early 2006, in St. Louis. Snow had contracted a staph infection following

Bob and Jan Arboit (left) with Jack Snow

his hip replacement surgery. Few people knew Snow better than Bob Arboit. They were classmates, baseball and football teammates at St. Anthony's High School in Long Beach, and roommates at Notre Dame. Arboit's father played football at Notre Dame in the mid-30's. Bob Arboit was a talented and popular catcher for the Notre Dame baseball team.

At Jack Snow's California service, there weren't as many people as I thought there might be. John Huarte, Nick Eddy and Vince Mattera—that was about it from Notre Dame. Then there were former Rams there, guys who never went to St. Louis: Marlin McKeever, Deacon Jones, Fred Dryer, along with their wives. There were probably only 100 people. The funeral was in St. Louis on Saturday, January 21. The service in California was the following weekend.

It was a typical graveside service. There wasn't a mass. Jack was cremated, and they had his remains there. The cemetery in Long Beach has this facility with a large chapel and a reception room, but Jack's reception was not in that room due to a prior funeral. Jack's reception was in the chapel, which was not very convenient because there were pews on both sides. J. T. (Jack's son, who plays for the Boston Red Sox) and his two sisters were up front greeting and talking to people. It was not easy to mingle with the people you knew because you had to weave your way through and around the pews to reach the other side of the room, and by the time you got there, they were gone or engaged with someone else. As a result, many who attended the graveside service and saw the reception arrangement chose to leave. It was sad from that standpoint.

Huarte said, "I've got to have some closure to this situation, Bob. Why don't Nick, you and I get away and go to a restaurant and just sit and shoot the breeze for a while?" I said, "My house is as close as any restaurant." John, Nick Eddy and me, and our wives, sat upstairs in the family room for hours telling stories and shooting the breeze while we ate. Oh yeah, we told some stories, and they were all true stories, give or take a lie or two.

When we go to reunions, people are just amazed about Huarte. I've always said, "John has always been the same way. You just have to know him." He is the most relaxed, easy-going individual you could ever meet. He's unpretentious—he knows who he is and what he has done and rarely talks about himself or his accomplishments. When Jack died, Jack's daughter called us forty minutes after Jack passed away. I immediately called John and left a message, "John, I know we've talked about expecting this, but it's never easy when it happens. I just got a call from Stephanie Snow, and Jack passed away about 45 minutes ago." I did not hear from him for two days. When he called, he made the comment, "Bob, I was home. I was sitting in my den reading when the phone rang. For some reason, before the recorder came on, I knew it was you, and I knew it was bad news. I listened to your message. It's taken me two days to get composed enough to call anybody and talk to them. The way I look at it, the guy who made me the Heisman Trophy winner passed away. I've always felt I owed him something for that. I'm going to go back to the funeral in St. Louis and see if I can get closure." He went back to St. Louis to the funeral, and he made notes, blow-by-blow notes. When he returned, he called me at my office. I asked, "How was the funeral?" He said, "It was a gray, damp day. The church was beautiful." I said, "Who do you think you are, Grantland Rice?" He started laughing, and then said "I was disappointed because it was a Rams show." I said, "What do you mean?" He said, "Well, there were three eulogies. His brother, Paul, spoke and never mentioned Notre Dame…

and Paul, like my brother David, is a graduate of Notre Dame. J. T. gave one eulogy…and never mentioned Notre Dame. Then, the guy who was a play-by-play guy for the Rams gave one and, naturally, never mentioned Notre Dame. I'm sitting there in a pew with **DICK SAUGET**, Jim Lynch, George Convy from our class, and Joe Yonto, the coach. That was the whole representation from Notre Dame—five guys. We sat in a pew—nobody ever mentioned Notre Dame in any of the eulogies. I was really disappointed."

At the St. Louis service, George Convy was sitting next to Huarte. Huarte said, "I mumbled to myself, after the last eulogy was given, 'Isn't anybody going to talk about Notre Dame?'" Convy said, "Don't worry. I took care of it." As they were rolling the casket out, the back doors of the cathedral opened and there to greet them was a bagpiper who started to play "The Notre Dame Victory March," in a dirge-like style. Convy had hired the bagpiper.

Huarte and I lived in Stanford, down the hall from one another, our freshman year. I knew him from playing American Legion baseball against him during the summers when we were in high school. I'd see him all around campus. You could be walking down the Quad in one direction, and he would be walking the other way. When you would walk past him, "How are you doing this morning, John?", you would not get an immediate response. It usually took 10 seconds and 30 yards…then, you would hear, "Oh, hi, Bob." It was like he was in another world.

He endeared himself to his teammates the very first day of spring practice going into our senior year. The first team meeting Ara held after Christmas—after Ara was hired—was in O'Shaughnessy Hall. Ara walked in and made the comment, "You can call me 'Coach' or

> **RICH SAUGET, ND '66**, had the rare distinction of being an official major league baseball player without appearing in a game. He was recalled from Triple-A, Richmond, and spent eight days with the Atlanta Braves. Bill Sharman, the NBA Hall-of-Famer, had the same experience with the 1951 Brooklyn Dodgers…even worse, Sharman was ejected from a game. In a late September game, umpire Jocko Conlan cleared the entire Dodger bench.

you can call me 'Ara.' Don't call me 'Sir.'" A ballplayer doesn't call his coach by his first name—you call him 'Coach.' The first day of spring practice, they huddle up for what was going to be the first play of Ara's reign. Ara walks back into the huddle and John says, "Ara, what do you want us to call?" I can remember Jack coming back from practice saying, "You will not believe what Huarte did today." Snow said, "Everyone looked at Huarte like, 'You gotta be crazy!'" Ara didn't bat an eye, didn't act like someone had never called him 'Ara' before. Ara told them what formation and play to run and that was it. From that point on, it was like, "This guy must be all right."

You've got to remember that Jack started 1963—our junior year—at wingback, and the only time he ever touched the ball coming out of the backfield, he went 44 yards for a touchdown. I used to tell everyone in the baseball locker room, "If they ever get Snow the ball on the outside, there's nobody in the stadium who will catch him." That was his claim to fame—he'd never been caught from behind. The 1963 opener against Wisconsin, he started it off with a touchdown, and caught a couple of balls. The next week, we go to Purdue. They threw the ball toward Jack six times and all six times he catches them. Jim Kelly, the All-American caught one of the two throws his direction. The following Monday morning, Devore calls Snow down to the coach's office.... I came back from class and Jack's packing his bags. I said, "What's going on?" He replied, "You'll never guess what Devore did." "What?" Snow said, "Devore said he was going to move me to wide receiver and get me out of the wingback position." Jack says, "Oh great." Devore said, "We're moving you behind Kelly." Snow asked him, "Why would you move me behind Kelly?" Devore's comment was, "We can't have you catching more balls than our All-American candidate." Jack walked out. He wanted to leave school. His dad spent two hours on the phone with him that night trying to convince him to stay at Notre Dame.

He didn't start another game after that Purdue game which was the second game of the year…he really only saw significant action in one other game…he and Huarte went in the fourth quarter of a rout. I really wouldn't want someone to do this now if I was coaching, but the two of them just threw the ball. Snow said, "We'd go in the huddle and Huarte would say, 'Jack, get out there and run a pattern, and I'll find you.'" Snow caught seven balls in that game. Then, neither played again...

Notre Dame goes to Michigan State. Sandy Bonvechio started the Michigan State game at quarterback. Notre Dame got inside the 20-yard line many times in the first half and didn't put a single point on the board. At halftime, it's 6-0. The second half starts, and they decide to put in Frank Budka at quarterback. Notre Dame runs the ball down the field a couple of times, gets inside the 30 or 25 several more times, still not putting up an points on the board. It's the early part of the fourth quarter. Michigan State is still ahead, even though we'd had all kinds of opportunities. Michigan State calls a time out. WNDU-TV pans across the Notre Dame sideline, and Hughie Devore, the interim head coach, is sitting on the bench between Snow and Huarte, talking. All of a sudden, Devore takes off his base-ball cap, throws it on the ground, gets up and walks away.

That night, when the team came back from East Lansing, I said to Snow, "I don't know if anybody has told you, but, during the fourth quarter, when Devore sat down and talked to you and Huarte on the bench, it looked like he got p----- off at something. He threw his hat on the ground and walked away. What was the conversation about?" Jack said, "You wouldn't believe what Devore did. He came down to Huarte and me and told us that the next time we get the ball, we're going to go in the ball game, and, if we lose, it's our fault." I said, "What did he get p----- off for?" Snow said, "Huarte told him to go f--- himself." ...so, they didn't go into the game.

I could tell you some Jack Snow stories that you would find hard to believe.

WHAT THOUGH THE ODDS
BE GREAT OR SMALL!

#45 DANIEL "RUDY" RUETTIGER

*Dan "Rudy" Ruettinger is the only college foot-
ball player to become a legend after his only
game, thanks to the autobiographical movie
"Rudy." The Joliet native lives in Las Vegas. He
does motivational speeches and is in the soft
drink business.*

You know when that dream starts. It starts back when we're
children. how dreams happen—they happen because you're
influenced by something. I was influenced by the game itself
and the loyalty my dad had every Saturday when Notre Dame played.
What I saw in my dad was hope. When Notre Dame won, it created
hope. That's what instilled that enthusiasm in me.

You don't realize anything about a movie until years later. When I
saw the movie *Rocky,* I said, "This is interesting." I watched the
movie *Rocky,* and Rocky "won," of course. It was that fiber of America. It just resonated against all odds. The guy is given a second
chance, and he starts getting excited about it. He's knocked down,
and the reality hits, "I really don't belong here." Then, he gets
inspired by someone or something, and he keeps working hard.
Then, he's in the ring, and what happens? He gets hit. He gets mad.
He hits back. He finds out he does belong there. That's the movie that
inspired me. That's the Rudy story.

Then, in 1989, the movie *Field of Dreams*—that's the imagination,
that's the fantasy. You mix the fantasy with reality. All of a sudden, I
have a movie. I start projecting that in my head. How do you go tell
people? You can't. People think you're crazy. People say, "Aw, you
don't know anything," or "It's not going to happen," or whatever you
hear. You're still going to hear it. The *Rudy* movie resonated from
movies like *Rocky* and *Field of Dreams.*

In the '80s, I was selling insurance door-to-door in a farming area around Washington, D. C., and I couldn't sell insurance. I mean, I was selling it, but I was having a hard time selling it that day. My attitude wasn't right. The last door I knocked on was a family. I said, "I'm not going to sell them insurance. I'm just going to tell them my story." I knew they were having tough times.

I told the family my struggles, and how I got to where I got. As I was telling it, it was almost like telling a movie. I was thinking of *Rocky*. I was thinking of *Field of Dreams*. I was putting all these in my head as I would tell the story. I could see the family being inspired by this. I said, "Maybe, I do have something here." That's when I really started getting serious about putting this together. "I do have a story." The more I told the story, the more people connected to it. It was such a big connection. It wasn't about a guy losing his leg. It wasn't about a guy coming back from a tragedy. It was about a common guy. We all deal with the reality of life's struggles. That's what they connected to. That's why I thought I had a movie. I saw people connect to the message.

I started writing it down. I wrote down little scenes. As I sat in insurance classes or sat in these seminars, instead of listening, I would write movie scenes down. Then, I would present them. "What do you guys think of this?" Everybody would get excited, but the reality is—how are you going to do it? That was the big question. I had no idea. Other than, I know this is a story everyone would love 'cause it's not about me or Notre Dame, it's about everybody. I knew the message was there. I went on my journey.

The making of the movie was bigger and harder than going to Notre Dame 'cause you're dealing with Hollywood and Notre Dame—two powers. Neither one of them wanted *Rudy*.

I went out to Hollywood. I asked a friend where the producers hung out. He told me the Carnegie Deli. Who's the first guy I meet? Jake Steinfeld, "Body by Jake." He just happened to be there with his entourage of people. I pitched him the story, and he liked it. Then, he told me he wanted to buy the rights, and he wanted to play Rudy. I said, "I don't think so." I said "no" to him because he didn't get the message. It's not about Jake. This is about a message. Jake was seeing it as an entrepreneur. He wanted to get in acting. He was a great guy. He's not Rudy. I didn't want to hurt his feelings, but I didn't want to get tied in like that.

I kept going. I went back to Notre Dame and met a guy by the name of Bob Gladieux, '69. He told me about his friend Ron Dushney. Ron Dushney told me about his friend Jason Miller. Jason Miller just happened to be a Pulitzer Prize winner writer of *That Championship Season*. He loved Notre Dame. He was either finishing or ready to finish the *Mary Thomas Story*, his mother's story. I went out to see Jason, and he liked it. He's a big Notre Dame fan. That went on for a year, maybe a year-and-a-half, and nothing happened. Finally, I went another route. I told Jason, because he led me to believe that this could be a movie that I was going to make sure he would have a part of that movie someway, somehow. He played Ara Parseghian in the movie. But, Jason didn't end up writing the movie script.

The people who act smart—those are the guys I don't want to be around. Dan Devine and I had a great relationship, even though we had to show him as a "heavy" in the movie. We talked about it extensively. He was willing to carry that cross. What we had to do was represent other coaches' attitudes, and we couldn't do that through many different scenes—we had to do it through one scene. He had to be the guy. He said, "Well, if it's going to help you, Rudy, in the movie and the message, I'm in." That was his attitude. Everyone looked at that movie like he was a bad coach—he was a great coach.

In California, I was selling insurance to earn a living. I worked for Ryan & Associates. I would go to car dealerships and set up their finance departments. That's how I survived there…. I went back to South Bend and worked for a car dealer. I lived in a condominium a couple of blocks from Notre Dame. That was neat 'cause I was right there. Absolutely nothing was going on now with the possibility of a movie. I had to refocus my energy to make a living. Every now and then, I would walk over to Notre Dame and tell the story, and I would get the same attitude, "We're not interested."

Then, I would tell John Stratigos, a hotel manager at the Jamison Inn in South Bend, my problems in Hollywood. He listened to me for two years, if not longer. He called me one day and said, "Rudy, you need to speak to my brother. He is really excited about what I've been telling him about your story. He loves your story. He thinks your story is "it." He can help you get that movie made." I said, "Really?" He said, "There's no guarantees, Rudy, but he can introduce you to the people that can get things like this done." I said, "Man, I'd love to meet him." He lived in Bloomington, and he drove to South Bend, and we met. He said, "You need to meet my friend, Angelo Pizzo, the guy who wrote *Hoosiers*." They were roommates at **IU** and they were involved in that movie…and away I went. I went to California to meet Angelo. Angelo never showed up for our meeting.

I thought, "That's it." But, because of that last bit of hope, I walked outside the restaurant, and there he was—the mailman. He was happy as could be. I said, "Man, where are you from to be this happy?" "I'm from Michigan." Now, think about that statement. He could be passing mail out in the snow, but he's in California. Maybe he didn't like his job, but he was happy. We just connected. I said, "I'm from Indiana." We started talking and before I knew it, the mailman was telling me where Angelo Pizzo lived. That's how the movie got written. I went over and knocked on the door and said, "You're late for lunch." He said, "How did you find me?" I said, "It's none of your business."

Listen to this. This is true. Never think about the facts or reality of this deal 'cause it will haunt you. It will scare you. You won't ever do it. There are too many obstacles. I always stayed in the dream and fantasy stage. I let the facts take care of themselves. That's how it got made. If you deal with reality, I'm going to tell you right now it won't happen. Reality is real. It won't allow it to happen. If you deal with fantasy and dreams and allow reality to happen, it works. It doesn't make sense—but it made sense to me, and that's how I did it.

I didn't listen to the negatives. That's it. I didn't listen to the obstacles. They were there right in front of me. It's true what they were saying. They were absolutely right, but I did not allow that to stop me.

One day, Johnny's brother called and said, "Did Angelo call yet?" I said, "No." He said, "I'll let him tell you. I'm not telling you." I said,

> **By winning percentage, Indiana ranks 12th in all-time Big Ten Football standings behind the University of Chicago.**

"What is it?" He said, "I can't tell you…but you'll be happy." Angelo did call me. He had sold the movie rights to Tri-Star Pictures. He went to lunch with a producer named Rob Free, which was a god-send. Rob Free also was tied in with Orion Films who did *Hoosiers,* and they were looking for another sports movie. They asked Angelo and David, "You know of any sports movies?" It was a good thing I'd been bugging these guys for two years, huh?

I'm telling you. *Rudy* is just a miracle. Think about it—why would they make a story of Notre Dame? At that time, sports movies didn't make that much money, and they were all a risk. Why would this thing get done? It was just people who believed in it and made it happen. You're not happy till you see it. You realize it's a movie when you see it up on the big screen. You realize it's working when the crew comes out and starts filming. It's amazing.

The first time I saw it was in the editing room. I was involved in all of it. We'd see a director's cut, a rough cut. I'm sitting there with the assistant editor, and David Rosenblum, a wonderful editor, says, "Rudy, go in the room there, all by yourself, and I'll have the assistant go with you. You guys sit there and watch it." It was overwhelming. I got caught up in the emotion of it. It worked. I said, "If this worked on me, geez, what's it going to do to people?" And, it's my story. It's kind of like it wasn't my story when I was watching it. It was Sean Astin I was involved with. I wanted him to win.

It was awesome to go back to Joliet, Illinois, my home town, for the premiere. You saw the old theater you used to go to as a child—now you're in there watching a movie with your family and friends and people you've never met before—2,500 people. It was an amazing feeling. You saw the people get caught up in the emotion of it. That was a key—seeing my family get caught up in the journey. They really got caught up in that moment of victory. Afterward, people came around wanting an autograph. They were crying and hugging me. It was an emotional moment. They thanked me. I heard a lot of thank-yous.

We had four premieres—L. A., New York, Joliet and in South Bend. We had a big premiere at the Morris Civic Center. We had a great turn-out, almost 3,000 people. Ara Parseghian was there. I was more nervous about him being there than anyone. He's one of those people in your life if you don't do right, he'll smack you. I wanted him to like the movie. I didn't want him to criticize the movie. Right? He loved it.

We filmed for 32 days at Notre Dame. They shoot a movie pretty quick. We heard remarks when we were there shooting. You'd hear people say, "That goofy Rudy. What the hell's he doing?" You'd hear all that stuff. I used their negative energy to get the movie made, anyhow, so it didn't matter what they said.

If I would have listened to those "whatevers," I wouldn't have the mother write me a letter saying how the movie *Rudy* has changed her son's behavior. He had leukemia at six years old. He had a bone marrow transplant and chemotherapy, and it triggered a bad behavior problem. They didn't know what to do with the kid. The grandmother sat the kid down and had him watch the movie *Rudy* with her. He's worn the movie out. He watched it for the last 10 years, and it's really changed his whole behavior. He doesn't even have cancer anymore. It's a thing of hope, of struggle, and these are the things. To have a mother come up to you and say, "My kid's playing basketball because of you. Thank you, Rudy. God bless you, Rudy. I love you, Rudy. He thought he was too short and now he's in the NBA, J. J. Redick." I had the Colorado Avalanche call me when they won the Stanley Cup to have me give out the Stanley Cups. They used the movie clips during the playoffs to inspire the team. So, that tells you, it's a culture thing. Thank God, it's not about me 'cause it would be boring, wouldn't it? It was the message.

People go to my web site, www.rudyinternational.com. A lot of people have said to me that they had a better story than *Rudy.* I just encourage them to do their story—to get it done. I tell them that I can't do it for them. I really don't know how I got mine done—I'm telling you right now. I don't know, but it happened. If you believe in it, develop it and do it—you'll find a way to get it done.

My life changed the minute I made the decision to do the movie, to be honest. Attitude has a lot to do with where you go in life and how you look at things. When my attitude changed, people saw my behavior. The best advice I got from Mike Leep, owner of the car dealership, was, "Rudy, you need to go out and spread this message. I know you're not going to leave on your own, so I'm going to just fire you. How's that?" I said, "Thanks. That's the best firing I ever had." He's a big *Rudy* fan. I told him the story when I was working for him. He loved it. He always brought me in, and I had to tell my story. Because of that, all the preparation I had from car sales meetings, from insurance sales meetings, that preparation paid off for my speaking. I've been doing that for 12 years and haven't stopped. I've been booked 60-70-80 times a year.

All my teammates at Notre Dame must have been astounded when this happened. Willie Fry was my best mentor in this whole thing. Luther Bradley and all these great guys who were in the trenches with me knew what a struggle it was. You don't hear too much from the All-Americans. We did have to take a lot of artistic license in doing the movie. We had to do that combination of the coach. And, the players—how we had to not show the players or name them, but we showed their attitude, if that makes sense. The groundskeeper guy was a composite of three guys. It was important that I get that janitor in there with those other people. Remember, after football games, I had to go sweep down the stadium.

In 1966,
ND beat USC 51-0
USC was lucky
to score 0

center for us. Notre Dame forced the inbound pass to go to Cunningham, who was way out beyond the top of the key. Cunningham takes a jump shot with the highest arc you've ever seen in your life. The horn goes off, the Notre Dame students charge the floor because they've just scored a major upset. Eventually, Cunningham's shot came down—right through the hoop—forced an overtime. Then, we won in overtime.

Another time, we went in there to the new arena. Our United charter was the last plane out of South Bend before a huge blizzard hit. Ten minutes later, and we would have been there for two days, but, as it was, our players all made their classes in Chapel Hill the next morning.

Another Notre Dame memory—I think it was 1987, and we were #1 in the country, and we went in to South Bend. Kenny Smith couldn't play, and we got beat. I think Notre Dame has beaten more #1-ranked teams in basketball than any other college in the country.

In 1991, my golf handicap was seven—the best it's ever been. I was a nine two years ago, and I'm a 14 today—at 75 years of age. I've lost a lot of yardage. Roy Williams has me working out three days a week. I never worked out for 50 years. Now, I've been lifting, and maybe I can get 10 yards back on my drives.

My shock! This is my ninth year out of coaching basketball—my first trip to Notre Dame seemed like last season instead of 43 years ago. I don't know where those nine years went. It just became fast all of a sudden.

When Joe Paterno
takes off his glasses,
does his nose come off too?

HEAR ME NOW, LISTEN TO ME LATER

JEFF JEFFERS

Jeff Jeffers grew up in Neosho, Missouri, rooting for Notre Dame and the St. Louis Cardinals. After graduation from the University of Tulsa, he failed his physical for the Marine Corps and headed to Notre Dame to study for his Masters. It is now decades later, and he's still in South Bend as the long-time sports guru of WNDU-TV.

In Neosho, Missouri, there aren't many of us. You grow up...and Notre Dame's the *house on the hill*. If you have any interest in football, and you're Irish-Catholic, that was like heaven. My senior year at Tulsa, a buddy of mine and I took a train, hitchhiked, took a bus *and* rented a car—which I'm sure there's still a warrant out for, but the statute of limitations has expired on that one—but we got from Tulsa to South Bend for the Air Force game. Little did I know that was Ara's last home game. I was sitting there in the 60th row of Notre Dame Stadium. I just had the feeling that so many people have had. It's like "This is the greatest place in the world."

South Bend is a fantastic place to raise a family. It's a neat media-market town that plays bigger in the fall in terms of my profession. You can do a lot worse. I've been to a lot of other 'so-called' college towns that I don't think hold a candle to South Bend.

At two-a-days in 2005, I realized Charlie was going to "turn it." At fall practice, I knew this guy was going to get it done. You didn't have a lot of guys walking around injured. There was an electricity to two-a-days that had not been there in years. He took no guff off anybody—big, small or in-between. He was imminently fair and imminently intelligent.

Guys like Weis win 'cause they're good coaches. They're better than the people they replace. It's not just Xs and Os. It's everything in addition to that. I became friends with all these coaches, but, that's after the fact. People say to me, "You're too close to be objective." I look at it just the opposite way.

If you'd ask Charlie Weis, "Are you good friends with Jeff Jeffers?" "Well, he's a friend." But, Charlie has very few good friends— Parcells, Belichick, Maura—his wife. You can say that for almost all good coaches. I would like to hope that I'm a friend of his. I covered Ty Willingham for three years—we never had a cross word, ever, ever. I don't consider him a close friend, but I consider him 'a' friend. I certainly admire him for a lot of things. Same thing with Bob Davie. We did not end well. We had some very harsh words with each other. It broke my heart because I like Bob. Time heals a lot of *misconceptions*.... Davie lives in Phoenix now. He and Joanne moved out there a couple of years ago. Charlie Weis bought his house here.

I had known of Lou Holtz when he was at Arkansas because both my parents are Arkansas grads. I knew how good a coach he was, and I knew how much he loved Notre Dame. When he was at Minnesota, I would go and interview all the Big 10 coaches at a summer meeting in Chicago. He and I never talked about Minnesota—we talked about Notre Dame. He would ask me tons of questions.

He gets the ND job. You knew, at his first press conference, much like Charlie, this guy was not screwing around. He had a job to do. He was going to do it. And, he was going to bring Notre Dame back. He's probably one of the most complex individuals I've ever met for a person who claims simplicity. He's brilliant. He's very mercurial with his emotions. His heart is diametrically larger. There are countless former Notre Dame players who got to law school or med school or in the NFL or into coaching because of one phone call from Lou Holtz. I love Lou Holtz. I learned more football from him than anybody else. I learned a lot about life.

He also drove me crazy. We taped his show on Sunday morning. You've got to remember—the game is played on Saturday. Notre Dame won three out of every four games they played under Lou. We taped at ten o'clock in the morning on Sundays. Lou Holtz would come in at 9:59:50 and put on his microphone and say, "Let's go." There was no prep time—you just go. You never knew how Lou looked at the game. There was one game they played against Air Force, which they won handily. I start out saying, "Well, it was a hard-fought game, and Notre Dame brings home the victory." "Do it again." "Was something wrong?" "Yeah, I lost two defensive tackles to broken legs. I don't think it was a very hard-hitting game. I think it was a cheap game." Lou's mind was so sharp on certain things. You never knew what kind of a mood he was going to be in. People forget that **HOLTZ** was the oldest of the big-name Notre Dame coaches. He left when he was 58, Ara was 51, Leahy was 45 and Rockne was 43.

Lou is one of those guys who burns brightly at first, and then burns out. I think the tenure Lou had here was probably a couple of years longer than it actually should have been. That was because of his love for this place. He wasn't going to let the pressure get him.

The loss to USC in '05 is pretty high on my list of hard losses. ...on the other hand, I can't really say that, and I'll tell you why—we won the recruiting war. Notre Dame gained respect. I'm not one of these guys who hates SC. I respect SC. There are other schools on the schedule, who will go nameless, I despise. USC always had good people. Do I want to beat them every year? H--- yes! I want them drubbed. That's why Lou's tenure was so great. The only game he lost to SC was the last one. They're classy people. Pete Carroll's probably a pretty good guy. You don't have the animosity you had back in the sixties when Ara and McKay were going at it. That was flat-out war.

Here's Charlie Weis in a nutshell. He got one Coach of the Year honor—he should have gotten them all. He accepts on behalf of the university, not himself. You have to remember, when you talk about Charlie Weis—he's a real Domer. You know what that term means.

> **In 1986, Skip HOLTZ played in 11 Notre Dame games as a member of the special teams. He carried the ball one time for one yard...Lou Holtz, Jr. co-wrote the movie *The Cable Guy* with Jim Carrey.**

That means someone who is thick and thin Notre Dame through and through. When you have someone like that, in addition to being as qualified as Charlie is—what you get is what happened in '05.

If Gruden had taken over for Davie? I don't like to think about that because that's a supposition. If it would ever happen that Jon would come here, it would be fantastic. I don't know if it will. Who knows? Who ever thought that Charlie would be here? One friend predicts that Gruden will replace Charlie in 15 years....

Father Jenkins—Notre Dame's new president is a great man, great man. Spiritual. Good leader. Made a very gutsy call and made it decisively and should reap every benefit he can get out of it.... George O'Leary—I liked him—good football coach. I was looking forward to covering the guy. The firing had to be done. I never talked to him when he had to leave. I've since talked to him. I saw him at the NFL Combine, when he was with the Vikings. He was still getting over it. He saw me and knew who I was, and he said, "Tell everybody I said 'Hi'." I thought, "Oh man. That had to hurt." I was very happy he did well. Yes, I would have let him go. Other schools could "get away with it" or at least "explain it" or "couch it." Not here....

Everybody asks, "Why is Notre Dame so arrogant?" Arrogant, what do you mean arrogant? I don't see any arrogance around here. I don't get that. Maybe I'm naïve. I see **MIAMI**—Miami doesn't have arrogant fans 'cause they don't have any fans. Their players were arrogant. There's a big difference. There's another school on our schedule whose fans are arrogant—no comment. I think there's a degree of wannabe there. Come on. We're living in the Disneyland of football here. Every day is sunny here. Not always—we know that. Any school would have made the deal with NBC in a heartbeat. It was never offered to them because this is a business. The only school that's going to garner the numbers necessary to sustain this contract is Notre Dame. Once you get the contract, it becomes self-sustaining. You saw what the numbers were like in Weis' first year. They were incredible. If the contract were up this year, I think Kevin White

> **Do you confuse Miami (Ohio) with Miami (Florida)?**
> **MIAMI OF OHIO** was a school before Florida was a state.

would be in a real good spot, but they're not—there are a few more years left. If NBC would drop it, you don't think FOX or ESPN wouldn't pick that up—they'd do it in a New York minute.

For every tenure that is down—I've been here through six tenures, Faust, Devine, Holtz, Davie, Willingham, Charlie—three good, three not-so-good. It's still Notre Dame. There's always been at least a bright spot somewhere within it which only perpetuates the momentum that gets you through the bad times. It's harder now because of the Internet. Notre Dame fans are now like a lot of other fans before. The SEC, Big 10, Big 12—instant gratification. Notre Dame fans weren't always that way, but they are now.

Thirty-two years and counting—my best memory? Right now. We're outside the TV station. We turn to the east, and there's the Dome. That's it. Everything else is subservient to that. People say that's a religious thing—I'm Catholic. No, no, no. It's not. It's a different place. It's a different place. I'm just lucky enough to be here.

Drove by the Kevin Rogers-Bill Diedrick Museum of Progress today. It's still not open.

HOOKED ON PHOENIX

JIM RATTAY

In 1998, Notre Dame ventured west to Phoenix where they defeated Arizona State in a lackluster performance at Sun Devil Stadium. Six weeks later, on the same field, Brophy Prep, the Jesuit powerhouse from Phoenix, was playing Desert Vista for the "Big School" state championship. Desert Vista had only been in existence three years and was coached by Jim Rattay, who had already won state titles in Ohio and Arizona. Rattay's son, Tim, had recently passed for 560 yards against Nebraska and would go on to a long NFL career. The star quarterback for Desert Vista was Tim's younger brother, John, a 6'4" lefty who would soon be the most recruited quarterback in Arizona history. After being snubbed totally by Notre Dame, John Rattay spurned 60 colleges when he signed with Tennessee. Sadly, his college career ended after three ACL operations in three years. His competitor, Casey Clausen, became only the second four-year starting quarterback in Tennessee's storied history. The other was **PEYTON MANNING**. *Clausen's youngest brother is the projected top high school quarterback in the nation in the 2007 class and verbally committed to Notre Dame in April, 2006.*

Desert Vista charged the field in gold helmets, pristine uniforms, while "The Notre Dame Victory March" boomed from the Desert Vista band. As one scribe wrote, "Desert Vista made the real Notre Dame look like a ragtag, disorganized, unenthusiastic and lazy outfit." Desert Vista won when Rattay connected on a 70-yard touchdown pass to his wide receiver—who went on to start for the Chicago Bears.

> **PEYTON MANNING's** father, Archie, is regarded as the greatest football player in the history of the University of Mississippi. In honor of Archie's uniform number, the posted speed limit on the Ole Miss campus is 18 mph.

Ken Maglicic, Notre Dame '65, played at St. Joseph's in Cleveland, and he was good friends with the foster father who took me in. I grew up in an orphanage called Parmadale, in Parma, Ohio. I was living with a foster family who were the best friends of the Maglicics. They took me to see Notre Dame games to see Ken Maglicic play. He ended up with Ara Parseghian that first year when Notre Dame was undefeated and went out to USC and got "homered" at USC. They called a holding penalty down on the 2-yard line on a dive play. I remember Woody Hayes saying "You go to the West Coast, and you're already two touchdowns down because of the officiating." ...I left this orphanage after my seventh grade year. This orphanage was a self-contained orphanage where we never saw the real world. When I went to this foster family, they actually had to walk my brother and me around the house to tell us what was what—"this is a spigot for a hose"—basic stuff. We had lived in this orphanage for seven years. I didn't have a clue about what was going on in the real world. Then, suddenly, we are going to these Notre Dame games. All Notre Dame colors! It's like the Wizard of Oz when it went from black and white to—all of a sudden—living color. All these people are out on the campus, the grass is so green, they're barbecuing and throwing frisbees and footballs, the intensity, the spirit of the stadium. Those people are like Notre Dame to the marrow of their bones. It was so exciting to go to some of those games. Ara was such a wonderful guy. He's like JFK—he's got that charisma. He had that look and he had that feel about him.

In the orphanage, I played a little football. Maglicic was my football hero guy. One time, he came back from Notre Dame and said that they got these new special shoes made out of kangaroo leather. They were really light, and you could run really fast in them. I remember saving up my money, and he got me a pair of these kangaroo-leather shoes. They were only guaranteed for eight wearings...'cause they were such thin leather. Of course, I wore them many more times than that. I wanted to do whatever Maglicic did. He was the last two-way player at Notre Dame. He was a great linebacker and pulling guard.

When I got my first head coaching job, I was 26 years old. I was at Elyria, Ohio Catholic High School. Guess what offense I ran—the Notre Dame Box. You remember when Knute Rockne saw how the

Rockettes would all shift. I got a really old book that had the Notre Dame Box Offense in it. I thought, "I'm the head coach, and I'm going to run that offense." I had this running back—God has been really good to me as a coach and as a dad—Brian Thomas, who was the Back of the Year in Ohio. He later starred with Dan Marino at Pitt. He was my big running back and this Notre Dame Box is fantastic if you've got a really good running back. We would do the shifts and everything. Isn't that cool? Nobody ran it so I had a huge advantage 'cause people only had one week to prepare for an offense they'd never seen before. At Mesa High School, here in Arizona, I brought out the Notre Dame box, and I put it in. Mesa High was horrible when I got there. Our first year, we were 1-9. The next year we were 9-1. All the East Valley schools were in one league, a ten-team league. We were picked preseason to come in last…and we won it outright…. running the Notre Dame Box.

When I got into coaching, I tried to pattern my teams after Notre Dame. I had a unique opportunity in that the principal here at Desert Vista, Joe McDonald, coached for me when I was the head football coach at Mesa High School. He wanted me to be the football coach at Desert Vista, which was going to be a brand new high school—because of the tremendous population growth in the Phoenix area. I had lost my eye and lost my teeth. I had a fungal infection so I had taken a leave of absence from Mesa High School. I was back just teaching and didn't know if my health was going to allow me to do the grind of being a head football coach. I said, "No, I don't really think that's what the Lord wants for me right now." He calls me again. He was a smart guy. He said, "If you'll be my head football coach, I'll let you pick out the colors of the school, and I'll let you pick the mascot." I thought, "Oh, Jiminy Christmas!" He goes, "I'd love to do the Notre Dame colors." He knew my weakness 'cause we had coached together for a year.

I said, "Well, you know, Notre Dame is the finest academic/athletic institution in America. He goes, "That's what we want. We want Desert Vista to be the finest academic/athletic high school in Arizona."

I took the job, and we started with just freshmen. We picked the Notre Dame colors. We had to vote on what our mascot was going to be. We promoted the 'thunder' 'cause the first song I ever learned in my life, because of my dad, was "The Notre Dame Fight Song—Shake Down the Thunder." Thunder became our nickname. Well, you have to have a mascot, so Thunder was our nickname, but Thunder wasn't a mascot. I had this big sign you buy at Notre Dame's bookstore of the Four Horsemen of Notre Dame, the picture of them riding on horses. I have that in my office. So, I said, "Let's do the stallions. Our actual mascot will be a stallion." That's where we got our mascot from—the Four Horsemen of Notre Dame. We tried to have a real horse on the sidelines. One of my assistant coaches actually owned a couple of horses, but the district wouldn't allow us to bring a horse into the stadium. So, unfortunately, we weren't able to do it. Our kids looked so good in their uniforms. The kids loved it. They had the blue socks and gold pants.

In order to develop a great tradition, you have to base it on a great tradition. In other words, for your future, you have to have a vision. All I said was, "This it not about Notre Dame or Catholic. This is about having the greatest academic/athletic tradition in Arizona." They loved that. The kids loved it. We've got the sign in our locker room as you walk out, "Play Like a Champion Today." Of course, I bought it from Notre Dame.

My oldest son, Chris's dream of his life was to go to Notre Dame 'cause he grew up with it. Chris was 18th in his class of 802 at Mesa High. He was Student Council President. He was captain of his football team. He scored the winning touchdown in the state championship game in Sun Devil Stadium. He was captain of the track team, which won the state championship. He was real active in church. The kid was the model Notre Dame kid. I had some friends who called for Chris, like Ken Maglicic and guys like that. You know what—he didn't get accepted.

After my son John's junior year, we went to Rockford, Illinois, for a 50th wedding anniversary party for my in-laws. John and I left Rockford at four one morning and drove through Chicago to South Bend. I wanted to take John to Notre Dame and let him see the Golden Dome and Touchdown Jesus and meet Coach Davie. We go there. The secretary told us Davie wasn't in but would maybe be there in an hour. We came back and waited. Coach Davie came in. He was a tall guy, and John's a tall kid, 6'3" at that time. I said, "Coach Davie, I'm Jim Rattay, head high school coach of the big school state champions in Arizona. This is my son, John, a pre-season All-American…." He said, "Good. Thanks. Bye." That was it—walks right by. We were devastated. We had gone there and waited and waited. He didn't even say, "Come on in. Let me call my quarterback coach or offensive coordinator, or somebody." You know, pass us off to somebody even if he didn't have time. He didn't talk to us. He didn't say 10 words to us. We were devastated. We would paraphrase the old joke: What happened when the pink elephant walked into Bob Davie's office? Nothing—he didn't see it.

We were there at Notre Dame all day. We went to the underground place where the cafes are. We visited the chapel. It was a dream come true for me to take my son there and walk through those places…and just be there myself…it's a mystical place. Notre Dame has a mystical charm to it.

Willingham would just stand there. He would just look. He's not talking to anybody. He's not talking with the coaches. He's not firing up the players. I'm a high-school coach, but, gosh, you've got to be coaching on the run, that presence Lou Holtz had. They used to say that you would never beat Napoleon if he was at the battle site. You've got to have that fire, that presence about you. That's the only thing about Willingham. I think he's a good person, and I think he's a decent coach, but he's not a Notre Dame coach. Notre Dame coaches have to have that spirit. They've got to have that fire in them.

Bob Davie was not a Notre Dame man. He was not a Catholic. He didn't grow up with Notre Dame. He was never a head coach in his life. I just felt that was a poor choice when they picked him for Lou Holtz. Go for the greatest guy you can get! I don't know what happened there. I just don't know what happened with him. Weis is a Notre Dame guy. He has woken up the echoes. I didn't think Willingham could do it. He's not a Notre Dame guy. He's another guy who wasn't a Catholic. It's not going to work. Notre Dame is a school that has to go to the marrow of your bones. When you recruit kids, you've got to sell them that you're special. You're going to put on the gold helmet…. The *Rudy* movie—I've only seen it about 20 times.

Here at Desert Vista, every kid that plays football at Desert Vista had to see the *Rudy* movie. Every year, we take our kids to football camp—90 to 100 kids—and one of the things we did there is we watched the *Rudy* movie together. My daughter could probably just say all the lines throughout the whole movie. The kids always love the movie. It's a great football movie. It's a great movie. Kids want to be passionate. Teenagers want to fall in love. They are infatuated with every good-looking girl who smiles at them. They want to have something their heart can grab onto. "Rudy" does that. That Notre Dame thing here—that's why we did it. That's how we made this school magical so fast—because we were the Thunder—we were special—nobody else was the Thunder—nobody had the gold helmets. We always told them we were always a touchdown up just because we walked out on the field, and they saw our gold helmets. We shook down the Thunder....

Look at it. Everybody is loving Notre Dame now. I've loved them forever.

Mr. Charles Weis
Class of 1978

MURPHY'S ROMANCE
MURPHY'S LAW

PAT MURPHY

Pat Murphy grew up in Syracuse, NY in a Notre Dame-crazed family. The former head baseball coach at Notre Dame now is the head honcho at Arizona State, the most storied college baseball program in the country.

From as young as I can remember, my dad instilled in all of us kids that Notre Dame was "the way," and that still hangs with our family today. I have two brothers who are die-hard Notre Dame fans. One brother who passed away, was also a big Notre Dame fan. My sister roots for them, and I root for them *very hard*. For all our lives, it encapsulated most of our youth. Every Saturday during football season was Notre Dame Saturday…nothing else went on. I'd run home from my Pop Warner football game, or literally, when I coached football at Claremont College, I'd have the headset on, and I'd have a radio underneath it. Any break I had, I'd get an update on the game—that's how important it was to me.

The first game I ever went to was in 1968, Notre Dame—Michigan State, when Theismann was the quarterback. I got to meet **JOE THEISMANN** and Ara Parseghian. My older brothers and I all piled in one hotel room in Elkhart. I'll never forget it. I was awe-struck. Ever since then, I've tried to make it back from Syracuse, New York, every time I could.

I hitchhiked on many occasions. It was a straight shot. In those days, hitchhiking was much safer. Many a trucker picked me up. It was surprising the number of people just going straight out I-90,

> **JOE THEISMANN** holds the NFL record for the shortest punt that wasn't blocked—one yard.

especially truckers. I was a junior in high school the first time I did that. None of us had functioning cars that could make the trip so hitchhiking was the only way we could get there. We never had tickets until we got there. We'd either drum up tickets—or we'd sneak into the game. We snuck into the games a lot. You used to be able to give the usher $20 or $30. I'd always try to bring a buddy. We hitchhiked to at least a dozen games. We'd just tell our parents we were staying at a friend's house, and we'd go out on Interstate 90 and go to the game and get back on Sunday. We'd always get picked up pretty quickly. I never stood out there more than an hour without getting a ride. We didn't hold up signs. I didn't look too dangerous. Usually, we'd leave on Thursday night, and tell our parents we had a day off from school, or maybe we'd leave Friday morning. I've made it in 12 hours hitchhiking. That's my record. That was two rides—one to Buffalo and then Buffalo straight into South Bend. One time I fell asleep on the way home and the guy took me all the way to Albany before I woke up.

In my orange bag, I'd take a little jar of peanut butter, peanuts, or whatever we could find. One time, we made peanut butter and jelly sandwiches with a plastic spoon on crusty old bread. My cousin and I slept in the Joyce Center that night. We got out there on a Friday night and didn't have any place to stay so we slept in the seats way up in the corner. When the security would come around, we'd just lie down in the aisle.... I was such a fan that I could identify every player on the team. That's how I got close to Rudy. I knew Rudy before he made the movie because I was one of the only people who ever came up to him and said, "Yeah, I remember you. You were a fifth-team defensive end, number 45"—Rudy just took a liking to me.

I hopped on a train one time in Erie, Pennsylvania, and that wasn't very smart. I was starved so I went in and got something to eat. When I came outside, there was a train, almost at a stop, going through Erie, and I just climbed on it. I'd heard my dad tell stories about hopping trains. That locomotive got going—it was zooming: I was so cold and so scared. I wasn't inside a car—I was holding onto a ladder. I probably stayed on it—well, it seemed like forever...I don't know how long, and the first chance I could, I jumped off. I could still see I-90, or what I thought was I-90. I could see the Thruway as I was hanging on for dear life. I thought, "I can't make it like this." It just scared the life out of me. That was one of the times I was by myself.

I tried to get into Notre Dame four times and got rejected—four rejection letters that I saved. It's kind of cool. I always say, "I wasn't smart enough to get in there, but they thought I was smart enough to coach there." I ended up at Florida Atlantic in South Florida.

When I was at Notre Dame, I had the privilege of meeting with Father Hesburgh a few times. He was so gracious and so wonderful. You feel like you're meeting with the Pope. Of course, Father Hesburgh and I are both from Syracuse. Father is 89 now and legally blind. He's been living on the top of the Library—which was named after him in 1987—and at the Holy Cross Retirement Home next to Moreau Seminary. He says Mass in his office 30 minutes after each home game. His brother, James Hesburgh from Syracuse, was a Notre Dame sophomore when Ted was named President in 1952. He's had 14 nieces and nephews graduate from Notre Dame.

If Gene Corrigan, the AD, was really looking for a great baseball coach, he would not have picked me. What made me a prospect to be the baseball coach at Notre Dame is that it was still a part-time job in those days. Being a part-time job, they were looking for some guy not to screw it up. Father Joyce told me they considered dropping the program at that time. They just didn't put a lot of emphasis into it. They had a great coach in Larry Gallo. He was leaving for the program at Wake Forest. Notre Dame was considering dropping baseball, with Title IX growing in importance.

I was coaching at Claremont in California. There was a young lady, playing volleyball, named Margie Penny. Her brother, Chris Penny, played baseball at Notre Dame. He came to her graduation. Everybody who knew me knew that Notre Dame encapsulated my whole life. He came by my office and said, "Coach, I know you've had success here. I don't know if you'd be interested but the baseball job is open at Notre Dame." I said, "I could never get that job." He said, "Well, I just wanted to let you know that it's open." I had asked to be a volunteer there the year before and Coach Gallo said, "You know, Murph, it just doesn't work. I just don't want to get you up here because we can't pay you anything."

But, Chris Penny's comment really got me thinking. I called Notre Dame the next morning, got Gene Corrigan, the Notre Dame athletic director, on the phone—and he'll laugh about this story if you talk to him—and told him straight up, "Gene, I'm going to be your next baseball coach. I love Notre Dame." Corrigan laughed and said, "Oh, you are, are you?" I said, "I'd rather be the Notre Dame coach than manage the Los Angeles Dodgers or the New York Yankees. I love Notre Dame." He laughed and he said, "Throw your stuff in the mail." I said, "Well, I've already done that, this morning, Federal Express." He laughed. I got on the phone with his secretary and said, "Look, I'm leaving for Holland on Thursday 'cause I was going to be the national coach for the Dutch team. I need you to understand that if I'm interviewing for this Notre Dame position, I'll stay home." I was to leave on Thursday, and this was Monday. "I need you to understand that I've got to move." She said, "Well, I'll do what I can." Jeanne Neely was the secretary, who had been there a long time. She appreciated how passionate I was 'cause she was so passionate about Notre Dame. I told her my whole story and how much I loved Notre Dame and how I grew up with it…that I had prepared all my life to be there. I had gotten turned down four times as a student, but I wanted to be there. Then, Brian Boulac got on the phone. I remembered he had been a football player and told him his number. I said to him, "Hey, Brian, I love Notre Dame, and I'm going to make a plane reservation to come up there tomorrow and you work it out that I can get in to see Mr. Corrigan." He said, "Pat, don't do that. Don't jump the gun. I'll talk to Gene and see what we can do." I waited all day. Sure enough, I made my reservations for Tuesday. I called them back early Tuesday morning. Corrigan wouldn't take my call. I talked to Jeanne and I said, "Jeanne, I'm getting on a plane. I need to meet with this guy." She said, "Let me see what I can do." I'm sure there was a bunch of chuckling going on. I got back on the phone with Brian and said, "Brian, I'm going to be there tonight. He said, "All right, I've got it set up for you. We'll interview tomorrow morning at 7:00." So, Wednesday morning 7:00—and I've got to leave by 2:30 to get back to California and get on the plane Thursday to Holland. Brian picked me up at the airport, and they took me all around. I met Roger Valdeserri, and after meeting Roger, I gave him a big hug, and he gave me a big hug. I vowed I wouldn't look at the Golden Dome 'cause I didn't want to become emotional, I just wanted to interview. I thought, "This is just right." Believe me, I was no more ready than the man in the moon. The interview was just smooth. They could tell my passion for the program. I interviewed with Boulac, Valdeserri, Tom Kelly, the former baseball coach, Father Beauchamp and Corrigan—all one-on-one. I just absolutely poured my heart saying, "I love Notre Dame." "I know a little about baseball. I've done pro ball. I've done international ball. I've done college ball at a really academic school." I thought that was a good qualifier. I'm was young— 26 at the time. "I don't care how much you pay me." They paid me $7,000. I taught five PE classes. We only had two scholarships, and I was okay with that. I didn't care. I just wanted to be at Notre Dame in any capacity.

When I was flying back to California, I felt I had a shot to get the job—Roger had hugged me. I was calling Jeanne Neely every day at home. I don't recommend it for everybody, but I knew that it was in my skin and in my stomach that I had something for that university. That university molded me into who I was as a child, and what I aspired to be every day of my life. It was more important than church. I didn't realize the entire irony of this whole thing, but it was more important to me than anything in my life. I just cared about Notre Dame.

Even though I wasn't ready, I did it…I became the head baseball coach at Notre Dame. I called Jeanne and a guy named Joe O'Brien, associate athletic director, got on the phone. He said, "Kid, we're going to give you the chance. I don't want you running around here thinking we're going to build a national power or anything, but we're going to give you a chance." I was still in Holland when I found out.

People back in Syracuse couldn't believe it. Nobody could believe it. Everybody thought I had to come up with some scheme to get the job. They knew I was a *get-out-there* kid, and they knew I would do anything to get the job, but they thought some scheme had happened. They didn't realize how it had come down. I was so elated that I went for a walk, and I just prayed every step of the way. I just thanked God. I promised Him I would go to Notre Dame and would give every ounce of energy to those young people. I really just wanted to be at Notre Dame. I thought I'd never leave. To this day, I can't give you a reason why I did. It had nothing to do with money. I would have made five times the money in '92 or '93 if I'd left. I just didn't want to leave. I couldn't separate myself from Notre Dame.

To be honest with you, it became a little bit about me. I lost sight of what Notre Dame really was there to teach. It made me grow up. People credit me with building the baseball program, building the stadium, getting a full complement of scholarships, putting us in the final 16 three straight years. The truth is, Notre Dame built me. I didn't build it. Notre Dame made me a candidate for all these jobs. Notre Dame has helped me more than I could ever help it. I had great people around me—Roger, Joe O'Brien....

I was able to get great kids and those kids built the program. I just pushed them beyond belief. They tolerated me. They came to that expectation that "this crazy SOB is going to be in my face—I'm going to show him I can do it." I pushed the kids to a level that was pretty inappropriate, in my mind, for Notre Dame student-athletes. I had them practice for hours and hours. Craig Counsell, of the Arizona Diamondbacks, talks about it to this day. I was really rough on these kids. If I had it to do over, I'd do it a lot differently, in a more humane way.

But, I will say this, "I never did anything to gain an advantage—other than to gain the advantage of having a player believe in himself more." I never cheated. I never went beyond the rules—none of that kind of stuff. I just wanted to win at Notre Dame...and for myself to be part of Notre Dame history. That's all I've ever wanted was to be part of Notre Dame history. In my little way, and in my own little mind, I guess I am.

Craig Counsell, Dan Peltier and Chris Mahalik were the ones who made the big leagues. Counsell just got so much better every year. He matured, and he loved the game. He had a little bit of an arrogance about what he could do—and I mean this respectfully. A "nobody was going to get me out attitude." He didn't have that goofy batting stance when he was at Notre Dame. I've talked to him a bunch of times about that, and he said he just developed it himself

Craig was my first guy, and I gave him a five-hundred-dollar scholarship. That kid earned every single bit of what he got. He signed for $1,000. I remember arguing with Pat Daugherty, of the Colorado Rockies, on the phone. The Rockies said, "We're going to give this kid $1,000 and if you don't like it, tell the kid to stay home." I love running into him now because I love telling Pat, "Hey Pat, you really overpaid Counsell, didn't you?"

Notre Dame stands for—the right things in life, meaning, fair, taking on what—whether the odds be great or small—any challenge, going for it. Those are the things my dad instilled me through Notre Dame. "It doesn't matter—you're at Notre Dame. You can do it." My mom and dad were still living when I became the coach there. My dad didn't like to gloat or boast, but I think he was very proud of me. I hope my family, for generations and generations, will always stick with Notre Dame because it's way beyond the football program. It's way beyond sports. I hope the men of the cloth continue to make great decisions, and I hope that it doesn't become corporate.

There is only one Notre Dame, my friend.

The BCS Bowls...
or as Bob Davie
called it—Passover

WHERE THE PAST IS PRESENT

JIM AUGUSTINE

Jim Augustine, 60, lives in Osceola, Indiana, just east of Mishawaka. He is a teacher at Virgil Grissom Middle School. "Augie" is a collector of Notre Dame football memorabilia, specializing in Knute Rockne artifacts.

I had polio as a child and was confined to Northern Indiana Children's Hospital right across the street from the Notre Dame campus. I was lying in my hospital bed, and could hear the crowd cheering. I would ask my parents, "What exactly is that?" They would say, "That's Notre Dame. That's the Notre Dame fans cheering."

My dad started taking me to games when I was seven years old. I always made him wait while I ran around the stadium and picked up all the extra ticket stubs. As I gathered up those football stubs after the game, once in a while, I would be able to pick up a program. I found an occasional pair of binoculars or a camera, but those things didn't interest me. It was only the ticket stubs.

My dad grew up right down the street from Knute Rockne. Most people mispronounce his name. It was "Ka-nute," not "Noot." Knute would come to his house and then walk over to my grandpa's house and they would talk gardening. The neighborhood boys played football with the Rockne boys. So, the love of Rockne has always been there. My dad passed away at a real young age, in his fifties, but my uncles always told stories about Bonnie Rockne. When Rockne was killed, his widow went around the neighborhood and gathered the kids together. My dad and friends and all my uncles rode their bikes in the funeral procession. Rockne's funeral was broadcast on CBS Radio and millions of people listened.

I recall my mom talking about having Christmas cards and gifts from the Rocknes. I've now got one of their Christmas cards. I've got the original paper, the *South Bend Tribune,* from the day after he died. My brother, who is a little younger than me, also collects Rockne. Studebaker released a car named "The Rockne" after his death. Rockne had worked for Studebaker for a number of years representing the company. Over the years, my brother has been on the quest for a Rockne, and in the last 10 years he's found two of them—bought 'em both.

I've got several pieces from *Rockne All-American*—one of the director's megaphones—one of the original scripts—some of the lobby cards that were in the theaters at that time and some of the advertising pieces. I've got one program signed by Ronald Reagan who played The Gipper and original tickets....I've got tickets and programs that go back to Cartier Field. Rockne once caught a young Joe Kuharich sneaking into Cartier Field...One unique thing I do have is the program and ticket from the "Kennedy game"—Notre Dame at Iowa—that was canceled because of the assassination in November of 1963. I don't know how many people took their tickets for that game back in and got their money. For a number of years, I couldn't find one of these tickets, but in the last five years, I've found three of them.

I've got each one of the Notre Dame *Sports Illustrated* covers, and every one of them is autographed. I've got the one with the movie, *John Goldfarb Please Come Home*, with Shirley MacLaine. I mailed the cover out to her in Hollywood, and she mailed it back to me, signed. Tony Rice is on the cover four times, the most of any Irish player. I heard that Lou Holtz didn't really want to sign his *Sports Illustrated* cover because they had just never given him good press. I caught him in a good mood one day. I'd heard him turn people down to sign it, but he looked at me, smiled and signed it.

> **More U.S. kids today play <u>SOCCER</u> than any other organized sport, including youth football. Perhaps, the reason so many kids play soccer is so they don't have to watch it.**

SHORT STORIES FROM LONG MEMORIES

I went to Notre Dame from Detroit, with orders not to play football because my dad had broken his sacroiliac back in the late 20s under Knute Rockne. He told me, "No football." I hadn't played in high school except for my senior year.

At Notre Dame, the guys talked me into going out for interhall football. In those days, football was very exciting because every hall had a team. They got all their gear from the old equipment that the Irish used. It was a big deal. We went out and played on what is now is part of the parking lot at Notre Dame. I was in Zahm my first year. I played offensive and defensive end. The first year we won the championship. The next year, I lived in a brand new dorm, Stanford. We played in the Stadium and won the championship for the second time. My junior year, I went to Dillon Hall and made All-Campus again. So, we had won the division three years and won the interhall championship three years at Notre Dame Stadium.

The spring semester of my junior year they brought in Joe Kuharich as the new varsity coach. I was dared to talk to him to see if I could get on the team so I did it. I started the Old Timers game and caught a touchdown pass from George Izo. My dad was there. I hadn't mentioned to him that I went out for varsity. He didn't even know I was on the team. He met me outside the locker room afterward and gave me a big hug and was very proud of me. That fall, I began as third-team end. I played nine of the ten games. Then, the Redskins signed me, and I had a great time playing there. In 12 months, I went from playing interhall football to signing with the NFL.

——PAT HEENAN, '60, on going from his interhall football teams to the NFL with the Washington Redskins

I was the first member of the family to attend college and I arrived in South Bend "outfitted" in the way my parents thought correct: in a Harris tweed suit that weighed about 20 pounds. It was a blistering August day where even the birds sought shady trees; some trees were thinking about chasing dogs. Lugging two huge suitcases from the campus bus stop to the main squad was a soaking agony.

who could kick." Ivan said to Coach Devore, "I kicked in high school." Devore asked, "Did you kick field goals, too?" He said, "Yeah, I kicked field goals." So, he kicked off, kicked extra points and kicked a field goal. It wasn't until afterwards that he confided that he'd tried three field goals in high school and had missed all three. So, while he had kicked them, technically, he had never connected on any. He was a good friend of mine, and it was ironic that we were listening to the game on the radio one week and the next week he's the star of the big game and got nicknamed Ken, "The Toe" Ivan after that. Nobody calls him that except me now, but every time I see him, that's what I call him.

——CAPPY GAGNON, class of '66

I got married in 1993. My wife was from Pittsburgh and she moved to South Bend. We rented a house owned by Notre Dame right there on Ivy Road. The people who had lived in the house prior to us were Rick Mirer and Demetrius DuBose. The house wasn't owned by Notre Dame at that time. It was owned by The Jamison Inn. Unbelievably, Rudy Ruettiger was working for Jamison Inn at the time as caretaker of their properties. So, I'm living there about six months, and the doorbell rings. I go answer it—there's Rudy standing there. He says, "Excuse me. There's a shed in your back yard that Rick Mirer and Demetrius DuBose have a few things stored in. Would you mind if I retrieved them?" I gave him a bear hug. I picked him right up off the ground. Rudy said, "Obviously, you know who I am." I was shocked that he was even there. I had already seen the movie. The very first time I saw it, I thought, "This could be me." The only thing I didn't do was graduate from Notre Dame. I've always loved the place…the Lady on the Dome. I tell everybody in Pennsylvania the reason I moved is something I can't explain, but, ever since I was a child, I've had this feeling like the Lady on the Dome was calling me. I know that sounds weird, but it's beyond anything I can put into words. There was a feeling like I had to be there. It's like a salmon swimming upstream against all the current—they had to get home. Something inside of me was telling me I had to come to Notre Dame.

——JIMMY ZANNINO, native of Central Pennsylvania

It was the 1970 Cotton Bowl against Texas. It was on artificial turf, and they were running that triple option. The game starts, and it's about 65 degrees, gloriously sunny. I'm backing up Joe Theismann. I'm standing up on the bench, thinking I was just going to watch the game. My hair was always a little longer than Ara liked it. I was looking around, "God, the girls are pretty here." All of a sudden, in the second quarter, there was a timeout on the field. Somebody goes, "Steenberge, come on in." I looked and Theismann was down. He had never missed a play in his whole career. He had hurt his elbow, hitting it on the turf. I looked down, and there were about 50 gold helmets in front of me. I'm going, "S---, which one's mine?" I just grabbed one with the right facemask and put it on and snapped it up. They give me the play, and, as I'm walking in, I realize I've got about a 7 ¾ helmet on, and I'm supposed to have a 7. We run an option play. I pitch the ball out, and the defensive end hits me in the head. My helmet does a 90-degree spin so that I'm looking out the ear hole. I got through the next couple of plays, took a time out and went and found my right helmet. The girls still looked pretty through the ear hole—a little rounder maybe.

———PATRICK STEENBERGE, former Notre Dame quarterback

Johnny Lujack was maybe the greatest Notre Dame player ever, and he still holds the Chicago Bears single-game record for most yards passing. Lujack was also the first "color" commentator on a televised football game. Charlie Callahan was my counterpart at Notre Dame, their Sports Information Director. Lujack married a St. Mary's girl whose father was the biggest General Motors dealer in Iowa. So, one day Callahan calls Lujack in Davenport, Iowa and says, "Do me a favor. My mother's eighty years old. Call her up and wish her a happy birthday." Lujack said, "I will do it under one condition—you don't call me for two years." And Callahan agreed. Two years later to the day, Lujack picks up the phone and Callahan says, "Time's up." Callahan's mother was called, but Charlie didn't call Lujack for two years because he said he would not.

Only Callahan would know that in the USC-Notre Dame game of 1948 where SC won 14-7 on a controversial interference call in the end zone that enabled Notre Dame to tie it up...Only Callahan would know the official was from Kansas, and he was a Quaker. Only

Callahan would know that—only Charlie...He would point out in the Ohio State game—the famous 1935 game you know, when Notre Dame scored late, four guys touched the ball and only one was a Catholic. Only Callahan would tell that....

One time, I asked Bo Schembechler, "If there were ten kids, Bo, and out of these ten kids, they had to pick between Michigan and Notre Dame, how many kids would you get?" He thought for about ten seconds and said "Three." Here's Michigan—three out of the ten, and Notre Dame would get seven....

When I was at ABC, Roger Valdiserri, the Notre Dame Sports Information Director (SID) told me one of the guys who wrote "The Victory March" was still alive; they were brothers named Shea. And they were from Holyoke or Hadley, Mass. One was still alive; I don't know if it was the one who wrote the music or the words. I said, "This is great." I went to a guy at ABC, the producer in charge of football—not Roone Arledge. I said "The guy who wrote "The Notre Dame Victory March"—one of them—is still alive. We should do a story on that guy." He said "It's nothing but a football song." This is ridiculous—"nothing but a football song." It's insane!

—BEANO COOK, ESPN, one-time Pitt SID

I knew Rudy. I was a freshman in high school when he was a senior. And a very good football player at Joliet Catholic. He was a guard and a linebacker. He was a real sparkplug and a fiery type guy. Back then, Joliet Catholic always had very small guards on their football teams. He also was a baseball player and did pretty well. Then, I lost track of the guy. He graduated in 1966. All of a sudden, I'm a senior at Notre Dame in '72, he shows up. That was when he got in there. So, my first year in high school was his last, and my last year at Notre Dame was his first.

His brother, Francis, was in the Rudy movie. He's a huge guy around here in Joliet. He's a city policeman and the weight-lifting coach for Joliet Catholic. He's the guru around here—a complete opposite of the guy who portrayed Francis in the movie. They took the liberties of changing him all around, just for the movie aspect, to make him look like a bad guy. Rudy is really a character. He's done very well for himself as a motivational speaker, which has been really phenomenal for him. When the *Rudy* movie came out, there was a preview on the first day of the movie right here at the big theater downtown, Joliet Rialto. We sold tickets, and it was a huge fundraiser for Habitat for Humanity. The movie was excellent. To somebody like me, I looked at it way too objectively and saw all the mistakes and all the liberties that Hollywood producers take when they're trying to do a movie. That lost a little bit of it for me. But, anybody else you talked to, it's just a phenomenal story about Notre Dame and the underdog. It was good for him, I'll tell you.

When I was a freshman, they still had pep rallies the last year in the old field house. They were great. **ROCKY BLEIER** had just come back from Vietnam where he had been wounded. He was limping badly, came back to speak at a pep rally. When he was speaking, there was 100 percent—not even 99 but 100 percent—dead, dead silence. You really could have heard a pin drop in that place. At that point, it was like, "How is this guy ever going to walk again, let alone play football?" That was very emotional and was a big moment.

The best thing about Notre Dame is the friendships and the camaraderie. It's the great friends and relationships you develop—and you keep—for the rest of your life. The other thing is that when you talk to somebody from Notre Dame, there's just that bond, that special relationship. There's a special treatment or respect that you automatically give that person. Not every Notre Damer is a great guy, but, at least, you have that bond right there no matter who it is. You meet football players now and you find out that almost all of them, without exception, are just regular people. They could have been big shots when they were back on campus playing football, but now they've settled into the normal lifestyle. Notre Dame helps them to do that.

——MIKE HANSEN, 56, a towering figure in the business and social circles of Joliet, Illinois

I got to know John Huarte really well because we were in summer school together in '64 trying to get our grades up. There were only

Robert "ROCKY" BLEIER, Jr. was given his nickname by his father who did not want his son to be called "Junior".

three players in summer school that summer and two of them were Huarte and Jack Snow. I had the food concession in that summer dorm hall so I was a bigger deal than they were. Huarte just couldn't have been a nicer guy. Up to that time, he was a guy who seemed to have some potential but never had done anything, and then he had a shoulder separation so was he ever going to do anything? Ara singled him out as the guy who was going to lead the team, and he sure enough did, and he has never changed as a person since. He was a low-key, nice guy then, and he's a low-key, nice guy today, a wonderful person.

Pete Duranko, who now is showing incredible courage as he battles **LOU GEHRIG'S DISEASE**, was a guy I admired as a student, but didn't know him well enough to be friends. Then, since we graduated, we've become friends. I admire him even more now. Freshman year, a buddy of mine and I are in downtown South Bend and were waiting on the corner for the bus to go back to campus. It was about 11:00 at night. A convertible carrying four huge guys pulls up at the curb. They had their tee shirts rolled up, holding cigarette packs. These were Fonzie-types of guys who had looked over and saw us 'cause we're wearing Notre Dame gear from head-to-toe. They've got a green light, but they wanted to heckle us. They called us "Rah-Rahs." They're giving us a lot of grief. My buddy and I are standing there taking this abuse and trying to figure out where to run to if they decided to get out of their car. I'm staring at the four guys, quaking, and not saying anything. I'm focused on them so intently that I don't realize that just at the moment, Pete Duranko comes up and he sees what's going on. He goes over to the car. He takes his shirt and he rolls up the sleeve and he flexes his biceps next to the guy who's sitting in the shotgun seat who's showing off his biceps. Duranko is like twice as big as the guy. Now Duranko starts talking to them…in a real polite way, but making fun of them. Now, they are as scared of Duranko as I had been of them. They had sat through a couple of light changes, but when the light turned green again, they want to take off…the guy pops the clutch and stalls the car. I just

> **Jacob Javits, Charles Mingus, David Niven and Catfish Hunter have all died of ALS—<u>LOU GEHRIG'S DISEASE.</u>**

thought that was great, so Pete Duranko was my hero from then on. He is a wonderful guy.

——CAPPY GAGNON

I was very saddened by the criticism of Paul Hornung. Paul Hornung loves Notre Dame and has done more for that school than anybody I know. He has worked so hard to try to get blue-chip athletes into Notre Dame, and he was frustrated, like everyone else, about the football program.

I'm fortunate enough to be able to sit in the press box of each game. During Charlie Weis' first year, the press box was electric. There was a sense that this was a different program, a different management situation. The management of the time clock, the management of play selection, time-outs, people on the field, etc. Many people in the press box were more upset about the spot where the official spotted the ball at the end of the Southern Cal game than they were about Reggie Bush pushing Leinart into the end zone for the winning touchdown. Many people, including Charlie Weis, said that happens all the time. Well, I said it doesn't happen all the time, and it doesn't happen on the last play that decides a game of that magnitude. If it happens all the time, I've got just one question for you—name at least two times it's happened and name the four people who were involved. I'll guarantee you that neither you nor anyone else can name two games like that. This wasn't an innocuous play in the third quarter at mid-field. This was the whole ball of wax. The officials absolutely blew it. They blew it, and it was hard to believe except for the fact they're PAC-10 officials.

——ALEX McMURTRIE, 57, "Mr. Notre Dame" of Richmond, Virginia

John Lujack is a good friend of mine. We play golf two or three times a month. About two years ago, when Tyrone was struggling, John said, "I'm gonna be 80 years old next year. Do you think, in my lifetime, we'll ever see Notre Dame in a BCS Bowl?" I said, "Oh, yeah, Johnny." He said, "Well, I'm not going to live to 120." I said, "You'll see it."

——PETER MURPHY, Palm Springs, California

I was dating a girl named Letitia Bowen, who played basketball for Notre Dame, my first two years there. She was a fantastic player. When she would go on the road, she would bring me back tee shirts from the schools where she played. Oliver Gibson, the All-American lineman, used to drive a Suzuki Sidekick. When he was in it, it looked like there were eight people in it. He used to let me drive it when I would go out on dates with Letitia. Otherwise, I drove a Pontiac Sunbird with the roof caving in, no heat. I had to keep a blanket over my legs…. Oliver wore corny clothes. His gear was wack. He didn't have any money. I would go to New York; Spike Lee had a store in Brooklyn. I brought back this New York Yankees black sweatshirt. I showed it to Oliver and he acted like he didn't like it. I couldn't wait to wear the sweatshirt around campus when it got cold enough. I was looking for it, and I couldn't find it. I go to the cafeteria…Oliver has it on. He is 6'3"—both ways. He is stretching out my sweatshirt. He acted like he didn't like it, but he's wearing my clothes. I can't beat him up so I can't fight him. I can't be mad at my roommate. I said, "What are you doing? I thought you said you didn't like it." He goes, "Everybody likes a sweatshirt, man." …A month later Letitia brought me back this tee shirt from Michigan. It was a nice tee shirt, and it was real tight. It was one of the tee shirts I would wear out to parties. I wouldn't sweat it up playing basketball. Oliver played on my team one year. I went out to warm up and look up and see Oliver in the layup line…wearing a Michigan tee shirt that looks very familiar. He has on the Michigan tee shirt that my girlfriend got for me. My girlfriend sees this, and she is mad at me. She sees this, but I can't beat him up. He can bench press both of us. What do you want me to do? That's the kind of stuff he would do to me. I got the last laugh. When he graduated and went to the NFL, I would steal his clothes. I've worn some of his stuff on TV, and I would shrink them if I could.

——OWEN SMITH, '94, actor—comedian

I hired "Rudy" Ruettiger twice and fired him twice. First of all, if you're around Rudy for any period of time, he has the ability to mesmerize. I took three people and Rudy to lunch one day. He sat down at this luncheon and told these people the story of *Rudy*. He didn't say 'I,' he always talked in the third person. At the end of the luncheon, three grown adults had cried during lunch, and they had laughed during lunch. He's good. He's really, really good. I haven't heard the guy speak since he went on tour, but he had the passion. The long and the short of it is he was really working hard on that movie deal and not working hard for me. It wasn't fair, so I said, "Hey, you've got to get fired." He said, "Why is that?" I said, "So you can go finish your book." He did. He got it done. He wrote the screenplay. That's how dreams are done. The guy had incredible focus—sheer focus on that book. Nothing came between him and getting that movie made. He wrote it all out. I'm sure he gave it to somebody else, and they edited it and all that, but Rudy had his own screenplay in his mind and he knew that it would work, and it really did. Everybody told him 'no,' but Rudy could not hear 'no.'

——MIKE LEEP, Gurley-Leep Auto Group, South Bend

I can't believe that Notre Dame had nerve enough to fire Tyrone Willingham…but I'm thankful that they did. Name one reason why Tyrone should not have been fired! He absolutely wasn't getting the job done…and he was *never* going to get the job done. I wish they would have fired Bob Davie after three years instead of giving him his five years. Davie's contract actually ended the same week Notre Dame played Ohio State in the Fiesta bowl. To some degree, Tyrone paid the penance for Bob Davie's sins. The fact of the matter is that in major college football, if you're a good coach, you get it done within three years. Leahy, Ara, and Holtz all won the national title in their third year at Notre Dame. I don't care if it's Bobby Stoops inheriting a horrible situation at Oklahoma and winning the national title the second year, or Pete Carroll taking over a moribund Southern Cal program and going for national titles back-to-back-to-back, or Nick Saban at LSU, or Kirk Ferentz at Iowa, or **URBAN MEYER**, wherever he's been. A good coach is going to turn it fast. If a coach doesn't win big in three years, he's never going to win big. The bottom line was that Tyrone's recruiting was horrible, his game-day preparation and game plans were terrible, his offensive coordinator had no clue—everything about it was disastrous.

Glenn Dickey, columnist for the *San Francisco Chronicle*, might have said it best on the day Notre Dame hired Tyrone. He said, "It's

URBAN MEYER, raised a Catholic in Ashtabula, Ohio, was named for Pope Urban.

the biggest career mistake that Tyrone Willingham will ever make because he'll be unmasked for the incompetent coach that he is."

———DICK FOX, Cape Cod, Massachusetts

Tyrone Willingham was one of the finest men I've ever been around—an absolute quality human being. I can't give a higher compliment to any person for his character than I would to him. The best example of that is how he handled his firing. He was fired, and the next day, his quote was something like, "I did not meet the standards that I set for myself." I was one of the last people to ever interact with him at Notre Dame when I walked him to his car after the football banquet a week after he was fired. He had come back to the banquet, which was closed to the public and was just for members of the athletic department and the players and their families. We did not know he was coming. He arrived during the banquet while the lights were down so no one even knew he had arrived until he started speaking. There was a film showing as he walked to the podium. Just before the lights came up, he started talking. People were looking around to see where the voice was coming from, and there he is at the dais. He was speaking—he had not been introduced—and was commenting on the film. He said it was a pleasure coaching these fine young men, etc. Then, when he finished, before you could react, he said, "Now, would everyone bow your head. 'Heavenly Father....'" He did the benediction. We were all stunned. Then, he got a standing ovation. Because I was responsible for security, I waited with him as he spoke with everyone individually. He posed for photos and shook hands and interacted. I walked him and his wife to their vehicle. I stuck out my hand and said, "Coach, it's been an honor to work for you." He interrupted me and said, "No, it's been an honor for me to work for Notre Dame." On the heels of being fired, which nobody can like— he's a proud man. I thought that was very impressive. Obviously, we have a better coach now, and I'm thrilled that we have Charlie Weis coaching for us, and he's a fine man, but it's very hard to beat Tyrone Willingham for the way he handled himself.

———CAPPY GAGNON, Director of Stadium Security

Chapter 5

Acts of the Disciples

The Gospels of Jared and Other Subway Alumni

ND SEPTEMBER SOXTOBER

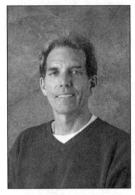

ED FARMER

Ed Farmer was an outstanding athlete at St. Rita High School in Chicago. He turned down full-ride baseball scholarships to Notre Dame and Arizona State to sign a professional baseball contract. Currently, he is the popular radio announcer for the Chicago White Sox.

My dad and mom would go to Notre Dame games when I was a kid even though my mom was ill. My uncle, Don Truesdale, went to school there. So, she started my brother, Tom, and me marching in with the Notre Dame band—where they assemble at the main building and then they play "The Victory March" and that two-step song they play all the time, "The Hike Song." We didn't *follow* the band in—we led them down the street. The Truesdale side of my family—that's the genes I have—are lunatics. The Farmer side is not going to do that. But, my mother's side, yeah, they're gonna do that. I still do it to this day. I go with the band into the stadium. They get me a pass that allows me to go on the field, and the guards know me. They have us march in front of the band. It's like Disney on Parade.

I'm not good in crowds…I'm good in front of crowds. I'm good behind the scenes doing the radio for the White Sox, but I get a little nervous when I'm in a crowd. It's not to a panic state, but it's certainly to a state where I'm looking around wondering what people are going to do. So, I'm a little uneasy. This way, I can go with the band. I never look up because I don't want to take anything away from the spectacle of what's taking place there with someone who might recognize me, which happens a lot. I'm 6'5 ½" and just walking along. If someone says, "Hello," I'll wave to them sheepishly and say, "Hello." This year, I took three Sox guys, and we all walked with the band toward the field. I can't sit in the stadium anyway because of the tiny seats. I also like getting in the tunnel at the end zone. When the team comes off the field, very few people hear the band play "The Victory March" inside that confined area. That really charges the team up as they go back up to their locker room.

Many times, I've said on the air—when I was asked for my greatest sports thrill—"Was it pitching in the All-Star game?" "No." "The World Series?" "No. It's being in the cement catacomb they call the tunnel of Notre Dame Stadium with the band halfway down and the team coming off the field and hearing them play 'The Victory March'." In there, you're amped up to a degree of decibel level that probably is off the charts. I was there for the Florida State game in '93. I was in the tunnel when the fight broke out between Notre Dame and USC when Lou Holtz was there in '89...and he was in it, too. He was trying to grab his kids, and someone threw him down. It started when the SC players ran through the Notre Dame players while they were doing drills, and they weren't going to take it.

Notre Dame is a great place. It's a wonderful place. The environment is great. It's what I think college athletics should be. One thing about the Notre Dame kids, when they get on TV or when they're interviewed, they can speak. And, they can speak in terms where people understand them.

I never had any regrets about not going to Notre Dame to play baseball—it wasn't the place for me. It just wasn't. It was a place for my father. It wasn't a place for me. I would have received a top-flight education. There's no question about that. The amount of schooling I would have gotten from going to Notre Dame would have been tremendous. The amount of teaching I would have gotten from the baseball coach would have been well below that.

In 2005, the White Sox were in the AL Playoffs in Anaheim hours after USC barely beat Notre Dame. The ND-USC game was shown on a big screen at Edison Field before our game. Everybody was watching it, and the crowd just went wild. They were rooting for SC. We came on the air at 7:00 Central Time, and the Notre Dame game ended an hour or less before we came on the air. In the fourth inning of our game, I was doing play-by-play and said on the radio, "I'd like to congratulate the USC Trojans for beating my Notre Dame team this afternoon in South Bend. Charlie Weis, whom I know, will take nothing from this loss. It's hard to look good when you lose, but I'm going to tell you something, folks, Notre Dame looked good losing today. Pete Carroll, I congratulate you. I plan on living a long life. That's the last time you're going to beat my team, either in the Coliseum or at Notre Dame, in my lifetime."

Some of the players of the White Sox have never been to Notre Dame Stadium, and they asked me what it was like. Fred Couples, when we went to the Fiesta Bowl—the Ohio State band comes out first, and they spell out script 'Ohio' and the sousaphone player comes out and dots the 'i' on each sideline. I said to Couples, "Do you like that?" He goes, "That's impressive." I said, "See the other end zone down there. That's my band." He goes, "Yeah." I say, "When they come out, you're going to forget everything you just saw. When they come out, and they play 'The Victory March,' everybody in this place, will be on their feet—that includes Ohio State's fans. Ohio State's people won't know why they're standing, but it's the greatest fight song in America...probably in the world." A few minutes later, Fred goes, "You're not kidding." I said, "Well, if we don't make it to the World Series next year, we're coming back here for Notre Dame and UCLA." He goes, "Count me in."

The Sox players, like Jermaine Dye, wanted to go to the Tennessee game in 2005. I've got friends who were going to the Tennessee game. It was my anniversary so I wasn't going. They said, "How good of an experience is this going to be?" I said, "Well, it will be the best experience in your lifetime." Dye was MVP in the World Series the week before. Afterwards, he said, "That's an unbelievable time—going to a Notre Dame game." And, it is. It's a privilege—number one.

I get complaints, "I don't want to hear Notre Dame stuff on a White Sox baseball broadcast." You've got 50 percent of the people who watch Notre Dame football who want them to lose. The other 50 want them to win. On a broadcast, when I say, "At South Bend, this afternoon, the score was...." I'll get a letter from Joe Smith from

Orland Park, Illinois, "I don't want to hear this." So, I called Joe, "I don't want to lose you as a listener, but you have to understand something. I'm trying to reach the majority and if this influences you in another way, I'm sorry, but I'm going to give the score."

I stopped a caller last year right in his tracks. He goes, "Willingham started out 8-0. Now, we're giving Weis this big contract." I said, "Well, if you look back and take a very, very good look at how we're 8-0, we had three offensive touchdowns in eight victories. You can tell me whatever you want." He goes, "Well, I just want you to tell me why Charlie Weis gets this huge contract and Tyrone didn't." I said, "Weis is a better football coach. Quite simple—he's a better football coach."

They've got that. Two years ago, not this past season, but two years ago, what did we hear about Brady Quinn? "He doesn't move well in the pocket. Notre Dame is going to have to look for a new quarterback. He doesn't do this. He doesn't do that." I heard the same thing about Maurice Stovall. If Stovall would have gone to Miami or Florida State, you'd have heard about him for three years. You'll hear about him with Tampa Bay now. We might as well throw in the kid from Valparaiso also, Samardzija, who caught a total of zero touchdown passes before he breaks the all-time record in one season. Weis takes the same players, and they look spectacular. They lose two regular-season games, one with one second to go, and the other against Michigan State in overtime.

So, when I was 10 years old, my mom took me aside and said to me, "You see who that is over there?" I said, "No." She was pointing to a Notre Dame football player. She said, "You see how quiet he is." I said, "Yeah." She said, "He doesn't have to tell anybody he's good. They know it. When you are playing baseball, I don't want to hear you ever tell anybody you're good." I said, "Mom, I don't think I'm very good." She goes, "They'll let you know when you're good." My mom had a wonderful way—she could shrink your head very quickly, and she could put you in your place without saying anything that was really that hard on you. Her brother went to Notre Dame so she loved the place. She would take the trip, and it was a way for my mom and dad to get away from nine children.

IRISH FEVER?
NO CURE

JOHN HRYCKO

John Hrycko is the embodiment of the American dream and of a prototypical Subway Alumnus. He owns a commercial printing company in Dowagiac, Michigan, near his beautiful spread in Eau Claire, Michigan. Born in France of Polish-Ukranian parents, he graduated from Western Michigan University and became a die-hard Notre Dame fan decades ago. The well-read Hrycko had three daughters married at the Notre Dame Basilica with Father Hesburgh performing the ceremony for the middle one. Two of his daughters graduated from Notre Dame. He has not missed a Friday football luncheon in years. Touring the Notre Dame campus with Hrycko is like being with a walking encyclopedia On a recent tour of the campus, a reporter notated just some of the interesting facts that Hrycko spouted. The following is a sample:

Frank Leahy made the seconding speech for Dwight Eisenhower's nomination...Jerome Heavens was the first Notre Dame back to gain 200 yards in a game...in 1977, he gained 1,000 yards, and then he lost six yards on his last carry of the season, so he didn't get the coveted 1,000 mark after all...only the Indianapolis Motor Speedway has more Indiana tourists than Notre Dame...over 700,000 people a year visit Notre Dame...in 1968, Michigan, my home state, averaged only 67,000 in their stadium, which, at that time, seated 101,001; late in that '68 season Moose Krause and Don Canham, the athletic director at Michigan, shook hands on playing a series, but the Michigan-Notre Dame rivalry series couldn't start until 1978...Rockne wanted the Notre Dame Stadium to seat 100,000 like Michigan's did...when Michigan's stadium was built Fielding Yost wanted a stadium that held 300,000...there were no Notre Dame home games in 1929...Father Corby was the chaplain of the Irish brigade at Gettysburg, and there is a statue of Corby at Gettysburg identical to the one at Notre Dame...Subway alumni came from the fact that back in the 20s, Notre Dame went to New York City to play Army at the Polo Grounds, Ebbets Field in Brooklyn, and at Yankee Stadium, hence the term Subway Alumni...Moose Krause is Lithuanian—he has a son, a priest, who teaches in a college out east—Moose's real name is Krauciunas—he died at Christmas-time back in '92, eleven years after he retired as athletic director—Moose was an All-American basketball player at Notre Dame three years in a row, and the only basketball player who accomplished that before Krause was John Wooden at Purdue; in the whole history of college basketball, less than 20 guys have done that...the Navy is the biggest source of research money for Notre Dame...Gerry Faust put up the "Play Like a Champion Today" sign in the locker room just before the 1981 season as a motivational ploy. It had nothing to do at all with Notre Dame's bookstore connection with Champion Products. Actually, the Oklahoma Sooners have had this sign and same tradition since the days of Bud Wilkinson...Willingham actually had Charlie Weis observe spring practice for a day in 2004 and speak to the team afterwards—Weis was not complimentary at all as he reviewed the team's effort that day...the alumni lottery for season tickets started in 1966. In '92, for the first time, Notre Dame returned more dollars in season-ticket applications than they kept.... Home football games for this coming season will mean about forty-five million dollars in additional income coming into the South Bend area.

Monk Malloy's basketball team in the annual Bookstore Tournament—when he was president of Notre Dame—was named *All the Presidents Men*...Notre Dame has had three guys finish second in the Heisman race...the Rocket was second in 1990, Theismann in 1970 and Angelo Bertelli in 1941....In 1983, Faust was 15 points away from a 10-1 record—instead he finished 6-5...in 1967, ABC televised the spring game nationally...Knute Rockne had no high school diploma...once in a pre-game speech, Dan Devine's dentures flew out—he caught them, and immediately put them back in...Bob Golic once had 26 tackles against Michigan when he was a junior... much of the *Rudy* movie was filmed at half time of the Notre Dame-Boston College game in '92..........

THE BUNCH,BACK OF NOTRE DAME

STEVE FILBERT

The best kept secret at Notre Dame on foot-ball weekends could be the Friday Night Smoker, held at The Santa Maria Knights of Columbus Council on Douglas Road, on the north side of campus. It commences 30 min-utes after the pep rally. The admission fee is only $5, the three speakers are usually excel-lent, and there's no expiration date on fun. The coordinators are Steve and Mary Filbert who labor arduously to continue the Smoker tradition, which began back in the 1940s.

We had a council on Michigan Street, right next to Memo-rial Hospital. When they talked about Smokers, they meant 'you couldn't breathe' Smoker. These fans would come in with their cigars. At that time, we got some really good names—the head football coach at Notre Dame would show up for at least one Smoker a year. Usually, Duffy Daugherty would come in for a Smoker. It would be standing room only in the hall at that time. As the other Councils were breaking away from our Council, form-ing their own, our membership dropped.

For our speakers, Ara Parseghian is probably the most popular.... A few years ago, we tried to change the name to the Notre Dame Pre-views, and it bombed very badly. I would call people up and say, "This is Steve Filbert with the Notre Dame Previews." They would go, "Who?" "What?" I'd say, "You know, the old Smokers." "Oh yeah, the Smokers." Finally, after a year of trying, I just gave up. I said, "Okay, it's the Smokers, but we don't allow anybody to smoke." Tradition is a hard thing to change…besides, if you laid all the people who smoke back-to-back around the world, 81% of them would drown.

SONG OF SONGS

- "The Notre Dame Victory March" has won multiple polls as the greatest college fight song ever. It was written in 1908 by two alums: John and Mike Shea. John Shea, who wrote the words, lettered in baseball at Notre Dame before taking his volley cheer on high in 1965 in Holyoke, Massachusetts.

- When Notre Dame beat sixth-ranked USC 23-14 in '73, USC Coach, John McKay, walked off the field humming "The Victory March."

- When ND defeated UCLA in 1974 to end the longest winning streak in college basketball history (88 games), UCLA star Bill Walton left the floor singing "The Victory March."

- Lou Holtz was schooled by the Sisters of Notre Dame at St. Aloysius in East Liverpool, Ohio. The school day commenced and ended with the playing of "The Notre Dame Victory March."

- In the late sixties, almost one-third of all junior high and high schools in the United States used some version of "The Victory March" as their school song.

- Because fans get so excited upon hearing "The Victory March," the Irish Guard's priority is to pave the way for the band and prevent fan interference as they march.... The Irish Guard has an annual standing date with the USC cheerleaders.

- Arguably, the second most famous fight song, Michigan's "Hail to (The Victors)," was written in South Bend in a house where the College Football Hall of Fame now stands.

- Rights to "The Notre Dame Victory March" are owned by Edwin Morris and Company, a division of MPL Communication.

A NOTRE DAME VOLUNTEER GITTIN' 'ER DONE

GARY YOUNG

Gary Young, 54, is a retired detective in Maryville, Tennessee—near Knoxville. His uncle, Ben Young, in Maryville, has one of the largest college football helmet collections in the country.

I go to a game every single year, and we always stay at the Holiday Inn in Niles, Michigan. I'll never forget one game as long as I live. Southern Cal beat us badly. I was coming out of my room to get some ice. There was a Southern Cal fan walking down the hallway. He was pretty inebriated and was really loud and obnoxious. He was blaspheming us, yelling and singing "Fight On"—that stinking song we all hate. He was bragging on the game. I am four or five rooms down from where he was when…all of a sudden, I see a door fly open. I can't really see the person, but this door opens…and a table lamp comes flying out and just coldcocks him. It was pretty severe. It knocked him flat out right there in the hallway.

People were just stepping over this USC fan. He looked deader than disco. It was strange. Finally, the guy came to, got up and just went bouncing off both walls going down through there again. It was just amazing. It was as if absolutely nothing had happened. People just stepped over him, like, "Okay. So, that guy's knocked out." Maybe they thought he was just passed out drunk. They hardly even looked down at him. It was over! Of course it would never happen, but I thought to myself, "Come up here and cheer against Notre Dame, and you're on your own."

It reminds me of that ESPN commercial. It's two guys at the rest home—both of them are on walkers. One is an Alabama fan and the other is an Auburn fan. One of them falls, and he's reaching for the other guy to help him get up. The man just walks right by him, and, then, he turns around and laughs. He's wearing an Alabama hat and the Auburn guy is still on the ground.

The Tennessee fans make fun of us for playing the service academies for years and years. I noticed, interestingly, that in 2007, we've got all three of them back on there. They'll say, "Notre Dame hasn't beaten anybody. Who have they played?" I know the Tennessee team is tough, but I know that when Tennessee plays somebody tough in the SEC, they usually lose. They kept talking about their "November Streak." Well, the reason Tennessee had a "November Streak" is they're playing Vanderbilt, Kentucky, and Memphis. They've got several *gimme* games. Now, in the shape Tennessee is in, no game seems to be a *gimme*.

The thing that has always amazed me about Tennessee is no matter what their season is doing, the Tennessee fans are more concerned with what Notre Dame is doing...even when they weren't playing each other. All they want to do is whine about Notre Dame—even when Notre Dame is not on their schedule and has absolutely nothing to do with who they are playing. They call in to the talk shows and bad mouth Notre Dame. It's just pure jealousy of Notre Dame. Notre Dame has had a little bit of tough sledding in the last few years. When you start looking at the number of Heisman winners from Notre Dame, and the number of national championships, Tennessee can't even compare. That sticks in their craw.

I have this good friend, who is just a real Tennessee fan. I've got a Heisman football signed—not stamped, but signed—by all seven Notre Dame Heisman Trophy winners. He was bad-mouthing Notre Dame one day. So, I came in and handed him an old football and said, "Here, I've got something for you." He said, "What is it?" I said, "It's signed by all of Tennessee's Heisman Trophy winners." Of course, there wasn't a single signature on it!

The worst was 1991, when Tennessee won 35-34 in South Bend. Notre Dame was ahead 34-7 at one time. Tennessee returned a blocked field goal. Long before Tennessee scored the last couple of touchdowns, it was like a snowball rolling downhill. You could see what was coming. It was just a matter of, "Oh, God!" It was horrible. I'm the type who just lives and dies with Notre Dame. I'm not one of these fans who says, "Oh, doggone it, we lost." I take it hard. The fact that it was Tennessee was salt in the wound. The fact that we had such a huge lead made it even worse. That's where I don't really understand Notre Dame fans as long as I've known them—if that game had been at Tennessee and things had been reversed—Tennessee fans would have been tearing the walls down. Notre Dame fans just don't seem to react.

I have been somewhat dismayed, particularly, in recent years. The average fan at a Notre Dame game is about 65 or 70 years old. They've had tickets since time immemorial. I always say they do the "golf clap." When Notre Dame scores, they do the real quiet golf clap. They are nowhere as fervent as Tennessee fans, who are just rabid, as are all SEC fans. Notre Dame can take it or leave it. They like it when they win, but there's no distress when they don't win. That was one thing that really bothered me. I was afraid we might never be back. Notre Dame compares to no one—our tradition and rich history. Yet, when I first saw that little rinky-dink stadium, after having seen Tennessee all these years, I could not believe that was Notre Dame's stadium…that was before the addition.

Part of it, I think, is the age of the season-ticket holders at Notre Dame—they are just too damn old. If you look around, I'll guarantee you that the people sitting beside you, behind you and in front of you are old enough to be greeters at Wal-Mart…and got money. They've got money they haven't even knocked the dust off of yet. The Tennessee crowd is a much more raucous, younger, more boisterous group of people.

If you thought the Maytag repairman was lonely, try being a Notre Dame fan in Tennessee.

SPORTS ILLUSTRATED

a *Time Inc. weekly publication*

25 CENTS
$7.50 A YEAR

PAUL HORNUNG

HE LEADS THE IRISH
AGAINST OKLAHOMA

SCOUTING REPORTS
ON THE TWO TEAMS

FOOTBALL
5th WEEK

TIME

THE WEEKLY NEWSMAGAZINE

NOTRE DAME'S LATTNER
A bread-and-butter ball carrier.

A VRRROOOOM WITH A VIEW

MIKE LEEP

Mike Leep runs one of the largest auto dealer empires in the United States. The Gurley-Leep group has 18 dealerships in the greater Michiana area. When the Notre Dame administrators or coaches need to travel on short notice, they often hop a ride on Leep's private plane. Leep winters in Ft. Myers Beach, FL.

I went to a Christian school. The Catholic school was a block away. Each of us thought the other ones were going to hell.

We were programmed to hate Notre Dame. We really, really were… and, so I did. But, when I moved to South Bend and went to that football game, that 1977 Purdue-Notre Dame game, it was really life-changing for me as far as my relationship to Notre Dame. I saw my first Notre Dame game in 1961 at Northwestern University when Ara Parseghian was the coach. He beat Notre Dame 12-10. He beat them three or four times in a row.

I played golf with Ara last Tuesday morning. He's 82 years old now, and he shot an 81. He winters in Destin, Florida. He's got all the memory. He is good. He remembers his players. He remembers the plays. He remembers the games. He remembers people. He doesn't remember to give me enough strokes. Of the Notre Dame coaches, Lou Holtz was the best golfer. I shouldn't say that. I played with Ara at a different time in his life than I played with Lou. Tyrone was a good golfer. Gerry Faust is the most improved golfer I've ever seen in my life. When I first started playing with Gerry Faust—and this is not an exaggeration—he'd shoot 125 or 130. Here's why you would know he'd shoot 125 or 130 because Gerry Faust kept score of every swing, no matter how embarrassing it was or how embarrassing the score was. But, now, Gerry shoots in the mid-nineties to high-eighties. He's really changed his game around.…I played Augusta National with

Lou Holtz. He was two over, and he was upset. He's a real competitor. He's a fast player. This guy does not like to waste a minute.

I've had a wonderful relationship with every head coach there except for Bob Davie. There's a reason for that. Here's what I would tell you about Bob Davie. First of all, I really do think he's done a great job on ESPN. Bob Davie never cared one iota for Notre Dame. All Bob Davie cared about was Bob Davie. That's just my humble opinion, and I'm just one guy on the outside looking in. I spent two years with Gerry Faust. I spent it with Lou Holtz. I was very, very close to Tyrone. I've been fortunate enough to be pretty tight with Charlie.

Bob Davie was the only guy that didn't bleed blue. He would say things like, "I don't care about the past. I don't care about Notre Dame's past. I just care about right now." I tell you, when you throw all that tradition out the window and say it doesn't mean anything, that's bulls—-. Kids play on emotion. They play on the past...and they play on the future. They don't just play on *now*. He never bought into it. It was all about Bob, just all about Bob.

Tyrone Willingham, a wonderful, wonderful man, had to weigh every word that he ever said before he said it because everybody was ready to jump on him...and they were.

Kevin White is the hardest-working athletic director in America—19-hour days. His wife is in there 100 percent with him. It is truly a team effort. She works as hard for the University as he does. If Kevin's at a function, she's at a function. He probably goes to 25 or 30 functions a week. He's the best we've ever had.

Living in South Bend is like living and going to heaven. You don't have to die to get there. When I came there, I really started growing my company. It's a wonderful place to do business. It's got good Midwestern values. With my son working, I get to be in Florida, and that's a good deal. I'm really blessed.

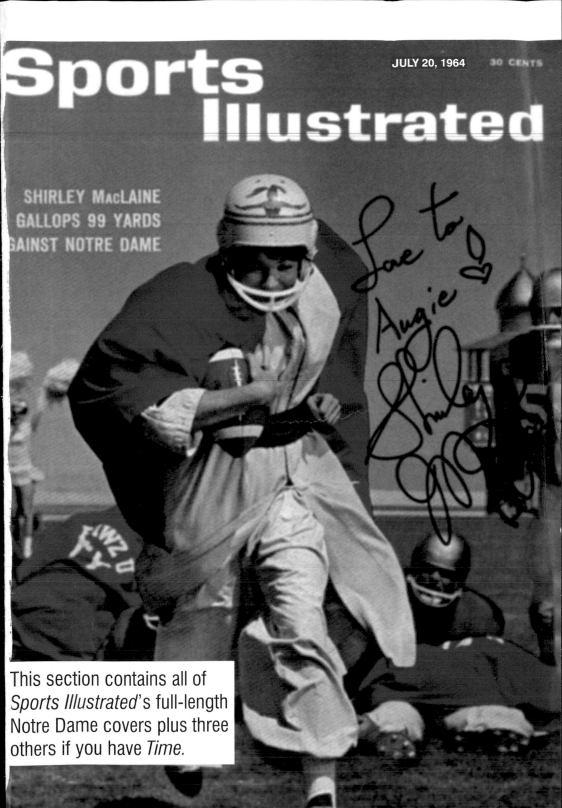

Sports Illustrated

JULY 20, 1964   30 CENTS

SHIRLEY MacLAINE
GALLOPS 99 YARDS
GAINST NOTRE DAME

*Love to
Augie* ♡

This section contains all of
Sports Illustrated's full-length
Notre Dame covers plus three
others if you have *Time.*

TIME

The Weekly Newsmagazine

COACH ROCKNE

"No chocolate, cocoa, greasy fried potatoes, pork or bananas."
(See Sport)

Volume X

Number 19

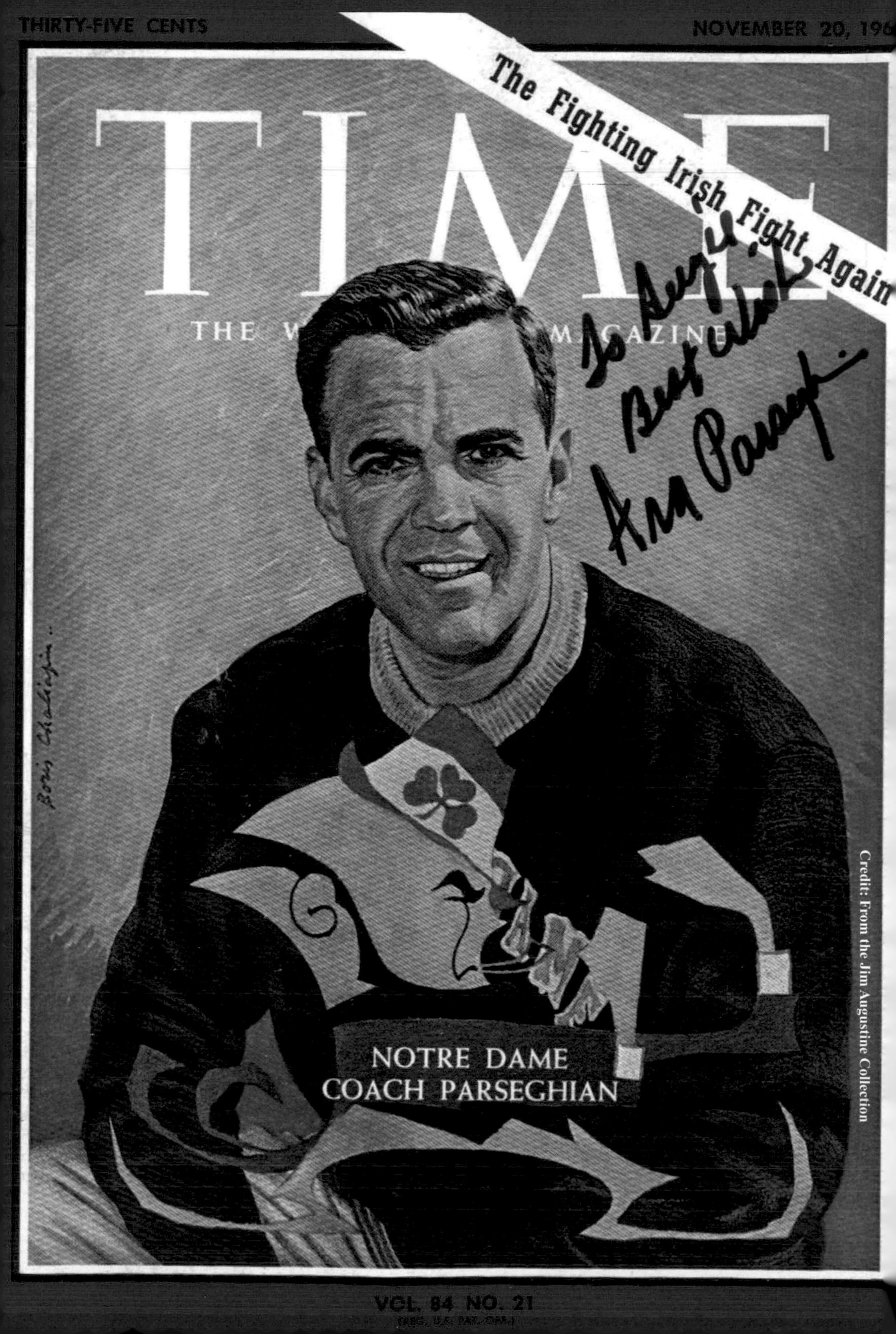

THIRTY-FIVE CENTS

NOVEMBER 20, 196

The Fighting Irish Fight Again

TIME

THE W   MAGAZINE

NOTRE DAME
COACH PARSEGHIAN

Boris Chaliapin

VOL. 84 NO. 21
(REG. U.S. PAT. OFF.)

OCTOBER 26, 1959

America's National Sports Weekly

25 CENTS
$7.50 A YEAR

SPORTS ILLUSTRATED

PREVIEW
THE BIG DUEL IN
PRO BASKETBALL

GEORGE IZO
NOTRE DAME QUARTERBACK

Sports Illustrated

NOVEMBER 2, 1964   35 CENTS

NOTRE DAME RETURNS TO POWER

QUARTERBACK JOHN HUARTE

FUROR OVER NO.

Sports Illustrated

NOVEMBER 28, 1966   40 CENT

NOTRE DAME RUNS OUT THE CLOCK AGAINST MICHIGAN STAT

Credit: Neil Leifer /SPORTS ILLUSTRATED

Sports Illustrated

NOVEMBER 7, 1966   40 CENTS

A NEW LEGEND AT NOTRE DAME

QUARTERBACK TERRY HANRATTY

Sports Illustrated

JANUARY 11, 1971

60 CEN

NOTRE DAME STOPS TEXAS
Joe Theismann Scoring

Sports Illustrated

NOVEMBER 5, 1973   60 CENTS

NOTRE DAME STACKS UP USC

Anthony Davis goes nowhere

Sports Illustrated

DECEMBER 9, 1974   75 CENT

WHAT A COMEBACK!
USC and Anthony Davis shatter Notre Dame

Credit: Sheedy & Long /SPORTS ILLUSTRATED.

Sports Illustrated

SEPTEMBER 30, 1974   75 CENTS

HEIR TO A TRADITION

Notre Dame Quarterback
Tom Clements

Sports Illustrated

SEPTEMBER 29, 1975   75 CENTS

DEVINE WEEK FOR NOTRE DAME

Quarterback Rick Slager

COLLEGE FOOTBALL '77

Sports Illustrated

SEPTEMBER 5, 1977 $1.25

THE IRISH WAKE THE ECHOES

Notre Dame's
Peerless
Ross Browner

Sports Illustrated

JANUARY 9, 1978   ONE DOL

THE IRISH
RAN WILD

Notre Dame's
Terry Eurick
Shocks Texas

JIMMY CARTER'S TOUGHEST RACE: EXCLUSIVE PHOTOS

Sports Illustrated

SEPTEMBER 24, 1979 $1.25

FLYING START
FOR THE IRISH

Vagas Ferguson
Leads the Way
Against Michigan

10094 0 39
724454

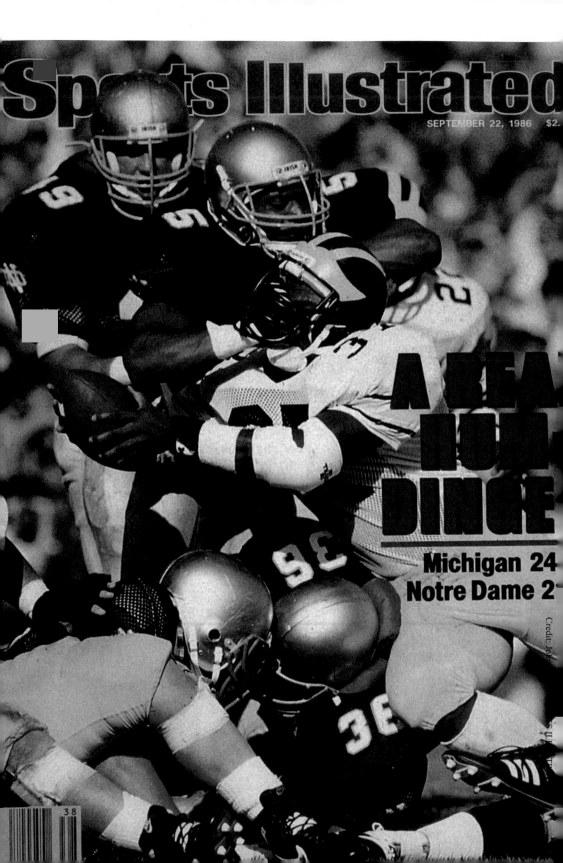

Sports Illustrated

SEPTEMBER 22, 1986 $2.

A REAL HUMDINGER

Michigan 24
Notre Dame 2

Credit: John

SI LP

38

Sports Illustrated

NOVEMBER 5, 1984 $1.95

'I'M GONNA MAKE IT!'

Embattled Notre Dame Coach Gerry Faust

4 5

COLLEGE FOOTBALL '87

OKLAHOMA IS NO. 1

SOONERS 4

AUGUST 31, 1987

Sports Illustrated

$2

NOTRE DAME'S
MR. T

**TIM BROWN:
BEST PLAYER
IN THE LAND**

**HERE'S THE CATCH:
A GALLERY OF
TOP RECEIVERS**

**THE GENTLE ART
OF 'HOSTESSING'
THE PROSPECTS**

**REMEMBERING
IOWA'S HEROIC
NILE KINNICK**

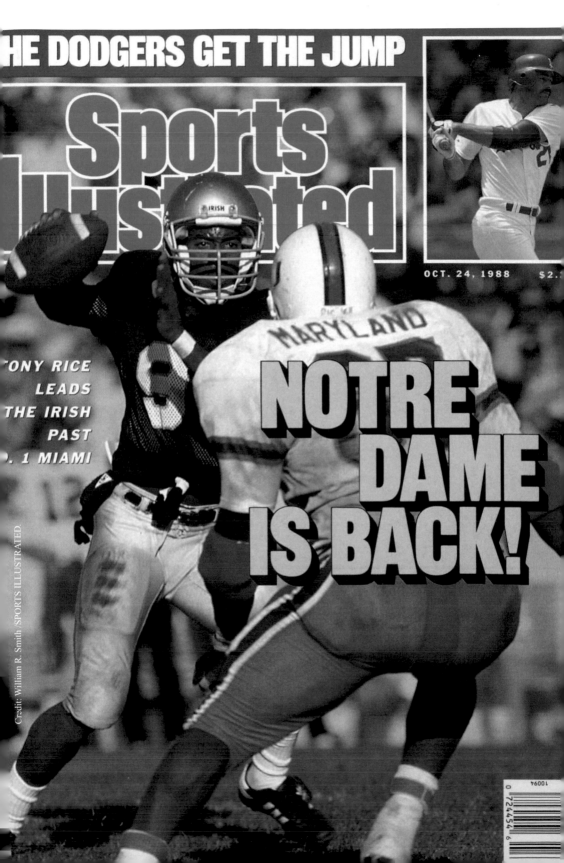

HE DODGERS GET THE JUMP

Sports Illustrated

OCT. 24, 1988 $2.

TONY RICE
LEADS
THE IRISH
PAST
. 1 MIAMI

MARYLAND

NOTRE DAME IS BACK!

DECEMBER 5, 1988

$2.25

Sports Illustrated

GREAT DAY FOR THE IRISH

NOTRE DAME'S TONY RICE

JAN. 9, 1989

$2.25

Sports Illustrated

IT'S A
CHAMPIONSHI
SEASON
FOR
TONY RIC
AND TH
IRISH

SEPTEMBER 25, 1989 $2.69

Sports Illustrated

ROCKET MAN

NOTRE DAME'S

RAGHIB ISMAIL

BURNS MICHIGAN

10094

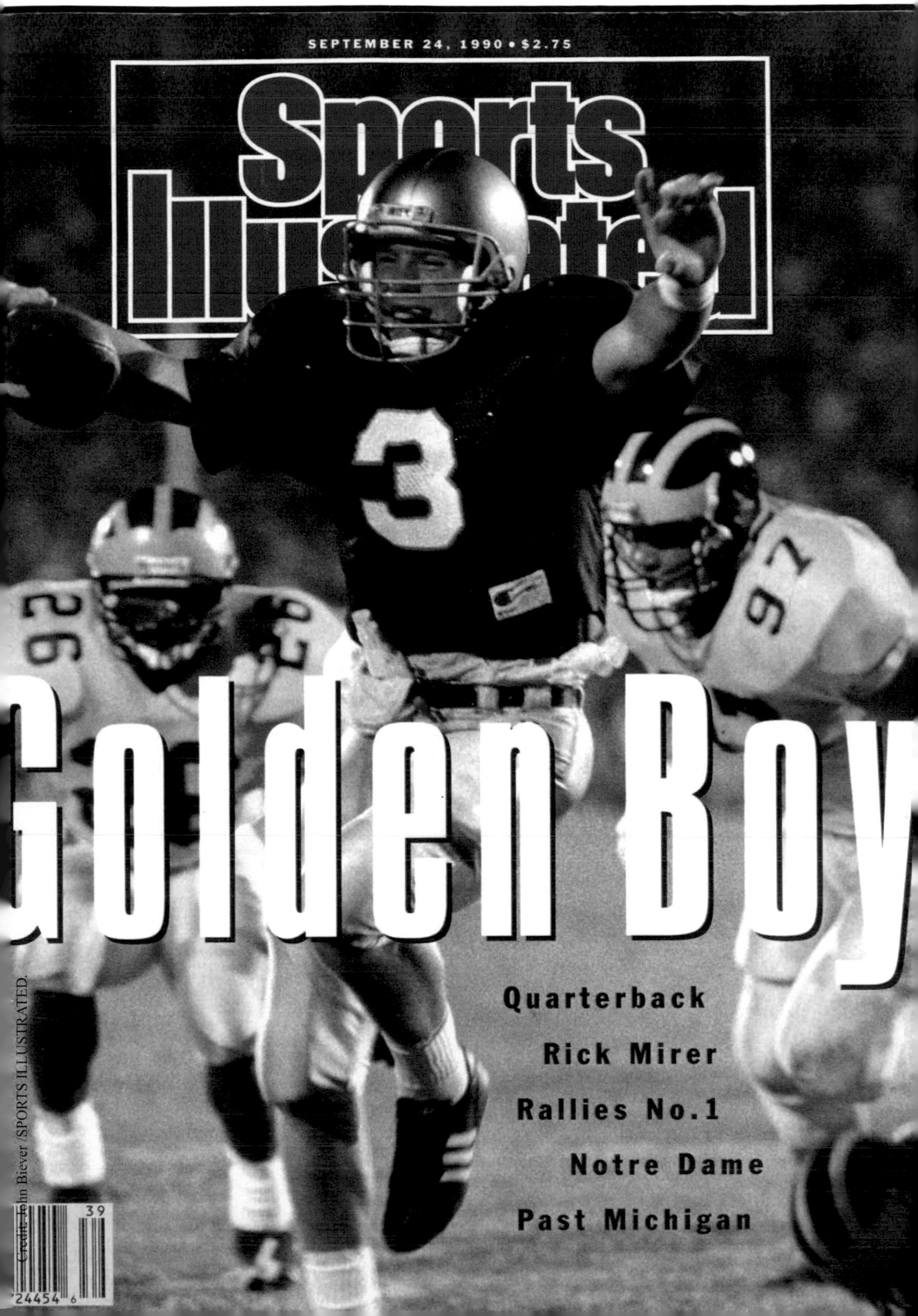

SEPTEMBER 24, 1990 • $2.75
Sports Illustrated
Golden Boy
Quarterback
Rick Mirer
Rallies No.1
Notre Dame
Past Michigan
Credit: John Biever /SPORTS ILLUSTRATED.

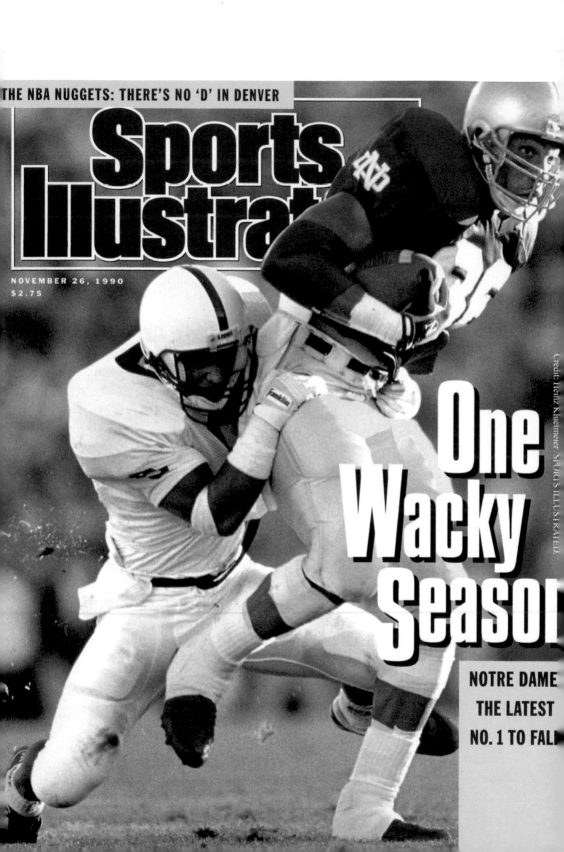

Sports Illustrated

NOVEMBER 26, 1990
$2.75

One Wacky Season

NOTRE DAME
THE LATEST
NO. 1 TO FALL

BRUARY 25, 1991 · $2.75

Sports Illustrat

READY FOR
LIFT-
OFF

Rocket Ismail:
The Next Megastar?

NOVEMBER 22, 1993 • $2.95 (CAN. $3.95)

Sports Illustrated

IRISH

44

WE DID IT!

Jim Flanigan and Notre Dame Outmuscle Florida State

0 724454 6
47
10004

College Hoops Preview

NOV. 29, 1993·$2.95 (CAN. $3.95

Sports Illustrated

Down Goes No.1 (Again)

Boston College Knocks Off Notre Dame

48

724454

SEPTEMBER 23, 1996
50 (CAN. $3.95)

Sports Illustrated

Now or Never

Can Ron Powlus finally become a Notre Dame legend?

BASEBALL MVPs: SI's PICKS

Sports Illustrated

RETURN TO GLORY

Notre Dame

WHAT A DIFFERENCE A COACH MAKES

Maurice Stovall (21) grabs a touchdown pass in a 21–17 Irish win over Michigan State

Sports Illustrated

ON CAMPUS

November 4, 2

WWW.SI.COM
AOL Keyword:
Sports Illustrated

Need a lift? Notre Dame will
give you a jolt, whether in the
raucous student section (right)
or the calm of the Grotto (p. 15).

The Perfect Week.

An Eight-Day Odyssey
Across College Nation

With stops at: **NOTRE DAME**, CAL,
TEXAS A&M and nine other campuses

Florida's PERFEC
AWFUL WEE

YEAH, THAT'S THE SPIRIT

To me, Notre Dame is special. It's a family of people, of brotherhood. I treasure that Notre Dame brings people from all different backgrounds, from all different walks of life, together in a common spirit—that camaraderie.

Not having been able to go to Notre Dame, I think, as we get older, just speaking for myself and some of the people I know who are "subways," we realize what a privilege it is to have a university like Notre Dame—what it does for the kids who graduate. The idea is that someday, somewhere, I want to help some kid who never thought he could graduate from Notre Dame do just that! I want to be part of that experience. I want it to mean as much to the people 20 years from now as it does to me right now. That's part of my love for Notre Dame. It's such a fabulous institution that it prepares people so well, as well as any other college in the country, and the idea that it's a family.

———**KEITH CROSS**, 33, Worcester, Massachusetts

Last year, when I left the field against Navy, and went upstairs to the press box, I looked out over the campus of the university. The trees were turning—that's always a special time for me because it takes me back to my youth. Anytime you can go to a sporting event, you're going to lose reality and be a child again for a while. Just looking out over the university and what it has become and how it has become that and what the education would have been like for me. Just that setting and looking out to the Golden Dome and seeing that, if there's a better place on a Saturday, for a football game in this country, if I go there, I'll know it. I'm not holding my breath.

———**ED FARMER**, Chicago native

There is no way I could put into words what Notre Dame has meant in my life. From my first moment, coming to Notre Dame, people have been incredibly good to me, like having a large, extended family. I can't even tell you the number of people when I was a student, who did great favors for me—teachers, priests, rectors, alumni, fellow students—just staggering the number of things that were done to assist me. Notre Dame is what we call the 'Notre Dame family,' and there is a lot of that family spirit about the place. I'm kind of a spirit, rah-rah kind of guy. I wanted to be part of something that has that. I'm the kind of person that when I have that in me, it motivates me. If you enjoy that, then you want to be part of Notre Dame, or you want to be a Marine, or you want to be an **FBI AGENT,** or you want to play for the Yankees—if you're into that. Or, you want to go to West Point. You want to be part of something that has a great tradition. If you're part of that, really, you feel it, it enhances your life. If you're not part of that, you look at people who do it, and you look askance at them. It's sort of the way liberals look at evangelical Christians. They think they're all crazy. They think there's something wrong with them because they are so content in their religious beliefs. I compare Notre Dame to—and this may sound kind of silly—believing in Santa Claus. If you believe in Santa Claus, there's nothing like it. Christmas is exciting, and you're just as happy as you can be. If you don't believe in Santa Claus, you think anybody who does has something wrong with them. A better analogy might be believing in Jesus. But, it's the same thing. If you believe in your Christian faith, then it sustains your life. If you don't believe it, then you think that people who do are somehow backward.

——*CAPPY GAGNON*, 62, South Bend

Notre Dame is everything in my life. Other than my family, which everybody has to exclude, Notre Dame is my life. Would you ever think, growing up, a little kid in Neosho, Missouri, I was going to get to work 32 years at Notre Dame? And, cover Notre Dame football and baseball and basketball? That's some pretty heavy stuff. I always said this—the people who are at Notre Dame are supposed to be here, for whatever reason. You can get all the benefits of going religious and blind luck you want, but people who stay here for any length of time or go to school here—they're supposed to be here. I'm sure there are people at other institutions and schools that can say

> **J. Edgar Hoover admired Notre Dame. During Hoover's long reign at the Bureau, the FBI hired more agents that were Notre Dame graduates than those from any other college…and he rarely gave them a pink slip. (The author couldn't resist that last remark. He'll show himself to the principal's office now.)**

that, but the only one I've experienced is here so that's the only one I can talk about. I firmly believe that. I firmly believe that God has blessed me to such a great degree that he has allowed me to stay here for as long as I have and raise my children in this community and be associated with the university, and I don't take it lightly. I've had chances to go other places. Most broadcasters, if you stick around a little bit, certainly should—either you're real unlucky or really bad. I just can't do it. I've never found anything that would match up to it. The job itself is basically the same—it's where you do it that's the difference.

——**JEFF JEFFERS**, WNDU -TV, 32 years at station

…I feel so fortunate in life personally. There was another experience I was able to share with my dad. On the last game of my senior season, we also had the opportunity to run out of the tunnel. They announce all the seniors at their last game. They announced us as well, and what a thrill to get—as a female—to have that opportunity to really be a part of that tradition was second to none. I also was able to bring my father down onto the field. The pomp and circumstance that surrounds game day—you're down on the field when the band comes in…. The singing of the National Anthem and the Preamble…. You just feel all of that excitement. You feel it in your heart. It really gives you chills. I was fortunate to be in that position where I could share it with my father, who had put me through this university for four years and dealt with all my tears and my excitement. To share that with him was so meaningful on that last day.

Notre Dame is just such a special place…. The players are so big. When they put the pads on, they're even bigger. The other thing is mental. I had the opportunity to be on the field for the Florida State-Notre Dame game in '93. The mentality of those guys was unbelievable. I was working with the offensive linemen that day, who were so mentally prepared and hyped. By halftime—these guys are sitting on the bench with Coach Moore—it was "You know what—we've got them. Their line is frustrated. They're yelling at each other. We've got them. We've got this game." It's just the most inspirational moment that you have when you realize who are the real leaders and just the power of being able to motivate and be caught up in that moment. It was unbelievable.

——**MARY THERESE (KRAFT) WILLIAMS**, '96, student football trainer

My basement is all Notre Dame, starting with framed pictures and bobble-head dolls and cheerleader dolls. When people see me now, they say, "There's Notre Dame Harvey." Everybody says, "You're the greatest Notre Dame fan." I say, "I'm not the greatest. We're all in the same boat. If Joe Blow's watching the game at home and I'm at the stadium, we're all there to cheer the Irish on." It makes me proud to be part of it. We're all part of that great university. That's the way I take it. I never went to school there. I wish I would have had the opportunity, but I have so much respect for people who graduate from that school. People say to me, "What makes you so proud of Notre Dame people?" The people I have met—people from Minnesota, Texas, California, Harrisburg, Pennsylvania who I could call right now and just have a conversation. It's the tailgating before and after the game. The reminiscences of talking about it—the Miami game of '88 or the Florida State game in '93, or the BC game that Gordon kicked the field goal to beat us. I was actually on the BC sidelines for that game. The friend of mine who's with the Carolina Panthers was the equipment manger for BC at the time. When Gordon went out to kick that field, I'm praying, "I hope you miss. I hope you miss." It was like seeing your best friend's wake viewing.

——BOB SUMNER, Wildwood, N. J.

When the band marches into the tunnel, I'm standing right there waiting for them. I've had people graduate from Notre Dame who have never, ever had a chance to stand in the tunnel for pre-game. I had met them when they were students, and they've come back and I've got them into the tunnel. The hour in the tunnel before the band gets there and after the band gets there and before kickoff is the greatest thing you could ever experience. I guarantee you it's something you will never, ever forget.

Let's say we're playing Florida State. Bobby Bowden walks right past you. Our first game this year, Joe Paterno. You're right outside their locker room, and you see their guys come out and do their stretches and their exercises, getting loose. All the VIPs are coming past you, going down onto the field. They get a pre-game pass. That's how I met Tommy Lasorda. There can be movie stars and businessmen and athletes. The USC-Notre Dame game is like The Who's Who of the College Football Hall of Fame. You're right there elbow-to-elbow with all those people. Then, the band marches in. It's so loud, and the drums are roaring. The music's blaring. They're playing "The Fight Song." You just feel like you want to cry. Half the band goes to the right side of the tunnel. The other half goes to the left side of the tunnel. They stand there until both teams come off the field after their pre-game warm-ups. Then, when Notre Dame comes up the tunnel, they're blaring "The Fight Song," and you're giving everybody high-five. The coaches give you high-fives. The players give you high-five. Then, when the visitors team comes up, the Notre Dame band blows the whistle three times, and then they all stand at attention and they intimidate the visiting team. You're not allowed to say a word, you don't even look at them, you just look right through them. It's very intimidating because you can hear a pin drop. The team actually has to walk right through our band to get to their tunnel. As soon as the last player for the visiting team gets in the locker room, the band runs down the tunnel and take the field. I tell people to bring a camcorder because you have to put it in a video—you can't even describe how cool it is.

————JIMMY ZANNINO, ND Stadium grounds crew

I had no desire to go to Notre Dame, but my father pushed me—I had no choice. It was my first Friday night on campus. My roommate and I were in our room in Cavanaugh Hall. All of a sudden, we heard this commotion. We didn't know what it was, but we left our room and went out on the Main Quad where we now see thousands of students and the band racing down the Quadrangle. We were totally unprepared for this. They came closer and went racing into the Field House. It was at that moment, when I was in the middle of that band playing and those people running, that I finally understood what my father had wished his whole life that I could experience. It had nothing to do with academics. It had to do with that tremendous sense of energy that came with "The Fight Song" and with the rally and with the players up there on the balcony. There was dirt on the floor, and there was 'that' smell in there. It was that whole experience. I was so grateful that he had insisted that I get that because he knew what "that" was and I didn't...until that moment....

Back in '64, Thanksgiving Saturday night, we were on our way to my uncle's house in Cornwall, New Jersey. I had a badge that said, "We're #1," on it. In the process of going there, Notre Dame lost the game to USC, which cost us the national title. I still had the badge on when we walked into my uncle's house. My uncle said, "Can I borrow that badge for a minute?" I said, "Sure," and took it off and handed it to him. He took it...went into the back of the house and got a green crayon...colored in the apostrophe in 'we're' so that it became 'were.' The badge now read "Were #1." I still have that badge. These Southern Cal games are killing me.

———DR. PAUL AHR, '66

I love Notre Dame from the standpoint that, when you're on the campus for the weekend of the game...and I tell everyone you have to go Friday 'cause you have to spend Friday on campus just walking around. There is no other campus in this country that you feel the traditions and the ghosts. There are times when you feel like people like Knute Rockne or George Gipp, or whomever, are walking right beside you. People just look at you goofy when I tell them that. Then, I say, "You have to go there to experience it, to know it, to feel it." Then, they finally go, and they call you and say, "You know what. You were right." People just can't convey it well enough for people to feel and understand it when you're talking face-to-face, off-campus. Once you're on campus, everybody knows. It's special in that regard. No other campus, no other stadium, gives you that feeling.

My favorite part of that Notre Dame weekend is the game itself and watching the student section. If it's the first home game, the students are wearing "the shirt." In my perspective, there is no more unified student section at a college football game like there is at Notre Dame. To me, they're as big a part of the game as the players and the teams and the game itself.

———STEVE WAITE, Michigan State Alumnus; writer

Chapter 6

The Promised Land

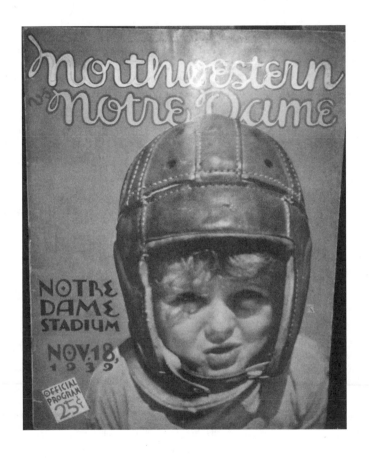

Sweet Home
Notre Dame Stadium

HE'S A MICHIGAN FAN FROM SAN FRANCISCO— NOT THAT THERE'S ANYTHING WRONG WITH THAT

TOM BRADY, SR.

In 1965, Tom Brady dropped out of the Maryknoll Seminary after six years. He took a job with North Central Airlines, where he met a spunky, gorgeous stewardess from Browerville, Minnesota, named Galynn. Their marriage produced three girls—all outstanding athletes, particularly in softball—and, finally, a boy named Tom. Tom Brady, of course, quarterbacked Michigan to 20 wins in his two years of starting there in '98 and '99 and has won three Super Bowl rings with the New England Patriots.

The author of this book has written almost two dozen sports books and none was more fun or more enjoyable as his "Tom Brady" book done in conjunction with The Sporting News.

I was raised a Catholic, went to the seminaries and Catholic schools all the way through. I always rooted against Notre Dame. They'd stockpile players. And, Ara Parseghian going for a tie in 1966! I said, "That's chicken. I never want my son associated with anybody that was not trying his best to win." They were just trying to tie and not win the game. I had two biases against them. One is, as a very early young kid, probably 1952, hearing the next-door neighbors listening to the Notre Dame football games on the radio. We didn't like those neighbors or anything they did. The second was Ara Parseghian being chicken and not going for the win in 1966. Of course, time has proven the wisdom of Ara's decision. I hated USC, too, because they always stockpiled guys, as well. When USC and Notre Dame would play, I'd root for them both to lose.

After Tom's junior year in high school, we sent a tape out to 54 colleges. I wouldn't let them send it to Notre Dame. I didn't want him to go to Notre Dame because of the bias I had. Tom didn't mind—he always rooted against Notre Dame, too. I swayed him in that direction. In retrospect, after going to Notre Dame, I think it is a magnificent institution that I would be proud to have my grandchildren go to, if that opportunity ever arises. Like, with Paul Harvey, there's always the 'rest of the story.' The rest of the story is in my own naivety, I had a bias against an organization that I think the world of right now.

Tom's first start for Michigan was to be the 1998 opener in South Bend. Tom didn't want to be intimidated by the whole aura of Touchdown Jesus and Fair Catch Sorin. One Sunday afternoon that summer, Tom was traveling back to Michigan from Chicago, where he had attended a Saturday wedding of one of his friends. He pulled off in South Bend, went in and drove around the campus. It was in late July. He was going to be starting there in about a month. He parked his car and then walked around campus and over to the stadium and walked around the outside of the stadium…just to take it all in. As he was walking around the stadium, lo and behold, he saw that a gate was open. He entered and went down on the field and walked from one end of the stadium to the other end. He went up the seats to the top of the stands on both sides of the stadium. He spent about 45-minutes inside the stadium just walking around and taking it in. It was starting to get late. He decided it was time to get going. He went back to the gate…the gate was locked. Now he says, "Aw, gee, this is not good." He knew this was a bad omen. He walked around trying to open the doors and trying to get out of the stadium. Nothing was open. He could just imagine the headline, "Michigan Quarterback Arrested While Trespassing at Notre Dame and Spends the Night in Jail." He knew that as soon as he would be back on campus, he would be in Lloyd Carr's office getting worked over. And, it would definitely be headlines on ESPN. He went around the stadium and tried to climb out over one of the railings. It was about 20 feet up. He figured he could hang down so he would only be about

12 feet to the ground. Of course, he realized that was not smart, because if he breaks a bone, he's not going to be playing there. Finally, he found a janitor's room that was open. He got in there and took a sledge hammer and went outside. There were ladders hanging on the outside walls of the stadium that were bolted to the bricks. He took the sledge hammer and broke a couple of the bolts on the ladders. Then, he got the ladder and carried it up to where he was going to hang over the stadium. He planned to drop the ladder down over the stadium wall and then climb over it. Every time he banged the hammer, it reverberated through the campus. He knew that he might get arrested by campus police.

So, on this Sunday afternoon, as he was coming down the ladders, summer session was in and people were looking at him saying, "What are you doing? What are you doing in there?" He had the fear of Touchdown Jesus in his heart. He ran to his car and didn't start breathing until he was halfway back to Ann Arbor.

Then, a month later, when Michigan was playing at Notre Dame, Michigan got down to the two-yard line and they brought Drew Henson into the game to run a sneak play. He fumbled the ball. We missed a bunch of field goals in the first half. At halftime, we were only ahead about 14-0.... In the second half, Notre Dame got the ball and went right down the field. Then, we fumbled the kickoff. Before we could blow our nose, it was 17-21. Michigan lost 36-20. We were sitting low, down about the 10-yard line. I was just so tickled that Tom got onto the field and was playing. I don't want to be sour grapes, but my thoughts were that had we not lost some of the momentum.... Notre Dame was very good, and the stadium is gorgeous. The whole opportunity to play at Notre Dame, for us—we were just blown away.

The next game, Michigan played Syracuse and got it handed to us. We were 0-2 and the fans were after Tommy's butt. They wanted to kill him even though the offense was moving the ball. We were at the Syracuse game, and the fans were booing him. That was very painful. At Notre Dame, we thought he had played pretty well, but the team lost, and he was extraordinarily disappointed.

The next year at Michigan—Tom's senior year—we beat Notre Dame. We came back in the fourth quarter, in the last few minutes, and scored with a couple of minutes to go. Michigan won 26-22. It is a battle every time Michigan and Notre Dame play no matter what the records are, they're always close. They're going to be stopping the rivalry. It shoots both teams in the foot. One team is going to lose early on, and you can't afford to lose early on anymore. You can't afford to lose at all.

At the end of Tommy's senior year, at the end of the Michigan victory over Alabama in the Orange Bowl, we were walking out of the locker room. Tommy had been throwing up on the sidelines during the overtime—he was just exhausted. Michigan was down 14 in the third quarter, tied it up, went down by 14 in the fourth quarter, and, then, tied it up and won in overtime. I walked down the tunnel and grabbed his duffel bag from him to help him a little bit because he was just really beat. Stan Parrish, a Michigan coach, came up and said to me, "You know, Tom, I've been coaching for 27 years, and I have never had more respect for somebody than I have for your son. I know what went on here, and I have the utmost respect." Any father would love hearing something like that.

Of course, after seeing and experiencing Notre Dame—even though it was in competitive situations—we have completely changed our bias. Notre Dame is truly a beautiful, wonderful place.

Charlie Weis is going to do well wherever he goes. Charlie is going to be a great fit at Notre Dame. It's a tough job—but Charlie's tough. Charlie's the man for the job. He's a motivator. You could see the kids Notre Dame had last two years ago were the same kids they had last year, and the level of play, the spirit, the energy came through on the television. I didn't see anything live, but it was very clear.

Tommy was interviewed on Sirius Radio this year right before the Super Bowl, when he was back. They asked him if he was going to root for Charlie. Tommy said, "I root for the people I really like. Yeah. I'm going to root for Charlie." He even said that he would root for Charlie when Notre Dame played Michigan this year. He really loves Charlie. It's a great relationship.

THE MARQUIS de SOD

CAPPY GAGNON

When Russell "Cappy" Gagnon left Gloucester, Massachusetts, and enrolled at Notre Dame in 1962, he had no idea that he would still be there four decades later. For the last dozen years, he has been in charge of security and game-day personnel at Notre Dame Stadium.

Twice, he has been elected president of SABR—the Society for American Baseball Research, a prestigious group of hard-core baseball fanatics. Before assuming his current campus duties, he was assistant to Pete Pitchess, the flamboyant, former sheriff of Los Angeles County. He followed that post as a key assistant to Gavin DeBecker, the renowned security chief for Hollywood stars.

Gagnon has authored Notre Dame Baseball Greats: From Anson to Yaz, *an excellent and detailed history of the national pastime at Notre Dame.*

When I was a kid growing up, I was not a Notre Dame fan—not until high school. I have no idea how that happened—it had to be more subliminal than anything. Seeing some Notre Dame games on TV was important—absolutely seeing those regular games on TV, as well as Lindsey Nelson on Sundays. Seeing the movie, *Knute Rockne, All American*. Hearing about Notre Dame people periodically like Dr. Tom Dooley, probably one of the more significant Notre Dame people that you hear about. I couldn't pick an exact time, and there was no real influence on me from family or anything like that....

It was my first pep rally as a freshman—at least one of the first. I'm in the old Field House with all kinds of goose bumps because of the emotion of students and the aura in the old Field House, the band marching in, the yelling and screaming, and the players coming up on the balcony. Everybody's clapping and yelling.

Looking straight ahead and talking to no one in particular, I said, "This is great!" The guy next to me said, "Yeah, I feel the same way." I look over, and it's Johnny Lujack. I just thought that was amazing that a Heisman Trophy winner, a famous guy, an older guy, a guy who had experienced all that first-hand, was getting the same enjoyment out of it as I was as an 18-year old…. Growing up in Massachusetts, before the **PATRIOTS**, the home team for anybody who lived in New England was the New York Giants. We got their games on TV. The announcing duo was Chris Schenkel and Johnny Lujack….

The greatest pep rallies were in the old Field House—no question. There was that dirt floor and the 100-year-old building, the atmosphere in those days was a little bit different and the players were up on the balcony. Maybe, it was because those were my first. Everybody was standing so it wasn't as formal as it is now. To me, those are the best. In the 70s, they stopped using the old Field House and tore it down. The Pep Rallies moved over to the Stephan Center, which was not good for acoustics or for the separation between the players and the fans, and it didn't hold as big a crowd either.

The best motivational speaker to me was Coach John Murphy, the football coach. In my freshman year, '62—when the team was doing poorly—there was an article in the *Scholastic* about dropping football and playing Ivy League football. It was critical of Notre Dame football. Murphy was an impressive guy, a military veteran. His brother was a World War II hero and might have even died in the war. Murphy—a big steel-jawed kind of guy with a powerful voice—was up there on the balcony, and it was just a tremendously moving speech. You can't convey it in a book, but I used to know the whole speech.

"It was World War II. I want to talk to you about a man. He was a Notre Dame man." That kind of cadence. *"He was my brother… Japanese soldiers."*

The New England PATRIOTS once played a regular-season home game in Birmingham, Alabama, in September 1968.

Another great speech was in my junior year, when the team came back from losing to Southern Cal. They held a pep rally when the team came back. The speaker was Lloyd Allen, the mayor of South Bend, probably the only Republican mayor South Bend's had in the last 100 years. He was a white-haired, very distinguished looking and stentorian-speaking person. There we are, and we're all sad because SC beat us with 1:33 to go with the aid of their officials—they stole the national championship away from us. Joe Farrell goes in and scores a touchdown with a dive play on the goal line in the first half to make it 24-0, which would have been an insurmountable lead. An official signals for a holding call. It was unheard of to have a holding call on a dive play at the goal line. In those days, the holding penalty was 15 yards. So, we don't score. In those days, most of the people at the pep rallies were just students. Now, the students are outnumbered by the fans at pep rallies. Lloyd Allen said something to the effect that someone once said, "It's not whether you win or lose, but how you play the game. Gentlemen, you played it magnificently." Speaking in a real rich-toned voice, the way he said that was great oratory….

Wayne Gretzky was a speaker at a pep rally. Because he was a famous guy, you can't advertise him as a speaker. If they're an advertised speaker, they get a fee, their agent gets a cut, and all that malarkey. He wasn't advertised, but the word leaked out. When the team comes in at the beginning of the pep rally, there were some people in the audience who knew Gretzky was going to be there. If it's reported anywhere, that a guy like Gretzky has flown into South Bend or been seen on campus, the word is going to get around pretty fast. At 6:30 when the team marches in and the lights are down, the spotlights are focusing on the team. People can see them as they walk in with the head coach. In those days, the leprechaun was the emcee. He said, "For our speaker tonight, I'm going to introduce him with just three words, and maybe you can help me—'The Great One.'" As he said that real slowly…by the time he got to 'Great' everybody was yelling it in unison.

There was a massive ovation. I'm not a big hockey fan anymore now that there are 500 hockey teams. I know he's the greatest player who ever lived, but I didn't follow hockey closely and, frankly, didn't know a lot about him. The only two things I remember from his talk are that he said because of hockey he'd never seen a football game in his life.

He said he sure had picked a great place to start for his first football game. Then, the last thing he said was that he'd had a great life, a great career but that he had only one regret in life—that he didn't come to Notre Dame to play hockey. Of course, that brought the house down with an enormous ovation—the biggest of any I've ever heard at Notre Dame. The remark was a standard 'sucking up to the crowd.' He didn't have to say it, but it was just wonderful the way he said it.

My job is to help get Gretzky out of the arena, so we had a limo waiting for him out back. I had four of the security people, and we were all ready to hustle him out. People just converged on us to get his autograph. He signed 50 or 60, which is a lot—I didn't want him to sign any because if you stop for one…in fact, I said to him, "Let's keep moving." He didn't say anything, but he just kept signing. Then, I said out loud, and this wasn't rehearsed, but it's a standard thing you do when you're with a celebrity who you want to get away, "Okay, folks, we've got to go now. Mr. Gretzky has an appointment." He turned to me and said, "No, I'm going to stay until I sign these autographs." We had a big guy on the other side of him, and the two of us put our arms around his back, and we locked arms so we could at least protect him from getting jostled and knocked around, and make it a little easier for him to do the autograph signings. He signed and signed and signed, and it went on and on and on. The more people who realized he was signing, the more people stayed. When it was finally over, he then turned to the crowd and said, "Is there anybody else?" I had never seen that in my life for a major celebrity. As we were walking to the car, he turned to me, and he said he didn't want to be like those celebrities who refused to sign autographs. That was his way of saying that was why he insisted to remain…. I was struck by how small he was. He's not tall, and since I had my arm around his back, I could feel his physique and he's not a large guy. Also, he had an incredible smile the whole time—just a handsome guy with a winning smile. He seemed like a genuinely nice person. He was very impressive.

There used to be a saying that "Nobody roots for General Motors." If you're #1, if you're the **YANKEES**, or the Celtics, or Notre Dame, you're legendary, so you generally have only supporters and detractors. I think that's true. It's like the U. S. and the world today. There's nobody neutral. Nobody has ever said honestly, "Oh, I don't particularly care about Notre Dame one way or the other." If anybody says, "Yeah, I'm a football fan, but I have no position on Notre Dame," they're lying to you.

I don't think we're arrogant. The charge comes from the fact that we take pride in striving to be the best. When you do that, you're going to get knocked down by people who can't understand that. Or, as I say, they represent places that don't make any pretense of that. Just to make an analogy, when a conservative or a minister gets in trouble for some kind of peccadillo, there are all kinds of talk about hypocrisy. When Bill Clinton was doing his thing all across the country, the same critics were silent. You're opening a bunch more charges against you when you profess to wanting to strive for excellence. A lot of people are uncomfortable because they feel you are saying you are better than they are. We never say that.

The accusation that Notre Dame hired a coach, George O'Leary, who lied on his resume—he never submitted a resume. When you're 55-years-old and have been coaching for 25 years, you don't submit a resume. He was hired on the basis of his body of work. It was silly that we got criticized on the George O'Leary deal. I can't see how. Did anybody criticize Georgia Tech? They hired him long before us. Nobody went back or wanted to take away their national championship or make fun of them. It's ridiculous.

If you're not predisposed to wanting to believe in something, you're not converted. It isn't that you're not open-minded, it's just that it's not part of your DNA. The guy who is trying to decide where to go to college, he doesn't care anything about the school, he just wants to know how good their history department is. That's a different kind of guy. You can't tell him what great school spirit Texas A&M has because he's already determined that their history department isn't that good. It's not that he's not open-minded, it's just that he doesn't

> **Thomas Edison sold the concrete to the <u>YANKEES</u> that was used to build Yankee Stadium. Edison owned the huge Portland Cement Company....Edison's middle name was Alva, named after the father of one-time Cleveland Indians owner, Alva Bradley.**

have the calling. He isn't of that flavor. He's not capable of getting that kind of feel. He doesn't have the rhythm.

Why did I return to South Bend to finish my career? My family was grown and on their own and all taken care of, I decided I could do something more selfishly just for me so I returned. It's like being a student again without having to do the homework. I could do all those things that I enjoyed doing when I was a student, except now they pay me to go to football games and basketball games and concerts. It's just unbelievable. I get to host events like that as people come to them, and I get to pass along some favors. One of the great things about my job is all kinds of people thank me for things I do for students or for people who come to the stadium. People will say, "Is there anything I can do for you?" I say, "No, listen, I don't want anything. Just pass it along. People were good to me when I was here. If I've done you a favor, pass it along to somebody else."

When you work for Notre Dame, it's such a great feeling. Hardly anybody works for Notre Dame because it's a job. It's more of a calling than a job. Even people in occupations on the campus that are not at the top of the food chain take great pride in the jobs they do for the university. You can have a good camaraderie working for Notre Dame and morale is very high.

Anything negative about Notre Dame just rankles me. I'm a believer. We're not a perfect place, and we don't claim to be—we just claim to strive for it. There's not much that we do that I think is not honorable. There are a lot of places that look the other way. We don't do that.

The BCS formula is actually a recipe for chili.

THE M.A.D.D. HATTER

TIM McCARTHY

May I have your attention please: This is a story about Sergeant Tim McCarthy, formerly of the Indiana State Police. Starting the final two games of the 1960 season, McCarthy made announcements near the end of the third quarter urging fans to be careful on their way home. After a tepid response, the next year he started ending his messages with a pun. Nearly 300 games later, he's still doing it. In 1978, McCarthy retired from the Indiana State Police to become sheriff of Porter County, halfway between South Bend and Chicago.

Back at the time when I started making the **P.A.** announcements, there were a lot of problems with fans having had too much to drink at the games. Most of those previous years, there was no toll road. So, the next season, I did a bit on drinking and driving. I said, "Remember the automobile replaced the horse, but the driver should stay on the wagon." At the time I gave it, for some reason, it seems like the stadium was quiet so it went over pretty good. I tried it again using a pun, and I've ended up doing it ever since.

I thought, "Hey, I'll just try using one of those punch lines and see what happens." I never realized it was going to be that popular. I got a

> The public address announcer for the Houston Astros (Colt '45s) in 1962 was Dan Rather. John Forsythe, the actor, was the P.A. announcer for the Brooklyn Dodgers in 1937 and 1938.

lot of my original sayings from a friend, Len Blady, who did traffic-copter reports for WGN in Chicago. Others I tried to think of myself. The ones that are really atrocious—the real corny puns—get a lot of boos. But, it got to where the cornier they were, the better people liked them. It wasn't that I was trying to be a comedian or anything like that, it was just a gimmick that worked because the idea was to do something to attract the attention of the people and make them aware of driving more safely on their way home. Now, in order to hear the punch line, they listen to the whole message. They absorb the whole thing, and the punch line gives them something to think about while they drive home. They may not remember the meat of the message, but that punch line is something that usually sticks with them.

My favorite game, over the years, was the 1977 Southern Cal game, the green-jersey game. Southern Cal was a heavy favorite. Up in the press box, I liked to stand up in an outer box where it was more in the open, and you could have a better feel of the crowd. A Southern California cameraman was standing next to me. He had never been at a Notre Dame game before in South Bend. He said, "My gosh, I can't believe the crowd noise. Is it always like that around here?" I said, "Man, that was for the band when they came out. Wait until the game starts." Then, when the team came out, the crowd never settled down. Ken McAfee, my favorite player was one of the stars of the game.

Chief Broderick used to be the head of the law school. On Fridays before every home game, he would have a pep rally in his class. He would walk in wearing an old blazer covered with Notre Dame buttons. He would invite guest speakers. The time I was invited, I was scared to death to go in and talk to those students. I had no idea what to expect. I'd written down notes for the things I was going to say—keep it short and sweet. He would introduce the speaker and the class would jump up and applaud and yell and whistle and shout and scream. He'd say, "Okay, thank you very much, Sgt. McCarthy." That was all the speaker did. The speaker didn't even get to say hello. The speaker never got to speak. He'd do that to every single speaker. They had a blast doing it.

What a lucky break I've had in my life, being able to go to all these Notre Dame games and, hopefully, maybe somewhere along the way, saving some lives.

MAY I HAVE YOUR ATTENTION, PLEASE?

These are some of Indiana State Police Sgt. Tim McCarthy's more outrageous pronouncements at Notre Dame football games.

- This is Sgt. Tim McCarthy for the **INDIANA** State Police: Fans, your police officers are always grateful for your careful driving in the heavy, after-game traffic. On the way home today, please continue with the principles of caution, courtesy and common sense. Remember, this message is not meant to give you the needle... only that you get the point.

- Please drive carefully and take your time because a traffic collision can be deadly. Remember, if you drive to beat the band, you may end up playing a harp.

- Don't let your day go down the drain by forgetting today's safety plug.

- Drinking drivers are like light bulbs: The first to get turned on are the first to burn out.

- Remember, any time your driving looks fishy, you could become the *catch of the day.*

- Please obey the laws, stay alert and, above all, do not mix drinking and driving. Remember, if you drive while you're stoned, you may hit rock bottom.

- Anyone who tries to bolt through traffic...is a real nut.

- Drinking and driving is the leading cause of traffic accidents. Please make certain the person driving your car is alert and absolutely sober. Drinking drivers are not very funny, but they can still crack you up.

- On the way home, stay alert, obey the laws and take your driving seriously. Remember if you horse around in traffic, you may get saddled with a ticket.

> When Steve Alford was a senior in high school in 1983 in New Castle, **INDIANA,** his high school team averaged more people in attendance per game than the Indiana Pacers.

THE BEST DAMN BAND IN THE LAND*...
AND WE'D DOT THE "i" TWICE
IF WE HAD ONE

LARRY DWYER

With apologies to Woody Hayes...and we'll brook no hullabaloo from the folks at dear old Texas A&M since the Fighting Aggie Band is not from this planet. Caneck?

Larry Dwyer graduated from Notre Dame in 1966 and never left campus. He is assistant director of the University of Notre Dame marching band—the Band of the Fighting Irish.

When I was a member of the band, it was, roughly, 100 guys. The spirit was great. There were bands, like Purdue, that would come here with 200—225 people and just really be able to wipe us...plus, they had the Golden Girl and the Silver Twins.

Notre Dame went coed in 1972 but two years prior, the then-band director, Robert O'Brien got permission to have St. Mary's college girls play in the Notre Dame band. He was hoping to get more players and instruments like flute, piccolo, oboe, clarinet and bassoon because often, girls play those instruments and guys tend more to brass instruments. He wished to make the instrumentation of the band fuller. The very first woman from St. Mary's who called up to be in the Notre Dame band was Rosemary Crock. Rosemary plays **SOUSAPHONE**. Robert O'Brien's plan worked quite well, and he did get a lot more students into the band on various instruments. It was always just ironic that the very first woman played the sousaphone, the biggest instrument.

> Before the band marches to the stadium on game day, the **SOUSAPHONE** section gathers by the southwest corner of the Sacred Heart Basilica. They sing "The Victory March"... and then they sing it backward...syllable-by-syllable.

There are 380 students in the Notre Dame band. The tryouts are two days before the rest of the students come to school in the fall. Most students arrive on a Friday, toward the end of August. Band members arrive two days earlier than that, on Wednesday. We have band camp on Thursday and Friday and final marching band tryouts on Sunday evening after dinner. We post the list of band members Monday morning, and usually have our first band rehearsal that Monday night just before classes start on Tuesday. Sometimes, our first home game is on the next Saturday. The brand new freshmen will be marching, right along with the whole band…so they learn fast.

The marching steps the **NOTRE DAME BAND** uses are different from that of most high school marching bands. We have flashier steps so even high school students who have had marching experience have to relearn things to get used to the Notre Dame style. Many students are from smaller Catholic high schools that may not have a marching band at all…. Deciding on our half-time show is a very interesting process. We start in the spring with student input, called the Show Committee. Any students who are presently members of the band, who are interested, get together. The students generally come up with a list of 40-50 different songs they'd like to do. During the summertime, the directors listen to those songs, pick the ones they think will best fit into marching band style and will work for Notre Dame fans.

We're trying to do a number of things with half-time shows at Notre Dame. First, we want to involve the student body so we do music that's fun. Sometimes, the Notre Dame band will set their instruments down and do a dance on the field to some of the songs that we do. That is designed to involve the student body. Since these are students playing for their peers, they want to do their best for them. But, along with that, we're also playing for parents—for alumni—we're playing for Subway Alumni. Sometimes, a show might have a traditional Sousa march or something like that which the older folks

> The **BAND** is four decades older than the football team. It is the oldest college band in continuous existence. Moose Krause once played the clarinet in the band…before Moose, Knute Rockne played the flute.

would appreciate more, along with some of the pop tunes that the students like. We try to balance different songs for different shows.

We look at which bands are coming to visit us at Notre Dame Stadium or when we're making away trips. We have some knowledge of what kinds of shows those bands will do. We always, if possible, try to figure out something that will top them or to just do a show that will be better than what we think they might do.

"The Notre Dame Victory March" has, at least two—maybe three, different versions to it. What's unique about our favorite CD is that one of the versions of the "Victory March" was recorded on game day. The band, 45 minutes before kick-off time, lines up in front of the Golden Dome and marches from there over to the stadium. If you've ever seen that march, you know that there's probably five or six thousand people lined up along the way. People are screaming and clapping along and having a great deal of fun as the band winds its way across campus. We got the idea, a couple of years ago, to actually record that live. We had a recordist with a microphone going along right in front of the band on that whole parade route from the Dome over to the stadium so you get to hear the drum cadences, the "Victory March," the "Hike Song," the "Victory March" again, 'cause we play it twice on the way over there, along with all the band cheers and just the crowd noise—actually recorded live. The CD is simply entitled "Notre Dame Victory March."

A couple of years ago, a 17-piece dance band, recorded a version of the "Victory March." It's okay, but it's not the way our band plays it. Our alums would get rather upset if we started messing around with "The Victory March." It's almost like something very holy and sacred around here. There are two parts to "The Victory March"— the verse and the chorus. The verse is the part that goes, "Rally, sons of Notre Dame." The chorus goes, "Cheer, Cheer for old Notre Dame." If I recall, the copyright has expired for the chorus. The verse is still in effect for another year or two, and then it's what's called public domain. Anybody can do anything they want to with it....

particular, oftentimes spends extra time working on their sticking and their cadences. On Friday night before games, the drums do what's called 'The Midnight Drummers Circle' right in front of the Dome. Several thousand students typically come out to see that.

Saturday is constant activity for the band. Starting at eight in the morning, we do a 'march out,' which starts at the band building and we march around the campus. We wind up going over to Loftus Athletic Facility to practice on the indoor football field. On game days, our regular practice area is covered with cars—it's used as a parking lot. Actually, we do three shows. We do pre-game, a halftime, and post-game shows so we have to practice all of those. After that is over, the band comes back to the band building. We have a meeting where we review all the information and go over what's important. Then, the students are dismissed for about an hour so they can go put on their uniforms.

The band plays 'The Concert on the Steps,'—90 minutes before game time. It's on the west side of campus on the steps of Bond Hall, which is the architecture building. It's chosen simply because it has really wide steps—it's big enough to put the entire 380-piece band up on those steps. We play a 25-minute concert where we do all the Notre Dame school songs, all the halftime music. We play the visitors' school song. We end up with "The Victory March." There are generally 8,000 at those concerts.

After the concert on the steps, each one of the sections in the band—by sections, I mean, the piccolos, the clarinets, the saxophones, the trumpets, the f-alto horns, the trombones, the baritones, the basses and the drummers—each one of the sections has some particular thing that it does. For instance, the drummers stay right over in front of Bond Hall and do about an extra 15 minute performance there where they go through all their drum cadences and drum cheers. The trumpets go over inside the Dome, up to the second floor of the administration building and make that big circle around the railing where they play the "Alma Mater" and "The Victory March." All that occurs in that extra 20 minutes between the end of the concert on the steps and when the band finally steps off toward the stadium.

LET THERE BE LIGHT

JOE CROOKHAM

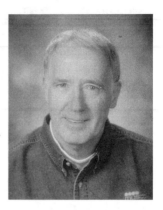

Guess what the cover story was on the sports page of the inaugural issue of USA Today, *September 12, 1982? It was about a Midwest man, Joe Crookham, who was about to drastically change the face of big-time college football. His company, Musco Lighting, devised a way to light college stadiums for night games, even though the venues had no permanent lighting system. The fact that Crookham was a pilot, who loved to fly, was an important factor in bringing to reality an almost impossible dream—a dream that first came to fruition one Saturday at Notre Dame Stadium.*

My friend, Myron, and I decided we needed to get into something where we had our own marketing control. We heard about a lighting company in Muscatine, Iowa, that was for sale. We bought the company and discontinued all the products they had. We shut down the foundry they had and bought the building. We decided six products would be a good mix, a cross-section of several things. The first product we developed was a sports lighting product, to light a ball field. It was the only product they'd had which made any sense at all. That was the first product we developed. I keep telling my partner that it's thirty years later, and he still owes me five products.

Knoxville, Iowa, has the Knoxville Raceway, and its famous World of Outlaws. NBC wanted to televise that race, back in '78 or '79. Their lights weren't adequate to do that. The people of Knoxville asked us about possibly lighting their track for them. I met with a farmer-based board of directors who really didn't have any idea what to do with a television contract offer. They didn't want to spend money to put lights at the track. After talking with them, my partner and I were trying to figure out what would be best. I joked, "Maybe we should put these lights up on a crane truck just for this event." Later, I was flying along, thinking about their problem, and I remembered that remark. The more I thought about it, I decided that may not be the dumbest idea I've ever had. Myron and I figured it wouldn't be impossible. The track wouldn't have to spend the money to permanently light the track, yet they could have the one televised event.

The next time I was in New York City, I looked up ABC, CBS and NBC in the phone book and called them and asked if they would talk to me about an idea for lighting for television. All three of them invited me to come over and talk to them. The guy at ABC said, "We've got a college football contract coming up. If that would enable us to add late afternoon and night-time games, we might be interested."

This was in the spring and summer of 1979. We had several conversations, and ABC got more serious about it. The only thing I knew about television was how to turn it on and how to complain about the programming. If I had a clue what we were getting into with this idea, I'd have gone and done something else. ABC was trying to decide whether or not this thing was really feasible. We made arrangements to go over to Kinnick Stadium in Iowa City and test it out after the football season was over.

We got one rental crane and put lights on it and the guy from ABC came out with us and we did a demonstration of it at Kinnick. ABC liked it so we took a lot of photographs of it and we started to work on perfecting it. This was only a concept of what we wanted to do.

For more than a whole year, nothing happened. Then I got a call from Don Bernstein at ABC on April 14, 1982. He said they wanted to do the Michigan—Notre Dame game that September—five months away. I asked when he'd need to know. He said Notre Dame had agreed to it, but I would need to talk with Michigan, and he would need to know "by noon tomorrow!" He said, "Any chance you can talk to them?" I said, "I guess I could fly up there. Will they be available to talk to me?"

At the Ann Arbor meeting, I got out the three-ring binder we made up from pictures we had made up of the trial at Kinnick. After our presentation, they said, "We were expecting something like carnival midway lighting, but this looks very substantial." I didn't bother to tell them it didn't exist anymore. They told us they thought it would be okay, so I went out of that meeting and called Don Bernstein. At that point, all that existed was one rental truck and a theory on paper. It occurred to me as I was going out to the airport in Lansing that I had never actually seen Notre Dame and that I probably should stop by there and find out what we had just promised.

Remembering the famous Iowa game at Notre Dame in 1953 when Notre Dame faked the injuries to stop the clock, I was still mad at Notre Dame. I had not gotten over that and had no use for Notre Dame. I stopped in South Bend and went by the campus and met with the AD there, Gene Corrigan. One of the dilemmas I had with this whole thing is, by the time we did the first game at Notre Dame, I'd fallen in love with the place. They are such nice, nice people.

We had arranged that two weeks before the game we would go over and light Notre Dame Stadium and go through a trial run. We were scrambling. I called Gene Corrigan three weeks before we were going to be there, "With all that's going on here, we think we'd be better off spending the extra time getting ready to go rather than coming to Notre Dame for a trial run." He thought about it for a while, and said, "We need to talk about that. Can you come over?" I flew over there, and that was about as long as that conversation was. I sat down, and he looked at me, and said, "What in the hell is this crap about not doing a test? I've got my neck stuck out a country mile. The alumni think I'm crazy for doing this game, and I've got everybody you can imagine all over the top of me on this, and you're telling me the first time I'm gonna see it is the weekend of the game. I don't think so." I had never seen the man even frown before, he'd been such a gentleman. I decided "He's serious about this." He talked to me about all the security and how they would have to redirect their traffic. We went over and did the test and everything was great. We were still wildly scrambling with it.

First of all, we had no financing. It was a four-million dollar system, and we didn't have four million dollars. Most of the financing we worked out was with the company that sold us the cranes. They were a large company and agreed to provide the leasing/purchase financing on the trucks and cranes. That was about half of the four million dollars. We got the rest from the bank in Muscatine. George Sheply, the bank president, was a big football fan. He agreed to lend us the rest of the money, about a million and a half.

The parent company of this whole thing was the Kidde Corporation. They ended up panicking at the thought of these cranes setting up over crowds of fifty thousand Notre Dame fans. They decided they didn't want to sell those cranes for that use. We were half-way through the project and everything was designed around these cranes. We had to have the cranes. Their final shot was, "Well, okay, we'll sell you the cranes, but we're not going to supply the financing." All of a sudden, three months into a five-month project, two million dollars in financing just dried up. When I told Shepley, he came up with the other two million dollars.

This is 1982, when banks and savings and loans were going broke. The next year, George called me and wanted me to come up immediately—the state bank examiners had just been there. George is a really nice guy; he's got a temper, but he's a really nice guy. He called me over to his office. I went in and he closed the door. He sat down and looked at me and said, "How in the hell did you ever talk me into this? Do you know what the examiners just did to me last week over this loan?"

I told ABC that we'd really like to have some sort of a promo at the start of a game. I know nothing about how that kind of thing gets done or the value of it or how to go about it. At the start of that game, they did a day-time shot of Touchdown Jesus and they zoomed down to the floor of the stadium. Keith Jackson starts out saying, "Up until now, college football has been a Saturday afternoon sport at Notre Dame," and they were showing a shot of the floor of the stadium, "but tonight, we bring you the night the lights went on at Notre Dame," acknowledging Musco Sports Lighting. They went to a wide shot of the stadium. Then, they did a tight logo shot of the side of our truck, and, then, pulled back and showed the whole truck. That was 1982. I've never had a year go by since that happened, and not have someone ask about that Notre Dame game. The risk was whether or not, with all the complexity of the challenge of doing it, something would fail. After the game, I took out a full-page ad in the newspaper "Thank you George Shepley for the help that made this possible."

CBS who had been a foot-dragger, came to us that Saturday night while we were still at Notre Dame and asked us to do the Penn State game the next week. They decided they had to play catch-up with this whole thing. So, we told them we would take a look at it.

A lot of the people are proud of what we do. I heard people brag about the fact that we were in Athens and Torino for the Olympics. We won an Emmy for technical advancement of lighting in television in '83. We were there 9/11 at the Trade Center. We lit the site through May of the next spring during all the search and recovery efforts.

On 9/11, we were able to call four guys who were in Rhode Island. They had just finished doing The Gravity Games there for ESPN that weekend and were getting ready to head back. We told them we really thought we should be at the World Trade Center. We said, "It's optional whether you want to go or not. There's a lot of danger involved in going down there, but, on the other hand, we think they need what we do." Without a lost beat, they said, "We're on our way."

Today, our company is unbelievably huge and very successful. We do hundreds of major events around the world every year. Thank God for Gene Corrigan and Notre Dame, where it all started.

What's the definition of gross sports ignorance?

144 Miami fans

BLEACHER CREATURES

A friend of mine by the name of Ralph Causey was from Mishawaka, Indiana. I was a Notre Dame fan when he moved East. He always promised me that someday he would take me out to see a Notre Dame football game. Here it is, 1988. We go to South Bend for the Miami game, but tickets are very hard to come by. We did the tailgate part and couldn't find a single one. We're standing out in front of the gates. It doesn't look like we're going to be able to get a ticket. Then all of a sudden, with two minutes to go, a girl came up to me and said, "Are you looking for a ticket to the game?" There are people with signs offering a thousand dollars trying to buy tickets. I said, "Yes, I am. How much do you want for the ticket?" She goes, "Well it's twenty dollars, or whatever the value of the ticket is." She said, "Tell my boyfriend I'm just not feeling well." So I get into the game myself, just the one ticket, and of course it was one of the most fantastic games. I was sitting in the end zone when Pat Terrell blocked the pass that would have been the go-ahead score for Miami. There I was. That was my first Notre Dame experience, which was incredible. After sitting next to her boyfriend, I came to understand why she was suddenly taken ill.

——JERRY QUINLAN, New Jersey, golf tour operator to Ireland

In 1952, the big game of the season matched the University of Oklahoma football team which was rated #1 in the polls and Notre Dame—a two-touchdown-underdog. Oklahoma had the longest win streak in college football, and if they beat ND, they would surpass the previous record held by the Fighting Irish. The hype for this game was terrific. It was Homecoming Week at Notre Dame. All the residence halls were designing displays to win the campus competition. The national media focused on the coming struggle. Everything was set for a great football contest.

In South Bend, game tickets were being sold at increasing prices— $50, $100, $150; and one of the students saw one sold for $250! There was rumor that someone got a new car in exchange for a block of eight tickets. The scalpers were having a field day! The week before the game, a major TV network decided to telecast the event. This was one of the first times a program change of this type was actually done. It was quite unexpected. Also, by this time, everyone who had been trying to secure game tickets decided not to bother. The prices being asked were simply out of sight. When people found out the game was on television, they all said, "I'll stay home and watch it on TV."

On game day, we walked over to Notre Dame Stadium to take our seats in the student section. As we approached the stadium, scalpers tried to sell us tickets. "Want a ticket for the game? Only $5. How about $3—$2?" Another scalper flipped open his coat revealing over 20 game tickets inside. "Buy a ticket—only $1." We didn't budge—we had our student IDs. Finally, one scalper said "Tickets—only a quarter!" The scalpers were hung. They lost a fortune on their ill-gotten speculation. If you had been at Notre Dame Stadium at the right time, you could have had a ringside seat for one of the greatest college games of the century—ALL FOR A QUARTER!

———**FRED DANNER**, Huntington, New York, retired engineer

The 1952 Oklahoma game gave us a host of stories on the field. But, the one that I think touched me most occurred behind the stands. It was the fourth quarter and the stands were emotionally drained, but still screaming.

It was the fourth quarter…a tie game and time was running out. I couldn't wait any longer, had to visit the facilities. As I went down the ramp, I couldn't believe my eyes. Hundreds of people quietly circling behind the stands, all going the same direction. You can guess doing what…saying the rosary. They could hear but not see the game. They continued the process until the cheering stopped. We had the ball so it meant the play was about to run. Dead silence. A few would work their way up the ramp, but most stood silent, waiting for the cheering to resume, meaning we were still in control. Then, the procession would start up again. I stayed for a couple of plays but this was more draining than being in the stands. Truly one of the greatest games ever.

As an aside, I can remember Mel Allen, at the pep rally before the 1953 Oklahoma game, telling us, even though he was broadcasting well above the rim of the stadium, our cheering had drowned him out several times during the '52 game. It was the first time he had ever seen it happen.

———**RICHARD HEUTHER**, Schenectady, New York (Zip code: 12345)

Before the Iowa-Notre Dame game in 1964, we had a blizzard. I was driving with my wife, and we had stayed overnight in Chicago. It had snowed a foot or more, and there were cars in ditches all over the place. Notre Dame didn't have enough equipment to clear the parking lots, and you just had to stuff your car in a snowdrift and make your way to the stadium. It was bitter cold—the high for the day was -10. I had a heater with me. Notre Dame had a wooden press box with open windows, a little lean-to affair, for the visiting stations. I turned on the heater, and it would light up, but I would put my hands against the filaments and not feel a thing. That's how cold it was.

———**BOB BROOKS**, Iowa radio announcer since 1943

Now Karen Knight, Bob's wife, is a sweetheart. She's a very, very dear lady. She has the most beautiful big, brown eyes you've ever seen in your life, and she has been wonderful to me. One time, we went to a Notre Dame-IU football game in South Bend. She kept wanting to buy me Cokes. I didn't want to drink any Cokes because I hate to use public restroom facilities. It was a very hot day and as we were leaving the stadium, I started to feel faint. I grabbed onto a rail and later collapsed on the ground. The Notre Dame security people were absolutely wonderful and when I came to, I asked one of the paramedics if they knew my nephew, Dr. Mike Thomas in Elkhart, which he did. I ended up at the Notre Dame infirmary. Karen was with me all the way.

———**HILDA VAN ARSDALE**, mother of basketball stars, Tom and Dick VanArsdale. Mrs. VanArsdale was a St. Mary's student when Rockne was killed.

We had 300 people at the 1988 Michigan game. Another guy and I were walking around the stadium looking for tickets. Most of my friends think I can find Bin Laden. I'm trying to check out every ticket taker on the gates to see if anybody will take money to get in the game. I walk up to one guy—later found out his name was Charlie—and said, "I'm looking for a guy...." He said, "You looking for the head n-----? You found him. You're looking to get in the stadium, right?" I said, "Yeah." He said, "Well, this is how it plays out." I should send him a Christmas card. We had to pay

$20—the game ticket was $22. So, we have these 300 guys—one guy pays six thousand dollars, and the other guys go through the gate. The three guys on the gate took in six large. Then, our friend, Notre Dame Harvey and 20 guys show up. They give the guy $200. The usher says to me, "Hey, does that guy think I can't count 'cause I'm black?" So, they had to give him the other $200.

For years, this guy got us in the gate. Say, you're going to go to Section 25. What you do is, you walk up to 25, and then you walk all the way around to the student section and just stand there. We'd have 300 people in the game who never had any tickets. But…that's over with. You can't sneak in any more. Somebody gave the guy up. I don't think Notre Dame prosecuted.

——**BILL O'LEARY**, 51, Philadelphia area funeral director

I'm third generation of Notre Dame, and it's funny—there's a scene in *Rudy* where the father goes to the game for the first time. He walks up that ramp and sees the field and said something to the effect that "This is the most beautiful sight my eyes have ever seen." I can remember, as a little kid, the first time I went in that stadium. I walked up the ramp, and all of a sudden that green field opened up in front of me. I can remember that moment like it was yesterday. Part of it had to do with the fact that I grew up in a rough area on the South Side of Chicago. We had a lawn in front of our house that was three feet wide. We had a hand mower, and you would go up and down two or three times, and you were done. When you went to the park, you played Pee Wee football, and it was on dirt and broken glass. There was no grass. When I went to Notre Dame Stadium and saw that beautiful green field, it just took my breath away. I will always remember the first time I saw that. It was just such a tremendous sight.

My earliest recollection as a kid going there was I saw Paul Hornung play. I suffered through those years with Kuharich and Devore. The only highlight was the Syracuse game in 1961. I remember when Joe Perkowski made that field goal to win the game. My father was a stern, phlegmatic Irishman. He had a poker face and was a man of few words and most of them were stern. When Perkowski made that kick, I saw my father howl at the top of his lungs. I never saw it before and I've never….

——**DR. JOE CASEY**, Chicago native, Florida resident

I had heard that USC had the defense for every Notre Dame play in the second half of the famous 1964 game at the Coliseum. The USC quarterback, that day, was Craig Fertig. Years later, I meet Fertig at Notre Dame. His nephew, Todd Marinovich, was quarterbacking SC. In '93, I'm sitting down at the far end zone at Notre Dame on a tarp. Here comes Fertig. I know who he is and asked, "Are you Craig Fertig?" He said, "Yes." "I'm Ed Farmer. I do the White Sox games on the radio." He goes, "Hey, how's everything going?" I said, "Tremendous. Can I ask you a question? When you guys came back in 1964...I heard a story that you had all the Notre Dame plays." He said, "I did. I gave them right to McKay, and we had the defense set immediately for whatever Notre Dame was going to run." I looked at him and said, "You know what. You can have all the signs today—you ain't gonna win this game." He said, "You're exactly right 'cause you guys are killing us on the line." We kicked USC 31-13 that day.

——**ED FARMER**, Chicago native

I watched the '77 USC game with Harry Caray. He was a guest of Dan's at the 49-19 green jersey game. Harry and Devine became close friends because Harry broadcast every one of Devine's games when Dan was head coach at Missouri. I *recall* more details of that game than Harry *saw* that afternoon. First of all, Harry had tailgated...heartily. He was in no way, shape, or form ready to attend a sporting event, let alone be on the sidelines of a Notre Dame-SC game. I will say this, "Harry was a gamer." He sort of sucked it up and went through four quarters, and then I helped carry him out.

Regis, Larry King, Tim Russert, Mike Piazza, Tommy Lasorda, Hank Aaron—he was great, Mark Prior...have been on our pre-game show on TV. Now, on radio, I can't tell you how many people we've interviewed over the course of when we were doing our talk show. Julia Roberts has been up there before; Jason Patric was with her. Farrah Fawcett has been in the press box at Notre Dame. A lot of celebrities are Notre Dame fans. Obviously, Regis is a huge fan. Tim Russert's a fan. Hank Aaron was sort of *not really sure*—but he left a Notre Dame fan. The same way for Kirk Herbstreit of ESPN—he became a Notre Dame fan in 2005, and he will be the first to admit it. He was on the sideline at the SC game and there wasn't too much journalistic objectivity coming out of his mouth. He was into it. He was into it because he knows how good a coach Charlie is.

There are tons of people in the entertainment business who follow Notre Dame religiously—Martin Sheen, George Wendt, Lara Flynn Boyle—a huge Notre Dame fan. There are more now because of Charlie, a lot more.

——JEFF JEFFERS, WNDU-TV

As a Notre Dame student, I was head coach of the St. Mary's flag football team. At a flag football game in 1964, we played Barat College from Lake Forest, Illinois. We played it in the Stadium at the conclusion of the UCLA game so there were 25-30,000 people left. We won 6-0 so I'm undefeated as a coach in that stadium. My assistant coach was Bob Conway who is now a Notre Dame trustee. They had played the year before at Barat College and won. The social commissioner had arranged through the university to have it in the stadium after the game. He was the guy who picked the coach, and he picked me. He told me he wanted me to do a good job because they wanted St. Mary's to win so we took it real serious. It was great fun. Every afternoon, Bob and I, and two or three or our buddies that also helped coach with us, went over to St. Mary's. We had trials and had 100 girls try out for the team. The school wasn't that big then—probably 700 girls.

——CAPPY GAGNON, Class of '66

Often in the third quarter, when Notre Dame was far ahead, and we were all bored, some student would get picked up, and they would pass him on their hands up toward the top of the stadium. Everyone would chant, "Over the wall. Over the wall." Generally, it's some skinny kid like me they would pick on. Some of my roommates would push me out there. The whole stadium is looking at you as they're passing you up. You're afraid you'll fall. After a while, there are some kids that are drunk or idiots and they're pushing back, trying to push you down. You could really get hurt. Other kids are grabbing your crotch, too, so that's really not pleasant. One time, we decided we would make a dummy and dress it in the exact same clothes I was wearing. We snuck the dummy into the stadium under our coats. The student section is passing me up. Everyone in the stadium is chanting "Over the wall. Over the wall." We get to the top, and I drop down for a second. We throw the dummy up and over. Then, you hear the stadium gasp…as this dummy goes over the wall. I didn't think too much about it. Then, two months later, I'm standing in dinner line. For some reason, the Stanford side of the North Dining Hall was closed, and I was in the Keenan line. There were two guys talking, one saying, "Boy, if I ever find that kid who threw that dummy over the wall and caused mom to faint…" I'm standing there—just dying. My roommate is there, and I'm trying to keep him from saying anything. To us, it was just a joke, and people would realize I wasn't really thrown over the wall. It happened so quickly. Across the stadium, it might have actually looked real enough that this kid's mother fainted, and he was still furious months later talking about it.

Later, we went out to see if we could find the dummy that had gone over the wall, and it was gone. Then, we went to the radio station and put out an all-points bulletin for the lost dummy.

——**JIMMY BROGAN**, '70, writer and comic talent booker for
The Tonight Show for nine years.

Does your alma matter?

Chapter 7

Revelations

The End is Near

(only 38 pages to go)

TOO OLD TO BE YOUNG
TOO YOUNG TO BE OLD

I. I. PROBST

Millions have seen the reality show, Survivor, hosted by Jeff Probst. Here's a fellow named Probst, who has hosted his own reality survivor story for more than a century.

I. I. Probst is an amazing fellow...a graduate of Notre Dame in 1926. He is 101 years old and sharp as a thumb tack on the seat of an electric chair. His son, Bob, graduated in 1958 and son, Bernard, received his degree in 1975. While growing up in Belleville, Illinois, Mr. Probst met baseball hall of famers Babe Ruth and Rogers Hornsby. Now, he lives in Florida...deep into the fourth quarter of his life and prayin' for overtime.

One thing that comes to my mind is that in 1924, Notre Dame played Butler. A special train came up from Indianapolis carrying rooters for both sides. After the game, my very best friend, Al, and I ran over to the streetcar station because we were wanting to get a seat before the crowd got on the cars. Two young ladies got on in front of us. My friend got up and offered one girl his seat so I was forced to do the same thing. One was a brunette and the girl in front of me was a blond. Al liked blonds so, as we got off the car to go over to the hotel, we switched partners. The girl that Al had first sat next to, later turned out to be my wife. We got married up at Notre Dame in 1927.

I met Rockne one time on a trip from South Bend to Chicago. My friend, Al, who was from the St. Louis area, too, and I got on the regular coach and sat down. This was during the Easter vacation. In comes Rockne, and he sits down right opposite us. The first thing he did, he said, "Good morning, boys. Why are you going to Chicago?" I told him that we had to catch the Illinois Central train that night to go down to St. Louis. We were so dumbfounded at being addressed by him that we didn't really continue the conversation. He brought a newspaper with him to read. As we got into Chicago, he said, "Well, have a good vacation. Good bye." That was the extent of any close relationship between Rockne and me. The last Notre Dame game I went to in South Bend was in 1973 against Northwestern.

When I was at Notre Dame, there were only 1,100 students. At that time, the Morris Inn wasn't even there. The whole campus has been enlarged. We started playing Georgia Tech the first time in my freshman year. Rockne did a very unusual thing. On the Friday afternoon before the game on Saturday, he sent out an invitation to the entire student body to meet in front of the Main Building. He was going to have a welcoming party for the Georgia Tech team. He did do that. He got up on the Main Building steps and introduced the coach from the Georgia Tech team. That man got up on the steps, and he really enchanted us with his southern accent. The next day, we played, and we won the game 13-3.

The last time we played Georgia Tech down in Atlanta, I was not able to go, but some of their fans threw fish at our team and out onto the gridiron. On the way out, after the game, Father Joyce, who was then executive vice president in charge of athletics, said to my friend, "This is the last time we will play George Tech." As it turned out, Father Joyce passed away a couple of years ago. Things have changed now so the team is now playing Georgia Tech again.

I never did get to see the "Gipper," George Gipp. He was a year ahead of me. There has always been this debate about whether Gipper, on his death bed, said, "Tell them to win one for me, Rock." I've got a clipping from a newspaper that was written by Ronald Reagan. He wrote to a sports writer that he knew. In it, he said that when they were making a film, Mrs. Rockne—this was after Rockne died— came out to California, and he met her. He asked her whether that was true. She said it was absolute…that Rockne told her that George Gipp made the statement on his death bed that he wanted them to win one for him. In the late nineties, I didn't care if they won one for the Gipper, I just wanted them to win one!

When I was a student there my freshman year, I was in Carroll Hall, which is now the Main Building. We lived on four floors. On the basement floor, we would have a medicine cabinet and a sink with water. On the second floor, which was the main floor, we had a desk. That was our headquarters. On the third and fourth floors, were the bedrooms—they were just a bunch of pipes with sheets hanging on them separating one party from another. Actually, one side of the building was Carroll Hall, and the other side of the building was Bronson Hall. Bronson was exactly like Carroll. After Notre Dame built some temporary buildings, they discontinued that. In our second year, they had built temporary buildings both for the freshmen and for the sophomores. My second year, I lived in Sophomore Hall, which was later torn down.

The 'Four Horsemen' were a year ahead of me. I personally can't say that I knew any of them; although we would pass each other on the campus. They were very friendly.

Joe Harmon was the back-up center to Adam Walsh of the 1925 team that went out to the Rose Bowl. One game, when Indiana played Notre Dame at South Bend, a special train came up from Indianapolis. Some of the fans were from the Cathedral High School down there where Joe Harmon had gone to school. When the game started, Joe Harmon wasn't in the lineup. He was sitting at one end of the bench from Rockne. The crowd right behind were all the Cathedral High School fans from Indianapolis, and they started to chant, "We want Harmon. We want Harmon." Rockne ignored it the first time. A couple of plays later, they said the same thing again, "We want Harmon." Rockne motioned with his finger to Harmon that he should come over. Harmon walked over to Rockne and Rockne said, "Go up there and sit with your fans. They want you." I didn't hear that, but the president of our class was in the group, and he's the one who told me the story.

Notre Dame is the most fabulous place. On Sundays, on our Hallmark Channel, they have 11:00 Mass from the Sacred Heart. I can't walk. I have to go in a wheelchair so I very rarely get to Mass on a Sunday…but I never miss that 11:00 Mass on cable.

Notre Dame really made a good choice with Charlie Weis. I'm going to drop him a line and tell him about this Georgia Tech deal. I'm very impressed with him. I watch all the games on TV.

LAMENTATIONS

THE LAST GOSPEL OF JUDAS

DON YAEGER

In 1993, Simon and Schuster rocked the Notre Dame Nation when they published the book Under the Tarnished Dome. *The book was written by Don Yaeger and Doug Looney, two writers with impressive resumes, outstanding reputations and award-winning work as investigative reporters. Yaeger is a graduate of Ball State University and a long-time resident of Tallahassee, Florida. He's not really a Judas, and it wasn't really his last gospel. His next book is* The Turning of the Tide, *about the culture-changing 1974 Alabama-USC game that led to Bear Bryant integrating the Alabama team.*

I had written a book called *Undue Process* about the NCAA and Jerry Tarkanian. In that book, there was a quote which said, "It's a shame more schools don't do it like Notre Dame—where they win, and they win honorably and they don't cheat to get there." A few months after that book was published, I received a phone call from a player on that year's Notre Dame team. He wouldn't tell me who he was, but he did tell me he had read the book. He had seen the quote, and he felt there were some things we needed to know. He said, "I played for Lou Holtz. I was never critical of Lou Holtz, but I feel as if the impression some people have of Notre Dame is not always correct." He wouldn't tell me who he was, but he called back later to give me more details, and it all checked out. I finally figured out who the player was.

It was a hard book to do. If there's an icon in college sports, it's Notre Dame. It was even more so back then, than it is today. In those days, steroids weren't the story they are today. We didn't understand the long-term, psychological and physiological nature of steroids as a drug. Most of the feedback I got from the book was extremely negative. Most often it was done, as Lou Holtz did, by claiming that they disagreed with the book's content, yet, with an acknowledgment they didn't read it. Unfortunately, you can't argue against ignorance. It was impossible to explain why the book, in my mind, was important, when people weren't ready to sit down and read it first.

One time, I ran into Dick Vitale at an airport and introduced myself. He said, "I know who you are. You wrote that awful book about Notre Dame." After he went on for a while, I said, "Did you read it?" He said, "Of course not. Why would I read garbage like that?" I said, "Far be it from me to have gone around last night after the game you broadcast and tell you what a horrible job you did if I hadn't watched the broadcast. That would be insincere and incorrect." Shortly after that, he sent me a really nice note and apologized.

If the book had been outrageously incorrect, Notre Dame would have sued like crazy. Notre Dame and Notre Dame people were not at all shy about suing over issues in which they think they've been wronged. You certainly can't blame them for that.

While passions run high about Notre Dame football, many of the smartest and brightest people that I have met in all of sports are connected to Notre Dame. Most are willing to approach the book with an open mind, even with all the criticism. There is no question the book created changes at Notre Dame. Several people with some relationship to the Notre Dame athletic department told me there was a renewed vigor about doing the right thing after the book came out. Notre Dame didn't want to deal with that type of criticism ever again.

The welcome mat has warmed somewhat over the years, and I've kept in contact with a number of the Notre Dame people who contributed to the book.

ARE YOU NOW OR HAVE YOU EVER BEEN A COLUMNIST?

PAUL FULLMER

Paul Fullmer, '55, lives the good life at the spectacular Eagle Ridge complex in Galena, Illinois. He keeps busy writing, grandparenting and fulfilling his duties as secretary of the Notre Dame class of '55. He is the author of the recent book, Presidents I Have Known.

*S*plinters from the Press Box, was always the column that the sports editor wrote in the *Scholastic*. I was the sports editor at Notre Dame, so I wrote it my senior year. When I left, I told the new sports editor, "Take good care of this column. It's been around the *Scholastic* now forever." He said, "I hate that name. I'm going to change it." I said, "You can't change it. That's legend." But, he did. I was a little ticked, so I got a job on a newspaper in Aurora, Illinois, and they said, "Do you want to write a column?" I said, "Yeah, I want to write a sports column." I named it *Splinters from the Press Box*.

I am class secretary for the class of '55, and we have about 300+ guys on our e-mail list. I decided to start writing *Splinters* again on the Internet for our class. The column now gets forwarded all over God's green earth by my classmates. A couple of months ago, I got a call from a guy who is a 'subway' alumnus. He runs a magazine called "*Irish Eyes*." He said, "We've been looking for an older alumnus of Notre Dame to write a column because all of us are young guys and none of us went to Notre Dame, even though we're all nuts about Notre Dame." *Splinters from the Press Box* is now in the *Irish Eyes* magazine…. It's been kind of funny. My brother is a priest and when he became a pastor, he sent me his first column from the parish bulletin. It was *Splinters from the Presidential Chair*. So, he stole a little piece of it, too….

When I was a kid in grade school, my uncle, a priest, used to take me down to games in the glory years when Connor and Lujack and those guys were there. It took forever to get to South Bend—three hours from Chicago—no Interstates. That was big-time stuff to get to go down with my uncle for that. I covered sports all through high school for the school paper, and, also, for the town paper. I was a stringer for the Chicago papers for that Catholic Conference out there in the suburbs. Tom Stritch, the head of the journalism department at Notre Dame and a nephew of Cardinal Stritch in Chicago. I said, "I'm here to be a sports writer." He said, "We don't train sports writers. We train journalists...."

In our time, the players had jobs. Lattner delivered our mail. We'd harass him, "Get here with the mail." He was such a great guy. A classmate of mine, Dave Metz, was VP for Communications at Kodak. He got an old black-and-white of the great Notre Dame-Oklahoma game from '52. He said he was going to have his guys at Kodak see if they could improve the quality of the film. It was the coach's film from Oklahoma—just the plays, one right after the other. Then he said, "For the hell of it, I'm going to write Regis Philbin to see if he'll do a lead-in." Philbin said he would read it. Metz was also a journalist so he wrote this great introduction for Philbin. Then, he got a pro to do the play-by-play. Then, he was getting greedy. He said, "Let's get some of the former players and get their stories about the game." I took Johnny Lattner down from Chicago, and we filmed it at WNDU. He got Dan Shannon, the hero of the game, Ralph Guglielmi, Tommy Carey and Dick Szymanski. This was 2004-2005, so it's available now. At the end of it, we have 45 minutes of interviews with the guys about the games. With Philbin on the tape, it's really turned out to be spectacular. I was a sophomore when Regis was a senior and I remember seeing him in musicals with Phil Donahue.

Years ago, the Notre Dame Club of Chicago started out giving out a 'Decency in Entertainment' award. It was a way to get somebody famous to come talk to our members, draw a big crowd and raise money for the club scholarship fund. We had a president of the club who went to school with Bob Newhart so we got Newhart the first year. He was in town for a show and his good friend asked him to come over and do this. He was absolutely spectacular. The first few years it wasn't too hard to get speakers. Then, we got famous

Chicago newspaperman, Irv Kupcinet, and he helped us out. He would tip us off as to who was coming to town. We really leaned on him. Half the time, the people thought they were getting an award from The University of Notre Dame, but it was just from the Chicago Club, and we never told them the difference.

We had Edgar Bergen. I remember Candace Bergen backstage when she was probably in her late teens. It was weird to see Charlie McCarthy being taken out of his box and put back in again. We had George Gobel once. Everybody said, "Watch out for him because this guy is a drinker." I'll tell you that little son of a gun—I was his shadow—I was going to keep him away from the bartender. Every time I would turn around, the son of a gun had a new full drink and he'd give me this s—t-eating grin. He knew what my job was, and I couldn't stop the guy. He was unbelievable. When he went on, I was really nervous about what was going to happen…but he was great…. Then, we got all kinds of flak. We gave it to Carol Burnett one year, and she had just gotten divorced. Somebody said, "How the hell can you give a decency in entertainment award to this broad." I said, "Hey, Carol Burnett's a clean entertainer." We even had Bob Hope. That was fantastic. He and his wife came in. The year I was club president, we had Jimmy Durante. We had it at McCormick Place. We'd had 1,000 people, and we had outdoor cocktails. It was a great night, about 65 degrees, and nobody would come inside. The waiters were ringing the bells for dinner, and nobody would come in. The staff came to me and said, "What are we going to do?" I said, "I don't know. These guys are out of control. They are having too great a time out on the lakefront." God took care of us. The temperature dropped about 15 degrees in 10 minutes, and, all of a sudden, everybody headed inside…. We've had some great stars and it never cost us a nickel. We'd offer to pay their way from Hollywood or wherever, and they'd say, "No, no, no. It's for Notre Dame." Times have changed along that front…. We'd get 1,000 for the Rockne dinner. It's still held, and they do well. We would also give awards to prep athletes at the Rockne dinner. Every high school would have a nominee, and they would all come with their coaches. That lasted into the early seventies. Then, of course, the NCAA stopped that. They say that was undue influence and told us we couldn't give out Rockne awards anymore.

WIT HAPPENS

OWEN SMITH

Owen Smith is one of the hottest rising stars in Hollywood. He has a recurring character in the show, "Everybody Hates Chris," where he also does punch-up writing and does Chris Rock's voiceovers when Rock is absent. Smith appeared in the early 2006 smash hit movie, "When a Stranger Calls." He was recently nominated for the College Comedian of the Year by The National Association of Campus Activities Directors. His web site is owensmithlive.com.

When I was going to Notre Dame, I didn't know where Notre Dame was. I grew up in Maryland. There was a Notre Dame all-girls school in Baltimore, but I thought the real Notre Dame was in New Hampshire. I knew they had gold helmets. When I found out I was going to Indiana, my family was nervous—"The klan is out there. I won't be coming to see you…." It was one of those things.

I grew up in Prince George's County, Maryland. That's the blackest county in America. It's right outside of Washington, D. C. My plan, when I got to Notre Dame, was to "find the baddest 'sister' there and make her my girlfriend and get through these four years." So, I start dating this girl who played basketball for Notre Dame.

I went to visit my girlfriend the night before the first football game. I didn't know about the whole parietals deal. Parietals mean at midnight, weekdays, you have to leave the room. No one of the opposite sex can be in your room at parietals. They throw you out, and they keep your money! But, you can stay in the lobby all night. I hadn't seen my girlfriend in a while so I'm with her hanging out in the lobby all night. We don't get any sleep.

The next morning, I go right to the football game without eating anything. I didn't know you had to stand the whole game. This is in

September, and I'm a freshman. I was standing there the whole game, and the sun is out in Indiana in September. It's gone by October, but it was there in September. I was standing the whole first half, and I hadn't had any food in my stomach for at least 48 hours. I'm getting to feel woozy so I left to go get some water. I passed out there in the line at the concession stand and fell into my girlfriend's arms. I was trying to be brave and strong. Being a basketball player, she was strong, so she caught me. She dragged me to the back wall. They got emergency people who gave me some water. I was so embarrassed. I felt emasculated. I sold my tickets for the rest of the season, and I didn't go to any more games because everybody was making fun of me. I took a lot of teasing from everybody for passing out and having my girlfriend catch me....

My mother told me two things. She said, "Don't be biased 'cause there's good white people and bad white people—just like good black people and bad black people." She said, "Get in there and work hard 'cause you deserve to be there just like anybody else. But, you'd better not bring one of those white girls home." That was her message. Then, my uncle said, "She didn't say you couldn't try one out. You can take one for a test drive, just don't drive her past the house."

During parents' football weekend, my mom came in from Maryland. It was so cold and was snowing. My mother has the worst luck with cameras. We call it the 'camera curse.' She always brings the camera, then the film pops out...or her finger is over the most important picture...heads are cut off—she consistently does this.

We had great seats in Notre Dame's end zone. It is really freezing. Mom had on this big, purple coat—purple, purple! She's taking pictures. "Click, click." She kept saying, "Oh, man, the people at work aren't going to believe this."

Now, it's halftime, and we don't know any better—we walk down on the field, and she's taking pictures of the Irish Guard. We're right there marching with them, "Oh, my God, no one's ever going to believe this at work." Click. Click. Click. Click. She was taking pictures of everybody. Security came and got us 'cause we were not supposed to be on the field. Because she's a sweet, older lady, they gave us a pass and walked us back to our seats. She's taking pictures of security accosting us. It was like, "Oh, they're not going to...." Click.

Click. Click. "Oh, they grabbed me." Click. Click. Click. She's getting all these pictures, and we're getting yelled at. She's feeling great and still saying, "The people at work aren't going to believe this."

We get back to our seats, and we're watching the game. The final seconds are ticking. They throw a pass to Reggie Brooks in the corner of the end zone. He catches it, and it puts us up by one point. The whole stadium stands up. They're going crazy. I was yelling, "Oh, Ma, did you see that?" I look over and all I see is a big, purple butt. I see her bent over digging down in the bleachers...she had dropped her camera. All I hear is "They're not going to believe this. No one is going to believe this." It was the curse. She had dropped her camera during the biggest play. We just left the game. She never was able to retrieve the camera—never got to see those pictures....parents' weekend! Camera curse! Everyone believed her....

I used to cut everybody's hair, including some of the ballplayers. It was great. They would always come over at any time asking me to cut their hair. It was real cool. I'd have a long line. I'd cut their hair and then, on football Saturdays, I would look at them on TV and say, "I did that." They'd pay me three bucks. It was the only way I could make a little money in college. Oliver Gibson, the tackle, had the hardest hair to cut. He's like the big brother I never had. He would hold up a mirror and watch me cut his hair. He said I made his hairline crooked, and we got in a big argument. He pulled out his driver's license. He was from Romeoville, Illinois. His hairline is crooked on his driver's license picture. I said, "I didn't do that, Oliver. I didn't know you then. I'm just following what's already been done." He was the biggest prima donna.

I was a fairly decent basketball player back then. I got scholarship offers from some smaller schools. The funniest basketball player was Jerome Bettis. I'm glad he finally won a Super Bowl ring—that's awesome. He brought the same amount of intensity to basketball that he brought to football. If he would score or block a shot, he would celebrate. The difference between most football players playing basketball is that they're so big, they don't have lateral movement. If you figure that out, you can beat them. But, they definitely dominate from the intimidation factor by their size. I'm 6'5" so I knew that, laterally, I could throw them off.

Being a black guy at Notre Dame was sometimes tough. The black population was 2%—that's like skim milk. You couldn't skip class 'cause they knew. I went from a situation where everybody was black. When you'd stop at the stop light, there were black people to the left of you, black people to the right of you. You go to the grocery store, same deal. My school was largely black, and we bused white students in. You could be anonymous where I grew up. I had no anonymity at Notre Dame. That was the only detriment. Once you adjusted to that, it was cool.

The bigger adjustment I had to make, aside from race, was just being in an environment where everybody was good at something. Everybody was a *big fish* where they came from. Then, when you get to Notre Dame, everybody was good at something. I remember they had a freshman welcoming party outside the LaFortune Center. They were playing music. Everybody had to wear a name tag showing what state they were from. When I left Maryland, I lied and said I was from Washington, D. C. because I thought it would be cooler and it would scare people. If you asked me about D.C., I couldn't tell you much about it…but, I would say, "I'm from D. C." They were playing all kinds of music, including some hip-hop music. Naturally, we blacks are supposed to be the best dancers of hip-hop music. All the black students were dancing in a circle. This one kid came up to me, and his name tag said, "Hawaii." He walked right up to me and did a move, and, then, I did a move. He had on a Hawaiian shirt, shorts and hiking boots. He walked right up to me again and did two back flips and splits and did some crazy move. I thought, "Man, I'm not even good at dancing out here. This is ridiculous." Here was this guy, who I guess was white, and he out-hip-hopped me right in front of everyone." That was crazy, man. I was humbled on many occasions. They do challenge everything you thought you knew. The beautiful thing is that there were people there from every state. I met women who had never seen a black person before, except on TV.

OLD TESTAMENT

RE: JOYCE

Rev. Edmund P. Joyce, C.S.C., deceased

Father Joyce retired in 1987 after thirty-five years as Chairman of the Faculty Board in Control of Athletics and the University Building Committee. Father Joyce passed away on May 2, 2004.

Father Joyce was born in Honduras, raised in South Carolina, and graduated from ND in 1937. Ned, as he preferred to be called, was an accountant in Spartanburg until he became a priest twelve years after his graduation. For many years, Father Joyce was an influential voice in the national NCAA, particularly in matters dealing with educational integrity of intercollegiate athletic programs. Because Father Joyce's close friend, retired Notre Dame President, Theodore Hesburgh, has traveled so extensively, Father Joyce logged more hours under the Golden Dome than any other person in history.

Near the end of the 1970-71 season, word had spread that Notre Dame Head Basketball Coach, Johnny Dee, was retiring. Army's Bobby Knight wanted the Notre Dame job. The author conducted this interview with Father Joyce in the late summer of 2000.

My memory gets worse as I get older, and I'm pretty old right now. I do remember Bobby Knight calling and writing me in 1971, expressing his interest in becoming the Notre Dame coach. He was still at Army at the time. But, we had already decided on Digger Phelps. When Knight contacted me, I didn't know who he was, certainly didn't know he was going to become a great coach. I'd had no contact with him prior to that. I have met him since and he always has seemed interested in Notre Dame—our program. I've been to several banquets when he's been there. In fact, Father

Hesburgh and I received an award from what they call "Youth Links" in Indianapolis. That's a big deal; we got $35,000, which I gave to charity. Bobby Knight was the one who presented the award. He's always been complimentary about Notre Dame. But at the time, I don't think I knew anything but that he was the coach at Army. It was a little bit unusual to get letters so I would remember it. Of course, as he became so successful I did remember it from time to time. Once he became successful at Indiana, we never tried to steal coaches from anybody else. He the most astute guy in the world and always has been when I've been with him—always very cordial and interested in Notre Dame and athletes. I think he stands for good things in athletics. I don't know how he gets himself in the scrapes he gets into with his players.

Digger had contacted us earlier than Knight, and I didn't have much to do with his hiring except to approve it. I didn't have any interviews with Digger or anything else but, on the face of it, he looked like a wonderful thing. He was very eager to come to Notre Dame and, of course, he had been successful at Fordham. He had beaten us that year when he shouldn't have and that caught my attention. So, I saw no reason not to go along with it. If we had hired Bobby Knight, Knight would not have been able to get away with that language or with any of the other antics. Either we would have converted him or he would not have lasted. Maybe, in this atmosphere, he might have restrained himself more, too. He may have been very good for us. He's obviously a wonderful coach, and is certainly interested in his players which we always want a coach to be, and is interested in their education. He has a lot of qualities that would have been perfect at Notre Dame if he could control his temper better than he did at **INDIANA.** Until now, I never discussed that we might have hired him; I was afraid I would be crucified by our alumni if it came out in public.

My personal relationship with Mr. Knight has always been warm and nice.

> **In the 1976 Ohio State-INDIANA game, the Hoosiers scored first. Indiana coach, Lee Corso, called a timeout. During the timeout, Corso had his team pose for a group picture with the scoreboard—showing Indiana leading Ohio State 7-0—clearly visible in the background. Corso featured the picture on the cover of the 1977 Indiana recruiting brochure. Ohio State won the game 47-7.**

IRISHPALOOZA

I came to visit the campus one summer when I was a junior in high school. Bill Meeker, of Arcadia, California, was the student who gave me campus tour. As soon as I walked through the Quad and looked at the Dome, I turned to my mother and said, "This is where I'm going to school." This was before I even talked to anybody. Years later, I was giving the campus tours one summer, and one of the people on the tour was a nun. She told me that she is the world's biggest Ara Parseghian fan and she would give anything if she could meet him. I said, "Oh, we just can't do that." She said, "How about—could we go by his office?" I said, "Okay, we can do that." So, we go over to the Rock, where his office was located. We were outside his office. You could look through the outer office into the inner office. Sure enough, there is Ara sitting at his desk. She said, "Oh, I'm the world's biggest football fan, and I love him. Could you ask if he could see me for just a second?" I said, "Okay, wait here." I go into the office. I said, "Coach Parseghian, sister so-and-so from New Jersey…" I'm starting to state the request, and I look around and she's standing right behind me. She told him she prays for him every day and shook his hand. Then, she said, "That's all I wanted. I just wanted to touch you." She walks out. I turned back to him and said, "Thanks coach, sorry to bother you." He was all by himself.

——CAPPY GAGNON, '66

Ron Reed played basketball and baseball at Notre Dame in the early 60s. He is one of 10 men in history to play in both the NBA and Major League Baseball. One day, Ron and I were in the bullpen together in Philly. He's 6'7" and at the time I was 6' 5". There was a basketball hoop, backboard and standard down the left-field line under the stands in the tunnel down by the batting cage. We'd go down there and shoot round. We were playing 'H.O.R.S.E.' He goes, "We need to play one-on-one." I said, "Believe me, you don't want any of me." He said, "You take it out." He's 10-feet away from me. I said, "I'm going to tell you something right now. I scored 37 points a few times in high school and, as a 13-year old, I had 51 points in a game, and I wasn't shooting three-balls. You need to come out here and get on me." He continued to refuse to come out so I took the first shot. If you made the basket, you kept the ball. 1-0…2-0…and I'm riding him hard, verbally…3-0…4-0. The stands came down at an angle so you couldn't really arc the ball to a tremendous height because you'd hit the cement stand support. It was 4-0. I said, "You know, if I beat you 21-0, when we get back to the clubhouse, I'm gonna do a lot of talking about your career at Notre Dame and in the NBA. I hit the next shot…5-0. The ball goes by the batting cage so I walk after it. I turn around, he is *on my chest*. His face is one-inch from my nose. I go, "What are we doing now?" He goes, "Now, we're gonna play ------- basketball." …he beat me 21-5. I couldn't get a shot off. He was very physical. The last basket he made was a reverse slam. He was walking back toward the clubhouse. The ball was just bouncing aimlessly on the cement, and I was standing there. He goes, "Hey, Skippy, bring the ball. Let's go." We got halfway down there, and he goes, "Did you like that?" I said, "Well, I didn't like the way the stars were coming down on me—you blocked everything I had." He goes, "You could shoot the basketball. The trick is getting the shot off."

——**ED FARMER**, former major league pitcher

At one of the pep rallies in the Stephan Center, I was on top of the backboard watching. I'm dancing and all the fans are loving it. I had a white Philadelphia Eagles jersey on. The pep rally is over, and we go over to the Linebacker Lounge. The next morning, we wake up and I still have on the same clothes from the previous night. We hadn't gotten in until about four o'clock in the morning. We wanted to go get something to eat and then change for the game. I go over to the diner across from the Holiday Inn. This guy comes up and says, "You were at the pep rally last night, weren't you? I saw you." I said, "Oh, you saw me up there on top of the backboard? How did you know me?" He said, "You've still got the same clothes on that you had on last night."

——**BOB SUMNER**, 46, Philadelphia, a.k.a. "Notre Dame Harvey"

There's a will-call trailer where the recruits pick up their tickets. There is a room for all the family members of recruits and a hospitality center. As a member of the athletic department, we're not really supposed to talk with them because it would be a violation of NCAA rules.

Last year, a guy named Zach Frazer was here on a recruiting trip from Mechanicsburg, Pennsylvania. I'd lived there for five years, and it was killing me not to be able to go over and say, "Hey, I lived in your hometown, man, you've got to come here." One of his assistant coaches knew a friend of mine. He came over and asked, "Are you Jimmy Zannino?" I said, "Yes." He said, "I'm from Mechanicsburg, and I've got this kid really thinking about coming to Notre Dame. He's a quarterback." I said, "Man, I would love to talk to him, but I'm not allowed to." Notre Dame is so by-the-book. They don't break any rules. We are schooled all the time on what we're allowed to do and what we're not allowed to do. Even though we're a foot away from these recruits, we've really got to be careful how we approach them.

Konrad Reuland was a California recruit, tall with blond hair. I was really surprised we got him because he just didn't look like the kind of guy who would be playing football in northern Indiana. He looked like an L. A. guy. I've seen them all. A lot of them are big. Whether we get them, or whether we don't, my philosophy is I don't want anybody who has to think about coming to Notre Dame. I want somebody who has dreamed about coming here all his life. I want the kid who wants to be here and he's going to put his four-years in—not somebody we have to give a banana split to every night just to keep him happy.

————JIMMY ZANNINO, ND Stadium ground crew

A Notre Dame football fan filed a lawsuit against…a tattoo parlor? Yep. Dan O'Connor visited a tattoo parlor in Carlstadt, N.J., and spent $125 to have a drawing of the university's leprechaun mascot tattooed on his upper arm. When he took off the bandage, the inscription read, "Fighing Irish." O'Connor's attorney said it would cost about $700 for a laser procedure to remove the tattoo, not to mention the pain and suffering. The parlor offered to squeeze the 't' into "Fighing." Said O'Connor: "You're not talking about a dented car where you can get another one. You're talking about flesh."

————From the **Author's book**, "Sports Fans Who Made Headlines."

My parents had told me that if I got a full-ride college scholarship, they would get a car for me. I was fortunate to get a scholarship. They bought a car for me and gave it to me after graduation. Then, for a Christmas present, they got me a license plate that said, "ND5" which actually turned out to be more of a pain in the neck. At different points in time, people bent the plate beyond recognition trying to steal it. Jon Gruden's dad recruited me to Notre Dame. Kathy Gruden was like my mom away from home, both at Notre Dame and at Tampa Bay when I was drafted as a rookie. Jon was like a little brother to me. I couldn't have my car on campus 'cause I was a freshman so I kept it at the Grudens' house and told Jon I didn't care if he drove it. So, Jon borrowed my car, a white Firebird, on a few occasions. He and my brother would drive around the town and have a high old time.

When I was at Notre Dame, Jon would come by and watch football practice. He was very close to Dan Devine as well. I went to some of Jon's high school games. He was a good player, very competitive. He was a natural leader; you could see that.

I was very excited when I thought Jon might become coach at Notre Dame. There couldn't have been a better fit because Jon absolutely loved, and still loves, Notre Dame. I thought it would be an absolutely perfect fit. Now, I was definitely a Willingham fan, as well. I think he's a class act all the way. When it was rumored that Jon was going to be the coach, I thought, "Unbelievable! They're not going to know what hit them." But, Charlie has done a fabulous job.

——BLAIR KIEL, Former Notre Dame quarterback

Back in the early 60s, Notre Dame would be on one or two televised games a year. We made up this elaborate poster which said, "Hi Mom and Dad, send $$. Tuition just went up 75¢ a case." We thought that was the greatest sign ever until about a half dozen years later, when Kentucky was playing Austin Peay (the 'eay' is silent) in the **NCAA BASKETBALL TOURNAMENT**. Austin Peay had a player from Brooklyn, a real talented guy named James "Fly" Williams. The great

> **Of the top twenty individual scoring games in NCAA TOURNAMENT history, only one name appears more than once: Austin Carr of Notre Dame. He has the single game record, three of the top five, and five of the top thirteen.**

banner from that game, held up by an Austin Peay student, was "The Fly is open! Let's go Peay."

My last three years at Notre Dame, we had three different styles of helmets. One year, the helmets just had the player's number in white paint on the helmet. The next year, we had shamrocks on the helmet. Then, the third year, Ara's first year, the helmets were just plain, shiny gold....A year or two later, a buddy of mine, Jon Spoelstra, a great guy and one of the top sports marketing guys in the country, had this great idea that we were going to sell pictures of Ara walking on water. We decided we were going to sell them after we beat Purdue in South Bend. There was a problem...we didn't beat Purdue. Leroy Keyes ran crazy on us. In the fourth quarter, we were trying to figure out a way we could doctor the pictures to make them look like Leroy Keyes was walking on water so we could sell them to the Purdue fans—but, obviously, that didn't work.

————DICK FOX, Falmouth Massachusetts

I went to **GEORGETOWN** in 1948. I had never seen Notre Dame play so I rode a train to Baltimore to see them play Navy. I got into the stadium and couldn't believe that Notre Dame played on the same size football field as the rest of the teams. You never pictured that on the radio, I always thought Notre Dame was bigger and better than anybody else—I thought they played on a bigger football field...Eventually, I got fabulous season tickets at Notre Dame Stadium. The first game I go to, this guy said, "What the h--- are you doing here?" It was Mike Leep, a big-time car dealer, sitting next to me. He said, "Where did you get the tickets?" I said, "I think God gave them to me and I will be coming here for the rest of my life." Leep said, "In that case, you're my best friend." He put his arm around me and said, "Whenever you come here, you'll always have a new car at your disposal." He has picked me up at the airport and has given me a car to use all weekend for 10 years now.

————BUBBY CRONIN, Portland, Oregon...once featured in an adidas commercial with the Leprechaun tailgating next to his private jet

Paul Tagliabue once held the career rebounding record at **GEORGETOWN**. That mark was broken by Patrick Ewing in 1985.

When I was a little boy, I just started to follow Notre Dame and have been a fan all my life. I'm 77 years old. I live and die with them. We always liked Notre Dame, and we were trying to figure out some way to show everybody around here that we were Notre Dame fans. Finally, my boys and I got the idea of getting a golden dome made. We put her up there on top of the silo and put a "Notre Dame" on top of it—got the Blessed Mother standing up on top. It looks pretty much like the Notre Dame Dome. I don't ever have to repaint it—it's put right into the roof. The gold was put right into the roof and the paint won't come off.

At one time, we've had a spotlight on it. It got a lot of reaction. Some people, who didn't like Notre Dame, said they were going to come over in a plane and drop a bomb down on it and blow the top off. We're in a town named Amsterdam, an area where they love Ohio State. People knew immediately what it was, and they started coming from all over just to get pictures of it. Mostly, they were people who followed Notre Dame and thought a lot of Notre Dame.

I have a business card with a picture of the Dome on it. I've had it re-done so many times, it's not as sharp as it used to be. The card has my name and "Silo Man" on the back. It's just fun. We've had season tickets for the Notre Dame games since '73. When I first started doing this, my wife thought I was crazy. But, it's been a lot of fun.

———ROBERT VAHALIK, Ohio farmer who put
"The Golden Dome" on top of his silo

My father and uncle went to Notre Dame-Oklahoma in 1957 when we upset Oklahoma. They didn't have tickets. My father and my uncle went into the Notre Dame team hotel, and they ran into a guy in a blue blazer. Dad goes, "Are you with the university? You wouldn't have two tickets for the game today, would you?" He said, "I do." He goes, "Can I see them?" He looks at them and goes, "These are on the 50-yard line. What do you want?" He goes, "I need five-fifty apiece." My dad goes, "I've got to tell you something. I've got a family of eight children in Chicago. I can't afford $1100." He goes, "No, I work for the university…$11. His name was Roger Valdeserri. I've known him my whole life. Roger was with me for the World Series last year. He lives right there in Paradise Valley. I had break-fast with him before the Fiesta Bowl. My father and he became close friends and my father gave him his business card and said, "I'm an electrical contractor in Chicago. If you need any electrical work, please call me." Roger needed a couple of switches changed, I guess, and my father sent down two or three of his workers, and they rewired his entire house.

———**ED FARMER**, Chicago native

Notre Dame is hated so much around thc country because they win. They sell more tee shirts, get more attention, always on national TV. Dick Rosenthal, when he signed the NBC contract, talked to me. He said, "Listen, this is the worst thing—and the best thing—that is ever going to happen to Notre Dame football. It's the best thing because it will enable hundreds, if not thousands, of kids to go to school at Notre Dame that would never have gotten the chance. The worst thing is it has raised the ire of everybody in college football that one school has, in effect, its own network. He was absolutely right. He was visionary on that. They're hated because they're Notre Dame. Everything Notre Dame does becomes legend. If you want to blame somebody, get in a time capsule, go back and blame that bald-headed Norwegian guy. Don't blame Charlie. Don't blame NBC. Blame Knute Rockne. It's a snowball going downhill. Sometimes, the snow melts a little bit. It doesn't roll quite as fast as it had before. It's never going to hit the bottom of the hill. Could you write a book about Miami fans that would sell anywhere outside of Dade County? No. You're going to sell hundreds of thousands of this Notre Dame book from one coast to the other. Michigan is a coast-to-coast team—the coast of Lake Michigan to the coast of Lake Erie—that's it. But, Notre Dame—you've got Notre Dame clubs in Afghanistan, for crying out loud. My son was in the Marine Corps and walked through the hooches in Iraq and saw Notre Dame flags. Notre Dame graduates and Notre Dame fans are loyal because—it's the Jon Gruden syndrome—it was the best time of their life.

Dan Devine had the greatest line—I'm going to have to paraphrase this—"There are fans that love Notre Dame…and, fans that hate Notre Dame…and, they're both pain-in-the-a---!" Think about it. He's right.

———**JEFF JEFFERS**, WNDU-TV

Easily, since I've been in the end zone, the loudest I've ever heard the crowd was the Southern Cal game in 2005. I remember the '88 game with Miami, the 31-30 game, that was very loud, but I was a fan back then. Notre Dame fans have a reputation of not being very loud.... The problem is we're playing against teams when we go to their field, a lot of universities have 30 to 40,000 students on campus. Notre Dame has 8,500 undergrads and 1,500 graduate students so right there—at other schools—you're talking 30,000 more young kids yelling for each game. Then, Notre Dame has the reputation as having an older, more sophisticated crowd. Trust me, when we're 11-0, and we're going for the national championship, that place can rock. Most of the time, you have to raise your hands to try to get the crowd going unless we're having a spectacular year.

You've got 40,000 kids in State College, Pennsylvania. We hold 81,000, and they have 105,000 so just in numbers, they're going to be louder. The Notre Dame students are every bit as faithful and avid as the Penn State crowd. The biggest comparison that's similar is their love for their football. I have ten friends, who are very close to me, who are die-hard Penn State fans. They're the same way I am. If their team loses, they don't even want to talk. They'll close themselves in their bedroom and just sulk and really be sad. Penn State is in the middle of the state. They don't have the Pirates. They don't have the Phillies. It's all they have. It's a religion. That's why when Notre Dame and Penn State play each other, I'm going to have my house half-Penn State people, half-Notre Dame people. I tell them, "You can stay here Thursday. You can stay here Friday, but when you wake up Saturday morning, just pack everything you've got and after the game just hit the Turnpike because you're not going to want to see me if we win, and I'm not going to want to see you if you win." I'm one of the guys who would have loved to have seen Notre Dame join the Big 10 just so we could spank Penn State every year. I'm nervous. Throughout history, they have eight wins—we have eight wins, and there's one tie.

——JIMMY ZANNINO, Granger, Indiana

Notre Dame has had a long tradition of college baseball and has produced all those major leaguers. We rank in the top 10 of all colleges as far as producing major league players. I was a student worker in sports publicity, which was what they called it back in those days, in 1964. I was paid for nine hours a week, and I worked about 40.

I loved looking through the files there. One day, I find this little paper that says Notre Dame Major Leaguers. I look at it, and, just by inspection, I notice all kinds of errors on it. I knew some guys didn't play in the majors so they weren't correct, and I also knew there were some guys missing. You couldn't really call it research, but I did a little head-scratching and came up with some names that weren't on there. I scratched out the names that didn't belong on there. I wrote a letter to *Baseball Digest*, and I gave them a summary. I said, "I've written an article on Notre Dame baseball in the major leagues, and here's a short summary of it." Herb Simon, editor of *Baseball Digest*, writes back and said, "If you get me 1,500 words by Friday, we'll pay you $50." Then, I had to actually sit down and write that article that I said I had written. I sent it to him, and I made *Baseball Digest*. In those days, minimum wage was $1.10 an hour, and here they gave me fifty bucks—that was enormous money.

From that day onward, I would just collect anything I could find about that topic and when I joined SABR (Society for American Baseball Research) in 1977, I was asked what my research interests were, and I mentioned Notre Dame. So, I started collecting research a little more heavily, and I would say to people, "I'm writing a book on Notre Dame baseball—Notre Dame men in the major leagues." It's easy to say you're writing a book, but you're not really writing a book until *you're writing a book*.

The people who actually sat down and read the whole book are amazed at the breadth of accomplishments by the people who've been at Notre Dame and then done something with baseball. People like Arch Ward, who created the All-Star Game. Or, Frank Shaugnessy, who created the Shaugnessy Plan, which saved the minor leagues. Stories like that.

——CAPPY GAGNON, 62, Author of *Notre Dame Baseball Greats*

When Tim Brown ran back the two punts against Michigan State in '87, I wasn't home so I had taped the game. I saved that tape and started taping all the rest of Tim Brown's games. Then, I taped the whole '88 season when Notre Dame won the national title. I was always wondering if I could get copies of the broadcasts from when I was a kid when Joe Montana won the title—the USC green-jersey game. Through my ad in Blue and Gold, I've gotten most major games since the '66 Michigan State game. ABC doesn't even have the first half of that game anymore so I only have the second half. I have the '73 Sugar Bowl when the Irish won the title.

I have a tape of every single game Notre Dame has played since '87 and all the major ones since '71, including all the bowls and Michigans and USCs. When I started, people would charge $40 or $50 for a game so I was unable to get too many older games. I put an ad in Blue and Gold saying that the people who needed the current week's game, or if anybody had any older games to trade, to contact me. Through trades, I ended up getting a whole catalog of games. Now, I tape games for ten bucks for anybody who needs a copy.

None of the networks sell a copy of the game. So, if you missed a game, or you were at the game and wanted to see a tape of it, nobody makes them available. If you call the University of Notre Dame and ask them where you can get a copy, they'll give you my name. They've never given me any hassle at all about doing this. I never make copies of anything that is available from another source. So, if NBC tomorrow said, "If you want a copy of this week's game, call us at NBC," I would not do it.

——ART MCDERMOTT, Lowell, MA

I was upfield, shagging flies one day during freshman baseball practice. Carl Yastrzemski was hitting, but I didn't know who he was at the time. The football team practiced at the far end of the field, and he hit this ball right into the football huddle. I ran over to pick it up. This assistant coach handed it to me and asked, "Who hit that, Yastrzemski?" I said, "I don't know. I don't know who he is." But, the coach said that to me.

I realized months later that the assistant coach was Hank Stram. About five years ago, there was an event that brought me together with Hank Stram. I said, "Hank, you may not remember this, but back in the spring of '57, Yastrzemski hit a ball into your huddle, and you knew who he was. How did you know that?" He said, "I followed him all through high school." I thought that was intriguing. Yaz was painfully shy and didn't talk a lot so a lot of people thought he was arrogant....

Later, Yaz and I became friends. In those days, if you wanted to spend a weekend off campus, you had to send a permission slip to your parents. They would sign it, giving you permission to go away for the weekend. Carl was deeply in love with a girl in Pittsburgh, and he wanted to go see her. He subsequently married the girl. He asked me if I would mind signing his dad's name to the permission slip, and then he would send it to Bridgehampton, Long Island, his home. There, some friend of his would mail it back—it would have the postmark of Bridgehampton. I signed it. He sent it on. He took his weekend. About a week later, I was walking to the cafeteria past Dillon Hall and met Father Glenn Boarman, a great priest—I was a pallbearer at his funeral. He knew everything on campus. He knew your innermost secrets. Nobody ever understood how he did it. He's coming on the diagonal from St. Edward's. I didn't know him at the time. He said, "Bill." I said, "Yes, Father." He said, "Do you have a minute?" I said, "Yes, Father." He said, "Listen, Bill. The next time you want to give Carl a weekend off campus, spell his father's name correctly." It was awful. I was so embarrassed that I didn't even go to dinner—I went back to my room. I was wondering what was going to happen now. Well, nothing happened.

—— BILL MCMURTRIE, 68, Boynton Beach, FL

The reason Northwestern has two directions in their name is they don't know if they're coming or going.

Peace Loving Villagers of Notre Dame

Why do you struggle against us? Why do you persist in the mistaken belief that you can win freely and openly against us?

Your leaders have lied to you. They have led you to believe that you are more powerful than we. They have led you to believe you can win. They have given you false hopes. They have deceived their own people.

We have nothing but affection for Notre Dame.

(signed) A free message from the
Michigan State University of America

Leaflets dropped by unknown Michigan State fans from an airplane over the Notre Dame campus in 1966, prior to the famous 10-10 "Game of the Century." The largest TV audience in history up to that time—33 million—viewed the game.

THE BOOK OF ~~WORK~~ JOB

IT'S LIKE PLAYIN' HOOKY FROM LIFE

JIMMY ZANNINO

Jimmy Zannino, a member of the Notre Dame Stadium grounds crew, grew up in the shadow of Penn State. The Lewistown native saw his first Notre Dame game at the age of 35—the classic 1988 Miami game.

What really prompted me to move to South Bend was my brother, cousin and I rented a Volkswagen bus in 1988. We'd never been to South Bend. We'd never been to a game. We broke down three times on the 600-mile trip on the way to the game. We went to see the Miami-Notre Dame game, which we won 31-30. I didn't even want to leave that day. The whole way back, I told both these guys, "I'm going to live here some day. I'm telling you I'm going to live here." I went back to where I was living at the time, Chambersburg. A couple of years later, in January, I got this *Blue and Gold Illustrated* in the mail. It said, "Spring practice starts April 10." I thought, "That gives me three or four months to get everything together. I'm gone." Everyone thought I was crazy. I wasn't married. My parents were deceased. I sold everything I could sell. I paid off all my debts. I didn't owe anybody anything.

On April 9, I had breakfast with my brother and two cousins, packed everything I could pack in the car…I drove to South Bend. I didn't know anybody. I didn't have a job. I didn't have a place to live. I was just determined to spend the rest of my life at Notre Dame. That night, I can remember getting off onto the shoulder of the Indiana Turnpike and seeing the Dome. I started to cry 'cause I couldn't believe I was actually going to do this. I was scared to death, but, yet, I knew it was something I had to do. I knocked on doors. I told people my story. I said, "My name's Jimmy Zannino. I want to spend the rest of my life here. Can you help me get a job?" People were calling each other on the phone from campus saying, "You've got to hear this guy's story."

Push came to shove, I actually got a job in the dining hall as a short-order cook. But, I wanted to work in the stadium all my life. At Notre Dame, you post jobs on the bulletin board. You go for those and you get interviewed. It took me seven years to get from the dining hall to the stadium. Three times I went for interviews at the stadium and got turned down.

I swear to God, the movie *Rudy* should have been called *Jimmy Z.* I watch that movie, and I cry. I go through a box of tissues, but so much of that movie was my story. Five years old—loving the Irish...wanting to get there...all this adversity. Once I get here, I can't get in the stadium. Three times they turn me down. On the fourth try, I get accepted. I've been out here for 15 years, and, God willing, I hope I'll spend the rest of my life here.

I'm on the grounds crew at the stadium. It is a dream-come-true job. We know all the coaches. We know all the players. I get paid to watch Notre Dame football games from the end zone. I watch *every* home game from the end zone...and I get paid for it. Can you believe that? Twenty years ago, I would have given my right arm just to see a game. Now, I line the field. I work there. Every morning, at seven o'clock, I report to the stadium, hit the time clock—that's what I do for a living. It's the greatest job in the world.

Interesting things are people you see at the games. I'm from a small town in Pennsylvania. The first 35 years of my life that field was just in a television set. I never even knew it was real. It was sur-real—unreal. Now that I'm out here, the biggest thing I have to keep myself calm about is all the celebrities I meet. I've stood beside Dan Patrick from ESPN, Jenny McCarthy from MTV, Tommy Lasorda. I was introduced to Tommy Lasorda as being the only Italian on the grounds crew at Notre Dame. At the time, he was tailgating and feeling pretty good about himself. He said, "Let me tell you something about those Italians." I said, "What's that?" He said, "There's only one thing Italians like more than eating." I said, "What?" He said,

"Talking about eating." Don Shula came down one night and talked with us for 20 minutes. The most interesting person I met this past year was when we played Southern Cal. **DICK EBERSOL**, of NBC, sat with me on the sideline the day before the game and told me his whole story. He told me about Roone Arledge getting him a job at ABC and how he became the president of NBC Universal Sports. He told me about the plane crash when his son passed away and his son who was a senior at Notre Dame. The coolest thing other than watching the game is milling around with celebrities and ex-players.

We actually lost a game once because the night before at the pep rally, Jenny McCarthy was in the stands of the JCC. Some of the students had cardboard cutouts of her and anytime someone would try to speak from the football team or the guest speaker, the whole student body was yelling, "Jen-ny. Jen-ny." This went on all night long. I still think it was a distraction because we ended up losing to Air Force the day she was there. She's Irish. She's from Chicago. She's absolutely stunning. It was neat that somebody like that would root for Notre Dame.

SHULA came down in the middle of the week. Sports Information had a couple of people giving him a tour. He came down and talked about the field and talked about football and about the Notre Dame tradition. He didn't have an appointment. We just happened to be down there working on the field, and he showed up. When somebody like that comes, we take the time to go over and shake his hand. It was a pleasant few minutes.

In the *Rudy* movie, the portrayal of what we guys do in the stadium was accurate. I'm sure a lot of the *Rudy* things were made for Hollywood, as far as whether he snuck in a window at night—I don't know about that. Whether or not the key was actually hidden on the

> NBC Sports President, **DICK EBERSOL**, recently paid $50,000 at a charity auction to have Carly Simon tell him the name of the subject person in her song, "You're So Vain." Only Simon, Ebersol and that person know the identity, rumored to be Warren Beatty, James Taylor or Mick Jagger.

> When **DON SHULA** retired, he had more victories than over half of the other NFL teams.

ladder—I don't know about that. I loved the fact that the movie was made and the way it was beautifully portrayed. I think Rudy deserves all the credit. Just the fact that a kid with a 'C' average ends up graduating from Notre Dame.

The first couple of years here were really hard. Before I met my wife, I had a lot of setbacks. I couldn't understand why God would let me come out here and not give me that stadium job. I got to the point, just like Rudy did, where I never thought I would get in. Then, finally, after thousands and thousands of prayers, I finally did. Now, it's like living in Disney World every day. It truly is heaven on earth. The campus is the most gorgeous place I've ever seen in my life. I'm actually classified as being in the athletic department. Every three months, our crew gets to sit on this thing called 'a town-hall meeting,' with Kevin White and 250 members of the athletic department. Each coach stands up and gives a "state of the union" address on how his team has done. I'm sitting there, and I've got to pinch myself because I can't believe that I'm included with all these people that I admire and respect. It's been the greatest 15 years of my life—it truly has.

Bob Davie, every single day, religiously, would jog around the track that surrounds the field. After his jog, he'd walk a couple of laps with a towel around his neck. He'd stand there and talk to us like we meant something to the guy. It was really beautiful to see a coach treat us with such warmth, affection and concern. We'd always talk about things like the grass looking good, or we'd tease him about the weather. He would actually invite us after practice sometimes to eat with the team if we wanted to. In the summertime, when they were going through two-a-days, he'd set aside a night for just our crew and our family to eat with the team, and meet some of the players. I really rooted hard for Bob Davie. I wanted to see him do well 'cause he was such a nice guy. I really, really liked him. He did have one very good year. Unfortunately, it didn't last....It was the same with Ty Willingham. Ty Willingham was like a father to all of us. If you would see Ty walking down the street, he would actually talk to you as long as you wanted to talk to him. I remember with Lou, it was "bing-bing-bing." He always had a place to go. He was always in a hurry. Ty Willingham loved being at Notre Dame, and he was the friendliest guy in the world, a super-friendly guy. I'm talking about

Tuesday, Wednesday, Thursdays when the camera wasn't on him. The guy was just a people-person. His whole coaching staff was the same way. Some of the coaches on his staff would actually go fishing with guys on our grounds crew. I remember meeting Kent Baer, defensive coordinator, the first day he worked at Notre Dame. I was opening the iron gate going down the tunnel. I started down. Here comes this guy out of the locker room. I shook his hand, introduced myself. We walked down to the edge of the grass...he actually got a tear in his eye. He said, "I can't believe I'm at Notre Dame." I said, "Wow, Coach, I'm flattered that you feel like that." He said, "Every coach's dream is to some day coach at Notre Dame. Don't, for one minute, think that's not true. Every college coach in America dreams of being at Notre Dame someday." He's from Utah, and he was overwhelmed. Maybe that's what's different about that coaching staff and this coaching staff. Those guys came here and it was bigger than life to them. It was huge. The regime we have right now is like, "Hey, baby, we want guys who are going to win football games. If you want to be here, we'll take you. If you don't, go somewhere else, but we're going to turn this thing around."

I didn't think Charlie would be able to turn it around that fast. I'm impressed with the wins and losses, but what I'm really impressed with is his work ethic. One of my responsibilities is snow removal for the sidewalk. I drive a plow truck in the wintertime for our crew. Sometimes I get in there at 4:00-4:30 in the morning, and Charlie's car is already there. I'm thinking, "Man, this guy's life is up in that office." He comes in at four in the morning. He leaves at eleven or midnight, goes home, eats a peanut butter sandwich and comes back. I've never seen anybody put so many hours into anything. He really is a workaholic. He is dedicated and truly believes that you can win at Notre Dame. A lot of people say academics—you can't win at Notre Dame with the type of kid that will come here. You can't talk to Charlie about that because he went to school here. He knows.

Before I worked with the ground crew, there was a story in '92—the Penn State game they called the Snow Bowl—when it was snowing so hard they had to get 100 brooms and every commercial break, they had to clean off the yard lines 'cause the referees couldn't see the lines on the field to mark the ball after the play. Since I've been here, a lot of college fields are experimenting with sand-based fields, compared to soil-based. This is the fifth year we've had a sand-based field. The first couple of years, the lineman were so big and so heavy, their cleats were digging up big hunks of sod. The longer we go, the root base is now becoming firmer so it's not a problem like it was in the early stages of the sand-base. We've been fortunate with the field. Now, we're going to go to an extra, seventh game. That's going to be stretching it because by the end of the season, the grass is pretty much non-existent in the middle of the field. We're concerned about the field—say you've got three homes games, back-to-back-to back. We use Kentucky Bluegrass in the off-season, and the germination takes 14 to 21 days. During the year, when we only have a week, we use rye grass. Even though the rye grass germinates, it can't reach full maturity because you've got three games back-to-back-to-back so it's constantly getting torn up. When you've got 80,000 people watching the game live, and 20,000,000 people watching on television, it can be trying at times to try to make it look appealing even though there are 22 guys, most over 250 pounds, tearing it up, so that's a challenge.

There are more people who root for Notre Dame in Pennsylvania than any other state in the country. That's because, in the Northeast, there are a lot of Italians and a lot of Irish plus it's an overwhelmingly, predominately Catholic state. Even when you go to Beaver Stadium, I've seen Notre Dame come there four times, and half the stadium roots for Notre Dame and half the stadium roots for Penn State. It is always going to be a tough ticket.

In the Boston College game, one of their players was taking turf from the field. They beat us, and they came into the visitors locker room and vandalized it terribly. They destroyed it. That's probably a reason why I think the next time we play them might be the last time they're on our schedule for a long time. You hear the story that all the Boston College kids are kids who couldn't get into Notre Dame so they go to Boston College. They resent Notre Dame for that reason. It's their biggest game on the schedule. To Notre Dame, it's just another game.

When USC came in 2005, it was really cool. Something I've never seen in my life, nor will I ever see again happened. It was Friday afternoon—the day before the game—USC shows up for their walk-through down on the field. There are 10,000 Notre Dame fans outside the tunnel. The buses can't even get to where the players have to get off. They had to let the players off over at gate E instead of where they usually get off at the tunnel. They had to walk a whole quarter of the stadium, out along the sidewalk. All the Notre Dame fans made a wall, and the USC players had to go right through the middle of all those fans. Our fans were loud and rowdy and were yelling, "WE ARE N D...WE ARE N D." Some of the USC guys were mocking them and singing along. You could see on their faces how intimidated they were. This was the day before the game. They're walking probably 250 yards to get to the tunnel. I was so proud of our fans and our students for being so loud. They were classy, too. Never once did you feel like anybody was going to step out of line. It was just good, clean fun. USC gets in, puts on their jogging clothes, and go down on the field. For an hour and fifteen minutes, it's closed to media and spectators. They have the field to themselves. At the last minute, our boss came up and said we had to go down and make an adjustment to some of the electrical wire along the side. USC was just coming off the field. Coach Pete Carroll was standing there with a football in his hand. I don't know what made me do it. I'm twenty yards away from him, and I yelled, "Hey, coach, give me one." He said, "One condition, you've got to take off." I took off running as fast as I could. He put one right on the money, and I caught it and spiked it. All the guys on our crew were applauding. I picked the ball up and went back to him and flipped it back to him. I thought that was pretty cool—the biggest game of the year for this guy, and he's so relaxed that he can do that. It was pretty neat he took the time to throw me one.

When I hear "The Fight Song," I'll be honest with you, I'm not making this up—I cry. It's hard for me not to cry. I'm a very emotional guy. I come from a small town. My dream was just to see a game at Notre Dame. Ever since I was five years old, Catholic boy, Italian boy, loved sports—I swear there is a God, and he lives in me because who do you know who can actually have a dream from five years old till now and you actually get the job you dream about having and you get to live it out the rest of your life. I truly am blessed.

WHERE WE GOING?
WHERE WE GOING?
I DON'T KNOW...YOU'RE THE ONE
DRIVING THE BUS!

HUGHIE BROWN

Every football weekend, hundreds of Citations, Lear Jets, and other private aircraft swoop out of the skies to make South Bend Regional Airport, the busiest FBO in the United States. Meanwhile, downtown at the Greyhound Depot, a solitary old man grabs his duffel bag and disembarks after a tiresome 16-hour ride from eastern Pennsylvania. He has 14 hours to spend at Notre Dame before he reboards for the punishing 20-hour ride back home, just in time for work on Monday morning. Hughie Brown, 71, has made this journey from Hazelton, Pennsylvania, for years. He has been a supervisor at The Bradley Caldwell Distribution Center for the last 22 years.

I get the bus tickets in advance. If you get the round-trip ticket seven days in advance, it's $130, after that, it's $227. It goes up quite a bit. You can't sleep on those long bus trips because the bus stops so many times. I have gone to dozens and dozens of games, and I've never met a person on the bus any one of those times who was actually going to a Notre Dame game. I buy my game tickets after I get there.

Greyhound leaves Hazleton, you go to Pottsville, then you go to Harrisburg. By the time you get to Harrisburg, you only lay over an hour. You leave there at 7:00. You get to Pittsburgh but when you get there, you have to lay over another hour. Then, from Pittsburgh, you go to Cleveland. When you get to Cleveland, you have to lay over three hours. You wait three hours for the bus that takes you to South Bend.

Actually, you're in these places maybe five hours. It's not the amount of time you're on the bus. It's all the in-between and all the stopping and going because they have to stop in so many places to be able to make money. They can't just go from Hazleton to South Bend and make money.

I went to the spring game this year. This is the longest trip I've been on by bus. I got up to go to work at 4:30 in the morning. I got on the bus at five in the afternoon. I got in South Bend at nine the next morning—16 hours. I left South Bend at eleven Saturday night and got home at 1:30, Monday morning. The bus broke down twice. First, they had windshield problems and then they couldn't get the door to close. It was a total of 69 hours from the time I got up to go to work until I got home. I went to work two hours after I got home.

When I was very young, we had a crazy family. To be able to listen to the radio—there were four of us—I had to crack the coal so I could listen to the Notre Dame game. That's the first thing I remember back when I was 10 years-old that always has stuck with me. We would go down to the strippings and pick the coal. If you live in a coal region, you're not supposed to pick the coal, but you go down there and it's like stealing…or borrowing, whichever. That was, to me, the start of Notre Dame football and being a nut about Notre Dame football.

The first game I went to in South Bend was the greatest experience in the world because when you see the Golden Dome, it's like you died and went to heaven. Unless you go to Notre Dame—I tell all my friends about the Dome, and everything about Notre Dame, but unless you actually are there to experience it…the first day you go there and see for yourself, see the beauty of it…it overwhelms you. Notre Dame—every time I go there and look at that Dome, I can't explain the word. I stop. I stop and I look. It's overwhelming. I was at the BYU game last year and people from BYU were looking at the Golden Dome, and they wanted to know if that was Touchdown Jesus. Everybody sees something different.

Since I've been going to Notre Dame, I've got six free tickets. It all depends on who you meet. It all depends on where you are—how lucky you are. I went to the Southern Cal game the time we played in 2003. I went to the Morris Inn, walked in and told the guy I needed a ticket. He gave me the ticket, and I went to give him the money. He said, "No, you don't have to pay me." His wife said, "Why are you giving it to him free?" He said, "When I was in the Linebacker Lounge last year, he bought me a beer." He remembered that. The most I've ever paid for a ticket was $500 for the USC game last year. My son flew me out to the USC game. When we were leaving the airport, I looked at the license plate on his rental car, and it said 972, and I said to him, "Within 10 days, I'll get your money back." On the 10th day, the Pennsylvania Lottery came up 972. I'm not kidding—that's true. I won $1,000—$500 for my son and $500 for me, but he wouldn't take the money. He donated the money.

Going to the Notre Dame games, I've been very lucky. I've met a lot of kids. Last year, David, a little boy in second grade sat next to me and his mother said, "Why are you letting him sit next to you? He'll talk your ear off." He sat next to me the whole game and we were talking and having a big old time. After the game, his sister said, "Will you take a picture with him?" I said, "Sure." Then, she took a picture, which I have in my room till today. I was going down the steps, and David started crying. He ran down and said, "You know what. This is the best day of my life." You know how it is, parents go with children and don't talk to them during the game.

One time, some little girls were selling candy. I told her, "I don't eat candy, but I'll buy one from you." She said, "What about my friends?" I said, "What do you mean, what about your friends?" She said, "I have four friends," so I had to buy from all the kids. This was on the Notre Dame campus.

At the USC game, there was a young lady there trying to be accepted in the school. She was from Michigan. We sat for 10-15 minutes talking about where she went to school and how excited she was about going to Notre Dame. When she was leaving, she said she was going to find out around Thanksgiving. I told her I would say prayers that she would get into Notre Dame. Talking to her and seeing how excited she was about the opportunity, that really meant a lot to me.

I talked to a guy from New Jersey and it was the first time he was ever at Notre Dame. He said, "When I get home, I'm going to sit on my couch and close my eyes and I'm gonna say, 'Was I really there?'" I said, "Yes, you really were here." But, the way he said it, he was so excited. He was in his fifties. That's the kind of thing that's so important.

Joey Getherall, the receiver, when he was a senior in 2000, spoke at one of the pep rallies. He broke down and started to cry. It was so emotional. You understood what seniors must really feel. He said that tomorrow he was going to run on the field for the last time, and he could remember running on the field for the first time and how exciting it was, and how he wished he could start all over. Then he broke down. That's what it's all about to me is feeling the way the players react, what they do and how young they are.

During the years, when Notre Dame was losing all those games, those bus trips were 50-something hours, but I have a different theory about it. I had a high school coach that told us, "When the gun goes off, the game is over. Shake the hand of your opponent. If you don't have enough respect to shake his hand, then you shouldn't play sports." So, I always follow his theory. Once the gun goes off, the game is over. I don't replay it. I don't say this, that, or anything else. The game is over, and I can't change it. That was his theory, and that's my theory. The thing with me is that I had a crazy year last year. I traveled 11, 722 miles—17,000 miles if you count the Fiesta Bowl.

My wife, Amy, got up one morning and she went to church. She said, "I just realized that if I die in the autumn, I have to die on a Monday. If I'm not buried by Thursday, you'll put me on ice until Monday." She actually, actually said that. So...she thinks I'm crazy.

The greatest game I ever went to was the Kansas game in '99. It was five days after I had my last chemo treatment. That was the greatest experience I've ever had at Notre Dame. The opportunity to go back that day. There'll never be another day that will be more fulfilling and that I really understood what Notre Dame means. I was very, very, very, very fortunate. I'm one of the survivors that God gave the opportunity. That was the greatest day I've ever spent at Notre Dame. I love Notre Dame.

Amen

TO BE CONTINUED!

We hope you have enjoyed the first annual *For Notre Dame Fans Only*. You can be in next year's edition, *For Notre Dame Fans Only: The New Testaments*, if you have a neat story. You can email it to printedpage@cox.net (put "The New Testaments" in the subject line), or call the author directly at 602-738-5889.

Or, if you have stories about the Chicago Bears, the Cubs, the Yankees, or the St. Louis Cardinals, email them to printedpage@cox.net (put the appropriate team name in the subject line).

For information on ordering more copies of *For Notre Dame Fans Only,* as well as any of the author's other best-selling books, call 602-738-5889.

Note: There were no actual Southern Cal fans harmed during the making of this book.

About the Author

Notre Dame alumnus, Rich Wolfe, is the #1 selling sports book author in America for the last six years. The only person to appear on both *Jeopardy* and *ESPN's Two-Minute Drill,* he captained the winning team in the recent National Sports Team Trivia Championship in St. Louis.

Other Books by Rich Wolfe

Da Coach (Mike Ditka)

I Remember Harry Caray

There's No Expiration Date on Dreams (Tom Brady)

He Graduated Life with Honors and No Regrets (Pat Tillman)

Take This Job and Love It (Jon Gruden)

Been There, Shoulda Done That (John Daly)

Oh, What a Knight (Bob Knight)

And the Last Shall Be First (Kurt Warner)

Remembering Jack Buck

Sports Fans Who Made Headlines

Fandemonium

Remembering Dale Earnhardt

For Yankees Fans Only

For Cubs Fans Only

For Red Sox Fans Only

For Cardinals Fans Only

For Packers Fans Only

For Hawkeyes Fans Only

For Browns Fans Only

For Mets Fans Only

Questions? Contact the author directly at 602-738-5889.